DAVID O. MCKAY LIBRARY

P9-ELG-260

DATE DUE

DEC 2 6 2007		
APR 0 4 2011		

Demco

DEC 8 2006

WITHDRAWN

MAY 0 6 2024

DAVID O. McKAY LIBRARY
BYU-IDAHO

CLASSROOM AUTHORITY

Theory, Research, and Practice

CLASSROOM AUTHORITY

Theory, Research, and Practice

Edited by

JUDITH L. PACE
University of San Francisco

and

ANNETTE HEMMINGS
University of Cincinnati

LEA

LAWRENCE ERLBAUM ASSOCIATES, PUBLISHERS

2006   Mahwah, New Jersey   London

Copyright © 2006 by Lawrence Erlbaum Associates, Inc.

All rights reserved. No part of this book may be reproduced in
any form, by photostat, microform, retrieval system, or any other
means, without prior written permission of the publisher.

Lawrence Erlbaum Associates, Inc., Publishers
10 Industrial Avenue
Mahwah, New Jersey 07430
www.erlbaum.com

Cover design by Kathryn Houghtaling Lacey

Library of Congress Cataloging-in-Publication Data

Classroom authority : theory, research, and practice / edited by
Judith L. Pace and Annette Hemmings.
       p.   cm.
   Includes bibliographical references and index.
   ISBN 0–8058–5160–7 (cloth : alk. paper) —ISBN 0–8058–5161–5
(pbk. : alk. paper)
       1. Classroom management—United States. I. Pace, Judith L.
II. Hemmings, Annette B.
LB3013.C526 2005
371.102'4—dc22   2005045476

Books published by Lawrence Erlbaum Associates are printed on acid-free
paper, and their bindings are chosen for strength and durability.

Printed in the United States of America
10 9 8 7 6 5 4 3 2 1

Contents

Foreword

Mary Haywood Metz
University of Wisconsin–Madison

This book describes and analyzes authority relationships in classrooms. Schooling and authority are among the most important, familiar, and transparent parts of the nation's social fabric. Yet both phenomena also are among the most misunderstood. Most adults are deeply familiar with U.S. schools after more than a decade of participating in them at a curious and impressionable stage of life. Many college graduates believe that, given a few weeks of pointers, they would be ready to step into the role of teacher. Nor is that idea just a fantasy. There are strong voices in our society recommending that more college graduates should move into teaching with minimal, or even no, professional training.

The common belief that schools are well-known territory has serious consequences. Many adults with little experience in schools beyond their childhood years feel justified in pounding the desk to insist that schools should be run as they think best. These include not just Monday morning quarterbacks in the general public or angry parents before school boards, but serious policymakers at the state and federal levels. Still, despite their agreement that schools are easily understood, such adults do not have a single vision of schools; in fact, they often drastically disagree about many important matters.

Schools are in fact far less transparent, far more complex, and far more subject to serious debate about both ends and means than they appear to their students or to adults who remember their school days. New teachers routinely find, to their deep dismay, that teaching is much more difficult and complicated than they anticipated. Even after a strong preparation in teacher education, new teachers find they have a great deal to learn on the job. Good-quality teacher education does give them resources with which both to start teaching and to learn more. Without professional preparation, they are likely to be overwhelmed and to fall back on inadequate and idiosyncratic personal resources.

The case is similar with regard to authority. Like schooling, adults have experienced it from the cradle and believe they understand it. But members of our society have fundamentally different understandings of what constitutes authority and how it should (or should not) be exercised. Consequently, challenges to classroom authority are endemic. New teachers find it one of their greatest preoccupations.

In the late 1960s, as part of my graduate work in sociology, I was given the task of closely analyzing several classic theorists who dealt with authority. At the same time, I had been, and continued to be, witness to repeated confrontations between university administrators and politically active students on Sproul Plaza at the University of California, Berkeley. As I read the theorists, I could see that in most of these confrontations the issue was not corruption of power, as the students thought, nor was it childish or illegitimate rebellion, as the administrators thought. Rather, it was the clash of different understandings of legitimate authority that had been ably analyzed by Max Weber a half century or so earlier. The confrontation was so acrid precisely because both sides felt that they were calling on a shared societal set of values that was a source of legitimacy for their actions. Members of both groups were, in their own eyes, acting as responsible agents of values to which the other group clearly owed allegiance. Part of the conflict lay in different definitions of shared values, and part of it lay in different understandings of the bases on which administrators could legitimately direct students' actions.

I was intrigued by the ways in which the abstractions of theory helped me to understand the drama of daily life. In doing ethnographic research for my first book, *Classrooms and Corridors,* I took those theoretical abstractions as tools to study relationships of classroom authority. I was not far into my study of eighth-grade classrooms, before I saw vivid instances of principled clashes between teachers and students based on differing definitions of authority relations, where each clung to their legitimate rights as they understood them. Precisely because everyone thinks they know what is right, disagreements are profound and easily become incendiary as all parties, even quite young ones, feel morally violated.

In the last 30 years, the study of authority in schools has fallen out of favor, as has the very word. But teachers must exert something very like authority if they are constructively to orchestrate the activities of more than 20 students spending 180 days together in a crowded room. Whatever they call it, they have to use it. At the same time, the "reading wars" and "math wars," and very different understandings about what multiculturalism is and how it should be part of schooling, all reflect deepening differences about the values in the name of which teachers can claim authority over their students.

In the current moment, reflective, empirically grounded discussions of actual classroom teaching and learning are far harder to find than are strident debates about sweeping educational policies. Standards, high-stakes testing, accountability, markets and choice, even career ladders and merit pay for teachers—none of these themes of the moment comes very close to engaging the daily dilemmas of classroom teaching, or of the relationships between teachers and students. Still, education happens, finally, in the classroom. Given an opportunity to learn, students make the ultimate decisions about whether they will learn. To understand whether education is succeeding, where it might be going wrong, and what exemplars can be found for educational improvement, one has to develop a fine-grained understanding of what happens between teachers and students, between each and curricula, and between individual students and their peers.

In this context, *Classroom Authority: Theory, Research, and Practice* comes as a breath of fresh air. The chapters that Judith L. Pace and Annette Hemmings have brought together in this book are both theoretical and deeply empirical. All are based on extensive qualitative research in classrooms or in the social spaces that surround and affect them. The authors recognize that classrooms are varied, highly complex settings. They share a concern with authority, with the variations in its forms, and with the ways that its various components may be contested and transformed in the process of the complicated lived reality of classrooms. These chapters reflect how relatively small matters and external forces can shape the life of a classroom by affecting the delicate balance in the many interactions that make a classroom's life a complex, reverberating social web.

Pace and Hemmings orient the reader to the theoretical discussion of authority and to the ways in which its variations and its implications were studied in the context of education since the late 1960s. Then, the chapter authors present a series of qualitative studies in locations that range from the fourth grade through college. As they elucidate a variety of social processes, they show us authority winding through them like a red thread. As the reader assimilates the separate chapters, he or she sees themes returning in different contexts. The similarities and differences among the settings and in the authors' perspectives build to help the reader gain an intuitive feeling for complexity and variation, order and structure, ambiguity and uncertainty in classroom life. Authority alone does not orchestrate the symphony of classroom cooperation; teachers use many, often tacit, forms of control. Students do not respond with on-and-off switches of compliance or disobedience, but instead respond with subtly nuanced, often ambivalent, inventiveness. Authority, along with other forms of classroom control, is highly interactive. In the intimacy of prolonged face-to-face relationships, it evolves and takes on forms entwined with a specific context and content. The reader also comes to appreciate that classrooms are both isolated and permeable. The schools within which they are set, and influences from beyond their walls from parents, communities, college admissions officers, and employers, all have an effect on daily life inside the classroom's boundaries.

These abstract statements only hint at the force of *Classroom Authority*. It is in reading these authors' vivid descriptions in conversation with their analytical conclusions that the reader's understanding will begin to grow. Teachers-in-training, practicing teachers, school board members, policy-makers, and educational researchers all will find much to reflect on as a consequence of reading this book.

Preface

The intent of this volume is to provide a better understanding of classroom authority through explorations of theory, prior research, and contemporary qualitative studies. The emphasis is on the social construction of authority and the crucial role that authority relations play in K–16 teachers' pedagogy and students' academic engagement and achievement. Although the general understanding is that teachers are entrusted with the formal right and responsibility to take charge in the classroom and students are obliged to obey, the actual enactment of authority occurs through complex negotiations between teachers and students that are influenced by numerous and often conflicting institutional, cultural, and societal factors (Metz, 1978). Among these factors is Americans' own ambivalence toward authority.

Since the political and social upheavals of the 1960s, authority in schools and classrooms has been an ideologically charged and controversial topic. Although debates over authority were, and continue to be, critical, probing discussions and in-depth examinations of authority *as it is actually practiced in classrooms and schools* have too often been neglected (Hurn, 1985). This book seeks to revitalize dialogue and research on classroom authority with attention to the contextual factors that bear on its social construction. It is aimed at teacher educators, scholars, policymakers, students of education, and practitioners who seek empirically based understandings of authority and its connections to classroom life and, ultimately, to the larger issues of educational quality and democracy in schools and society. Contributing authors offer insights on a variety of key questions: How do teachers engage students in curriculum, communicate expectations for academic performance and conduct, evaluate students, maintain order, and generate learning? What are the dilemmas they face, and how do they manage them? How do teachers negotiating authority with students representing diverse racial, ethnic, class, and gender social locations actively weigh the demands of schooling against their own interests, aptitudes, understandings, and experiences? How do external factors, such as national and state reform movements, school policies, and community and parental pressures, influence the ways in which teachers and students construct authority relations?

What are the consequences of how authority relations are actually enacted in and out of classrooms?

The book begins with an introductory chapter that grounds the reader in social theory on authority; presents groundbreaking qualitative studies of classroom authority; describes ideological debates over authority in schools; and discusses implications for research, practice, and policy. This chapter is followed by six field-based qualitative studies that illuminate the dynamics of authority across a spectrum of K–12 and college settings. These studies feature a variety of methodologies, theoretical lenses, and interpretive perspectives that the authors used to gather and analyze data. The emphasis in all of them is on the nature, negotiation, and implications of authority relations between teachers and students. David T. Hansen's epilogue pulls together this research by elucidating new findings and vital themes that expand our vision of what classroom authority means, how it is constructed, and why it is so important.

This book does not purport to be all inclusive of issues pertinent to classroom authority. Our hope is that it will stimulate further work on authority and schooling that considers the impact of contemporary culture, politics, and economics on the teaching profession and educational system. Since our studies were conducted, these factors have become increasingly important and have contributed to blurring the lines between authority and power sometimes to the detriment of teaching and learning.

SUMMARY OF CHAPTERS

The book begins with a foreword by Mary Haywood Metz, whose own 1978 classic study of classroom and school authority served as a deep source of inspiration for this book. In chapter 1, "Understanding Classroom Authority as a Social Construction," we provide a foundational overview of theoretical conceptualizations, ideological positions, and qualitative research on the social construction of authority in schools and classrooms.

The next six chapters present qualitative studies conducted by educational scholars working from sociological and anthropological perspectives. They are organized in order by level of schooling. Chapter 2, "Authority, Culture, Context: Controlling the Production of Historical Knowledge in Elementary Classrooms," investigates links among classroom authority, elementary school culture, the production of knowledge, and standardized testing. John S. Wills portrays a fifth-grade social studies teacher as she engaged low-income Latino, Black, and White students in the production of historical knowledge against the backdrop of state-mandated testing. Wills identifies the teacher's exercise of authority as a form of positive control and analyzes a "typical" social studies lesson in which the teacher provided students with ample opportunities to assume active and meaningful roles in shaping accounts of history. The teacher's approach fits within a coherent and caring school culture that supported her "unambiguous" authority over curriculum, instruction, and students. However, state-mandated testing in reading and math created a dilemma for the teacher between superficial coverage of social studies curriculum and the more time-consuming task of building students' understanding of history. When pressed to rush through history lessons, students complied with little or no complaint, but they were relegated to less meaningful roles in the production of historical knowledge. Wills's chapter raises a critical question that demands further attention: How does standardized testing (and other external mandates) undermine the joint production of classroom knowledge and positive authority relations?

Chapter 3, "Playing with Pedagogical Authority," is an examination of how students played with authority. It is based on a study conducted in a Jesuit middle school established to prepare Mexican immigrants for admission to elite high schools. The authors of the chapter, James Mullooly and Hervé Varenne, offer a critique of Bourdieu and Passeron's 1977 model of pedagogical authority. Using ethnomethodological techniques, they describe moments of playing with pedagogical authority in an eighth-grade reading lesson and illustrate how mutually constituted authority can be fun or made fun of. Mullooly and Varenne's theoretical emphasis on the fact that people do play with authority exposes school actors' practical awareness and agency in ways that a broader focus on *habitus* or *hegemony* can make invisible. They show how play highlights indeterminacy and unpredictability in the enactment of school authority patterns. Although moments of playing could be interpreted as unsuccessful challenges to the teacher's authority, Mullooly and Varenne suggest that they are examples of students' acknowledgment of it and their position in relation to it.

Chapter 4, "Saving (and Losing) Face, Race, and Authority: Strategies of Action in a Ninth-Grade English Class," explores authority and the construction of the "achievement gap" by examining the classic tensions between order and engagement, the mix of strategies used to manage them, and unintended consequences. Judith L. Pace presents her case study of a White female teacher in a racially mixed, lower track ninth-grade English class in a college-preparatory high school. Although the teacher expressed dedication to raising achievement of her Black students, she is frustrated by those who appeared to have given their consent yet constantly received low grades because they refused to do their work. In her analysis of the classroom discourse, Pace uncovers the dynamics of what the teacher perceived as a "semblance" of engagement and underlying resistance to her agenda. She explains how the teacher's contradictory enactment of authority is based on culturally shaped "strategies of action" (Swidler, 2001) that blended encouragement and face-saving politeness (Brown & Levinson, 1987; Cazden, 1988) with pressure to conform to the social norms and competitive values of the school. Although these strategies fostered a semblance of cooperation in class, the emphasis on grades, rigid boundaries, and control of knowledge generated various tensions that evoked a mixture of student responses that unintentionally perpetuated the construction of underachievement among Black students. Pace's narration and analysis of classroom events indicate the importance of attending to authority in teacher education and professional development in ways that foster new strategies of action based on better understandings of students, racial issues, and authority.

Chapter 5, "Authority in Detracked High School Classrooms: Tensions Among Individualism, Equity, and Legitimacy," focuses on authority in detracked classes. Janet Bixby investigates authority relations in two ninth-grade U.S. history classes that are part of a detracking program at Hillside High School, an academically competitive, college-preparatory public school. The detracking movement that fostered this program was derived from an egalitarian impulse that challenges the reproduction of social inequalities through school structures (Oakes, Wells, & Jones, 1997; Wells & Serna, 1996). However, Bixby shows how the students, especially students of color, who were supposed to benefit the most continued to lag behind. Although the two teachers enacted authority relations based on their professional expertise as subject matter experts, they also responded to various dynamics that perpetuated differential achievement. Among these dynamics were the pragmatic code of "making the grade" within the exclusive cliques of high achievers; elite parents' use of their status and knowledge to pressure teachers to raise their children's grades; and school administrators' pressure on teachers to raise minority student achievement. The teachers defended their legitimacy by participating in the development of strong departmental units that reinforced their authority based on subject matter expertise. These units established powerful norms for curriculum and instruction even though teachers readily acknowledged that they were not effective with low-achieving students. Bixby's chapter raises questions about the limited efficacy of detracking reforms that change the structure, but not the culture, curriculum, and pedagogy, of classrooms. It also poses issues concerning teachers' beliefs about their role and whether these need to change in order to successfully work with socioculturally and academically diverse students.

Chapter 6, "Moral Order in High School Authority: Dis/Enabling Care and (Un)Scrupulous Achievement," is an inquiry into the moral order of schools. Annette Hemmings reminds us that classroom authority is a relationship between teachers and students enacted in "the service of a moral order to which both owe allegiance" (Metz, 1978, p. 26). In actuality, however, school moral orders are highly negotiable and subject to varying degrees and kinds of commitments. Hemmings offers a broad definition of school moral order that is broken down into three analytical dimensions: (a) worthwhile curriculum, (b) proper pedagogy, and (c) good character. She then presents a contrast between the moral orders of Central City High, a school that served mostly low-income, inner-city Black youth, and Ridgewood High, a school located in a predominantly White, upper-middle-class suburb. The moral order at Central City High was one of dis/enabling care where teachers cared for students as disadvantaged youth but appeared not to care about them as capable learners. At Ridgewood High, teachers were guided by a moral order of (un)scrupulous achievement that prompted them to be scrupulous in their efforts to prepare students for college but unscrupulous in how they catered to students' demands for unblemished report cards and less strenuous schoolwork. Although there was significant variation between moral orders, teachers' enactment of authority relations in both schools was affected by paradoxical understandings that had mixed consequences for students. Hemmings's chapter invokes further questions about how schools can address the particular needs and interests of their constituencies as well as educate young people for the public good.

Chapter 7, "Standards and Sob Stories: Negotiating Authority at an Urban Public College," is an account of how college teachers deal with the incessant demands of students to adjust their standards. Randi Rosenblum presents her study on the negotiation of standards that occurred between students and faculty outside of the classroom at an urban public college. She outlines three general strategies and positions faculty adopted in response to students' "sob stories": (a) flexibility (the Supporters), (b) inflexibility (the Standards Bearers), and (c) bounded flexibility (the Ad Hoc Majority). The Supporters viewed rigid adherence to rules as a misuse of teacher authority and were therefore quite flexible, whereas the Standards Bearers were inflexible because they felt that negotiations with students undermined their authority and lowered standards. The Ad Hoc Majority were in the middle; they adopted a strategy of bounded flexibility in their case-by-case responses to students. Rosenblum links faculty strategies to their beliefs about their role, student accountability, effective pedagogy, and the often-conflicting moral imperatives of equity and excellence at a public institution of higher education. Her work indicates the need to explore negotiation of standards and its meanings and consequences for both faculty and students.

Our book concludes with an epilogue by David Hansen, who articulates the major themes, issues, and questions generated by these studies. His discussion makes it clear how important the topic of authority is for educational researchers and practitioners who seek better theoretical understandings of, empirical research on, and more responsible and responsive practices related to classroom teaching and learning.

ACKNOWLEDGMENTS

We are deeply grateful for the help and support of colleagues and editors who helped to make this book possible. Mary Metz, with her ongoing interest in authority and generous mentorship, brought us together and encouraged the project. She and David Hansen not only agreed to write the Foreword and Epilogue but also served as discussants for our symposium, "Social Construction of Classroom Authority: Research and Dialogue," conducted at the 2004 annual meeting of the American Educational Research Association. The symposium was a forum for book contributors to present drafts of their chapters, and Mary and David in their commentaries provided sagacious insight into how authors might think about and improve their work. Reba Page gave us advice on creating an edited volume and feedback that was critical to our introductory chapter on authority. We also appreciate the wonderful editorial guidance of Naomi Silverman; her assistant, Erica Kica; production supervisor Sarah Wahlert; and other members of the staff at Lawrence Erlbaum Associates. Thanks to all of you for all that you did.

REFERENCES

Bourdieu, P., & Passeron, J. C. (1977). *Reproduction in education, society and culture*. London: Sage.

Brown, P., & Levinson, S. (1987). *Politeness: Some universals in language usage*. Cambridge, England: Cambridge University Press.

Cazden, C. (1988). *Classroom discourse: The language of teaching and learning*. Portsmouth, NH: Heinemann.

Hurn, C. (1985). Changes in authority relationships in schools: 1960–1980. *Research in Sociology of Education, 5,* 31–57.

Metz, M. H. (1978). *Classrooms and corridors: The crisis of authority in desegregated schools*. Berkeley: University of California Press.

Oakes, J., Wells, A. S., & Jones, M. (1997). Detracking: The social construction of ability, cultural politics, and resistance to reform. *Teachers College Record, 98,* 482–510.

Swidler, A. (1979). *Organization without authority*. Cambridge, MA: Harvard University Press.

Swidler, A. (2001). *Talk of love: How culture matters*. Chicago: University of Chicago Press.

Wells, A. S., & Serna, I. (1996). The politics of culture: Understanding local political resistance to detracking in racially mixed schools. *Harvard Educational Review, 66,* 93–118.

Chapter 1

Understanding Classroom Authority as a Social Construction

Judith L. Pace
University of San Francisco

Annette Hemmings
University of Cincinnati

Despite authority's fundamental role in schooling, there are ongoing debates that reflect divergent belief systems as well as confusion over what authority is and how it ought to be enacted. To arrive at a better understanding, authority must be recognized as a complex social relationship that unfolds in schools and classrooms through various kinds of interactions that hold varied meanings for teachers and students. It must be understood, in other words, as a *social construction*.

The purpose of this chapter is to provide a framework for the studies in this book and conceptual tools for understanding classroom authority as a social construction. We argue that classroom authority is jointly negotiated through the symbolic actions of teachers and students and is shaped by local contextual forces and larger social, political, and cultural factors. Our conceptualization of authority challenges a number of misconceptions, such as the view that authority is synonymous with coercive power, something that teachers possess, enforceable through top-down sanctions, or equivalent to discipline. Both common-sense assumptions and academic suppositions perpetuate conflicting views of authority as good, bad, coercive, nonexistent, stable, universal, and so forth. In contrast, we make the following five essential claims:

1. Classroom authority in its truest form depends on teachers' legitimacy, students' consent, and a moral order consisting of shared purposes, values, and norms.
2. Authority is multiple in its forms and types and the ways in which it is interpreted.
3. Authority is enacted through dynamic negotiations between teachers and students that often involve overt or subtle conflict.
4. Authority is situated in various arenas—such as curricula and classroom discourse—and is shaped by multiple interacting influences, including varying perspectives on educational purposes, values, and norms; school ethos and policy; teachers' knowledge; institutional features of schooling; and historical context.
5. Authority is consequential for classroom life, students' achievement, teachers' work, and democracy.

In this chapter, we review the classic social theories that support these claims and lay out the fundamental elements of authority. We proceed with an overview of key empirical studies that examine classroom and school authority as a social construction. The rest of this chapter is organized around several themes that reinforce our argument for how classroom authority should be understood. We acknowledge that many more writings on authority could be included in our review, notably philosophical discussions of authority, but they lie beyond the scope of this chapter.[1] The chapter ends with implications for research, policy, and practice.

ESSENTIAL ELEMENTS OF AUTHORITY: LEGITIMACY, CONSENT, AND THE MORAL ORDER

Authority is often associated with coercive power that works against the democratic ideal of freedom. Authority is also equated with trust and respect and is considered necessary for the stability of community life. These contradictory understandings make it imperative to revisit classic theories in order to provide definitions of authority that shed light on how it differs from, yet is related to, power. In doing so, we relate abstract social theory to everyday classroom life.

Legitimacy and Ideal Types

In the second decade of the 20th century, sociologist Max Weber laid the theoretical foundation for authority and in particular the essential element

---

[1]For example, see David Nyberg and Paul Faber's edited collection of essays in *Teachers College Record*, fall 1986 (Nyberg & Farber, 1986).

of legitimacy. Weber (1925/1964) defined *authority* as the probability of a person gaining voluntary obedience from others. The right of that person to give commands depends in large part on others' belief in his or her legitimacy. Authority, in other words, is a relationship of command and consent based on the legitimacy of those who lead and the voluntary obedience of those who follow. Other sociologists have explained that this relationship serves and is justified by a moral order that comprises shared purposes and goals, values and beliefs, and norms (Metz, 1978; Selznick, 1992).

Weber's (1925/1964) foundational contribution to the conceptualization of authority is his delineation of three ideal types of authority rooted in different sources of legitimacy. This framework has been applied to analyses of authority relations in schools (Grant, 1988; Hurn, 1985; Metz, 1978; Pace, 2003a, 2003c). *Traditional authority,* the first type, is based on long-standing traditions that grant legitimacy to certain people with superior status. A person with superior status serves the traditions through his or her commands, and loyalty from subordinates is to be given in return. Teachers exercising traditional authority act *in loco parentis* and expect to be obeyed simply because they occupy the role of teacher.

The second type, *charismatic authority,* occurs when heroic or exemplary individuals with exceptional qualities garner unusually high prestige. Charismatic teachers evoke emotional attachment from students. They are not bound by official rules, and their legitimacy lasts as long as they satisfy students' needs and inspire commitment.

The third type, *legal–rational authority* (also known as *bureaucratic authority*), stems from rules and regulations based on legal procedures and policy. A person in authority occupies an "office" and has the right to issue and enforce commands that support an established order. The teacher's role is that of a boss, and students are the workers. It is important that bureaucratic authority may actually depend on power, which may very well involve the use of rewards and punishments. Although bureaucratic authority may generally be accepted as legitimate, the threat of power (e.g., bad grades or detention) suggests that what is gained is compliance rather than voluntary consent.

Other sociologists have identified *professional authority* as a fourth type distinguished by the use of individuals' expertise to achieve consensual aims (Blau, 1974; Parsons, 1964). In the role of professional expert, teachers' command of subject matter knowledge and pedagogical skills are their most important claim to legitimacy.

Although the differences between ideal types are crucial, Weber (1925/1964) pointed out that in the real world they do not exist in their purest forms. Those who exercise authority usually appeal to mixed claims to legitimacy. Pace's (2003c) research found that this is especially true of teachers as they constantly respond to complex situations. Such observations are explicated in classic social theory not only through conceptions of legitimacy but also through the notions of consent and the moral order.

Consent

Like Weber, sociologist Chester Barnard (1950) emphasized that authority rests on—indeed, depends on—consent. Rather than stressing the superordinate's legitimacy, Barnard explained four simultaneous conditions necessary for consent to a particular message of authority: the subordinate (a) understands it, (b) sees it as not being inconsistent with organizational purposes, (c) believes it is compatible with his or her general self-interest, and (d) is mentally and physically able to fulfill it. These conditions are essential to classroom learning, as students must find the teacher's agenda acceptable and attainable to genuinely become involved in it.

Political theorist Carl Friedrich (1958) asserted that true consent is based on agreement, rather than merely obedience. He maintained that "authority rests upon the ability to issue communications which are capable of reasoned elaboration" (Friedrich, 1958, p. 29). Superordinates should be able to justify what they are asking others to do. This implies that teachers need to be clear about their purposes and be able to articulate them to students. Such purposes are integral to the moral order of schools.

The Moral Order

As a scholar of education before the turn of the 20th century, sociologist Emile Durkheim (1956, 1961) emphasized the importance of *moral authority*. He understood such authority "as that influence which imposes upon us all the moral power that we acknowledge as superior to us. Because of this influence, we act in prescribed ways" (Durkheim, 1961, p. 29). According to Durkheim, moral authority depends on teachers who express genuine confidence in their own ability to inspire students' respect. Part of their role is to represent and uphold the social and moral order, which he defined as rules for good conduct. "The teacher," he wrote, "is the interpreter of the great moral ideas of his time and of his country" (Durkheim, 1956, p. 89).

Several decades later, philosopher Hannah Arendt (1954/1977) decried the loss of authority in modern society and urged the preservation of tradition, including moral standards, to ensure continuity and stability. She argued that the purpose of authority in education is to provide guidance to children in a world that has existed for a long time but is strange to them. The teacher is morally responsible for preparing youth "for the task of renewing a common world" (Arendt, 1954/1977, p. 196).

Mary Metz (1978), who in her ethnography of two junior high schools wrote the most systematic, comprehensive, and insightful analysis of school authority, brought together theorists' work on legitimacy, consent, and moral purposes in her conceptualization:

Authority is distinguished ... by the superordinate's *right* to command and subordinate's *duty* to obey. This right and duty stem from the crucial fact that the interacting persons share a relationship which exists for the service of a *moral order to which both owe allegiance.* This moral order may be as diffuse as the way of life of a traditional society or as specific as the pragmatic goals of a manufacturing organization. But in any case, all participants have a duty to help realize the moral order through their actions. (p. 26)

Genuine authority does not exist when legitimacy, consent, or shared purposes and values are missing. This distinguishes authority from coercive power and other kinds of control. Metz (1978) identified different resources teachers use to maintain control. When students are forced with the threat of punishment to do what they do not want to do, it is *coercion.* When students' cooperation is gained by offering them incentives, it is *exchange* (see Powell, Farrar, & Cohen, 1985; Sedlak, Wheeler, Pullin, & Cusick, 1986; Sizer, 1984). When teachers use their personal relationship with students to persuade them, it is *influence* (see Swidler, 1979). Of course, these other resources for social control are commonplace in classrooms and are often mixed with authority. This makes it all the more difficult, unusual, and yet important to tease out authority using a valid theoretical construct and to recognize that there are different kinds of authority.

Problematizing Legitimacy, Consent, and the Moral Order

Classic social theory lays out ways to understand the essential components of authority; however, difficult questions persist about how legitimacy is defined, and by whom; what is true consent versus compliance; and what constitutes the moral order. Additionally, the distinction between authority and power can be very ambiguous, because authority is defined by some scholars as legitimate power (Swidler, 1979), and sanctions—or reference to them—are often used to gain cooperation. More pointedly, neo-Marxist education scholars have argued since the 1960s that the institution of schooling exists within social and economic forces shaped by capitalism, a system of unequal distribution of wealth. They claim that capitalism depends on particular forms of socialization, in which students are schooled to carry out unequal roles in a stratified work force. As we discuss later in this chapter, some scholars have argued that these larger forces, encapsulated in the industrialist ideology of social efficiency, have determined the purposes, values, and norms that dominate schools, as well as what constitutes school knowledge. The institution of schooling is set up to exert power over teachers, which impedes their ability to construct authority with students. The current standards-based reform movement involves coercive mandates that erode teachers' professional legitimacy and voluntary consent of students.

We also explore later another vital factor in definitions of legitimacy, consent, and the moral order: culture. Many researchers in the last 30 years have brought to life the very different cultural understandings people from different backgrounds have about the meaning of education and how it should take place in schools. Valenzuela (1999) examined this phenomenon and its consequences for Mexican American students.

Our social constructivist orientation indicates that all conceptualizations of authority must be understood as "historical construction(s) shaped by diverse traditions that contain their own values and views of the world. In other words, the concept of authority . . . has no universal meaning just waiting to be discovered" (Giroux, 1986, p. 24). Although we assert the importance of constitutive criteria for authority, we recognize that interpretations of those criteria are variable across individuals, groups, institutions, and historical periods. This finding is quite clear in ground-breaking studies of the social construction of authority in classrooms and schools.

SOCIAL CONSTRUCTION OF AUTHORITY IN CLASSROOMS AND SCHOOLS

Mary Metz: Classrooms and Corridors

The most instructive study of authority in classrooms and schools is Mary Haywood Metz's (1978) classic book, *Classrooms and Corridors: The Crisis of Authority in Desegregated Secondary Schools*. Metz was the first scholar to treat authority as a social construction. Rather than posing universal ideas about authority based on general surveillance of schools, Metz (1978) mapped out the highly variable, complex, and historically situated terrain of interwoven arenas that shape and are shaped by authority relations between teachers and students. She described in detail the moment-to-moment, face-to-face interactions in which authority is constituted. Metz's (1978) thick descriptions and larger analyses emerge from systematic, sociological, ethnographic research. Her work is rooted in social theory and makes major contributions to it, by clearly showing how authority is a relationship jointly constructed by teachers and students through actions that have social and cultural meanings. These relations are connected to the embedded and historically situated contexts of schooling and society. Metz (1978) illustrated how authority is interwoven with other strategies for control in the fabric of classroom life.

Metz's (1978) two research sites, Chauncey and Hamilton, served a large cadre of students from upper middle class families and a population of poorer children many of whom were Black. They were "typical" in that they were structured to offer conventional academic programs, and yet, despite their similarities, there was notable variation in authority relations that could be traced to influences both inside and outside classrooms.

Inside influences included teachers' own conceptions of learning and teaching, the types of authority roles they attempted to establish, the other resources they used to gain control, and their subject matter. As important, if not more important, were students' orientations to schooling; their academic abilities; and sociocultural identities, especially race and social class. External influences included schoolwide factors such as tracking, faculty culture, administrative leadership, and the larger school ethos. Local community and national influences also were crucially important. Both schools were located in a university town at the forefront of the social and political rebellions of the late 1960s. Events within the community coupled with the national political climate had a major impact on authority relations. They certainly affected Chauncey and Hamilton teachers' conceptions of, and approaches to, authority.

Teachers' Conceptions and Approaches. Teachers confronting conflict and contradictory educational ideologies adopted differing approaches to their role. Most were split between what Metz (1978) characterized as *incorporative* and *developmental* approaches. Incorporative teachers tended to be older and more conservative. They viewed the moral order as involving the transmission of standardized content consisting of tried-and-true knowledge, skills, values, and norms. Some invoked the traditional model of *in loco parentis* authority and insisted that students obey simply because they were told to obey. Others relied on legal–rational forms of authority by which students were expected to follow directions as if they were carrying out the orders of a future boss. Developmental teachers were younger and more liberal. They interpreted the moral order as the development of the whole child. Their curriculum was open ended rather than fixed, and they attempted to identify students' prior knowledge, experience, and interests, to make education more relevant. They saw their role as facilitators and responded to students' challenges by explaining how their commands would help them to learn and realize their individual potentials.

Teachers' conceptions and approaches were also very much affected by tracking systems. Tracking is the common practice in secondary schools of placing students in differentiated classes and programs based on academic ability and vocational orientation. The practice not only has had enormous implications for curriculum and instruction, but it also has greatly affected the manner in which teachers attempt to position themselves as authority figures.

Tracking. In Metz's (1978) study, student attitudes and teachers' approaches toward authority differed significantly by track level. Low-track students generally accepted the conditions of authority but found school irrelevant and expressed antagonistic attitudes through physical disruptions. High-track students had specific ideas about how schooling ought to be conducted. They were generally invested in learning yet verbally challenged teachers whom they regarded as incompetent or as fair game for intellectual one-upmanship. Teachers were more controlling in low-track classes, giving students individual seatwork that made academic performance private, highly structured, and unchallenging though safe for those students who were academically insecure. They were more discussion based in their approach with high-track classes, and they created with those more confident students an intense yet open atmosphere.

Regardless of their differences in approaches, teachers in both schools confronted what Metz (1978) described as a "crisis in authority." This crisis, which is still felt today in many schools, was fueled at Chauncey and Hamilton by race, policy, and faculty cultures.

Race, Policy, and Faculty Culture.   The crisis of authority had its origins in the conflicting demands of maintaining order and promoting engagement among young adolescents, but it was fueled in the 1960s by the protests of university youth and mounting racial conflict. Desegregation brought Black and White public school students together in places where racial integration had never been tried before. Interracial tensions flared in the spring of 1968 when Martin Luther King was assassinated. Instances of student disorder increased and became quite apparent at Hamilton, where the facility was much larger and teachers' approaches to authority varied. At Chauncey, underlying currents of student anger and resistance were hidden from view, mostly because faculty members presented a united front. Teachers who experienced difficulties in their classrooms were reluctant to admit they were having problems, because the school culture was such that they would have been blamed. The crisis was thus hidden behind a façade of apparent orderliness. However, as other groundbreaking researchers describe in their research, crises may be much more apparent in schools and not as easy to hide.

Other Groundbreaking Studies

Whereas Metz (1978) examined authority within the confines of conventional schools, Ann Swidler (1979) studied Group High, a free school that enrolled mostly White middle-class students, and Ethnic High, which served racially diverse low-income and working-class students. Faculty and administrators were influenced by the ideological belief that teacher domination and student subordination interferes with meaningful education and the realization of a just, democratic society. They deliberately eliminated formal authority. Rather than giving direct commands or imposing professional expertise, teachers relied on their personal influence and charisma with the hope of forging closer ties with students.

Although this shift gave students more freedom to express themselves and participate in democratic decision making, it also put teachers in highly tenuous positions. Students, especially those at Ethnic High, put up resistance because they felt their easygoing teachers were failing to do their jobs. Teachers found that personal appeals were the only strategies available to gain students' cooperation in the pursuit of educational goals. "The effect of [these strategies]," Swidler (1979) explained, "was to put a tremendous premium on a teacher's ability to make himself charming, interesting, or glamorous enough so that intimacy would be an enticing reward" (p. 66). Teachers became exhausted to the point where they literally resigned from their jobs.

These groundbreaking studies from the late 1960s and early 1970s show the critical importance of examining, through the lens of authority (or the lack of it), the complex dynamics of classroom relations and their multiple and inter-related influences. Metz's (1978) and Swidler's (1979) work shows that research on authority must be historically situated. Grant's (1988) book, *The World We Created at Hamilton High*, carries this endeavor forward, again by examining challenges to authority in a desegregated high school during the 1970s and 1980s. He argued that the identification of schools as responsible for social inequalities resulted in a general loss of trust and consent. Traditional authority gave way to more bureaucratic forms. Teachers who could no longer depend on unquestioned obedience and who were unprepared for a racially diverse population found themselves in a predicament as their legitimacy was questioned. The decline in the 1960s and 1970s of the teaching profession's status, and of adult status more generally, contributed to this. Teachers tried to win students' cooperation with their personality and offers of friendship. Weakened authority led to a less moral and intellectual school ethos. In this book Grant advocated for the importance of authority:

> The teacher must have a capacity for engendering trust and an ability to engage in the creative confrontation that is at the heart of all good teaching. She must have the courage to make demands on a student, to insist that he rewrite the same paragraph until it begins to make sense and do work that is often difficult from him—and sometimes boring. (p. 143)

Although he, too, explained that families, policy, and culture influence authority, he placed the greatest responsibility on teachers' character.

Pace (1998, 2003a, 2003b, 2003c, chap. 4, this volume) has studied the social construction of authority relations and their connection to academic engagement in four classes in an ethnically diverse metropolitan high school. While building on Metz's (1978) study of authority in crisis during the late 1960s, 30 years later Pace has found that overt exercise and questioning of authority has given way to indirect assertions and challenges. Correspondingly, teachers now use a broader array of strategies, such as politeness, humor, and grade inflation, to maintain generally cooperative yet ambiguous relationships in which discord lies beneath the surface. Also different from the distinct teacher roles Metz (1978) found, Pace (2003c) observed that teachers manage conflicts between order and engagement as well as between maintaining standards and appeasing students by using hybridized forms of authority that mix traditional, bureaucratic, and professional roles while masking authority with the semblance of egalitarianism. There are enormous pressures placed on teachers that stem from challenges such as heterogeneous yet tracked classes, unattended gaps in teachers' curricular expertise, tension between competitive and egalitarian values, and the press for positive rapport. Teachers use various strategies to deal with these challenges, but they often produce ambiguous expectations; compromise serious involvement with subject matter; and exacerbate ambivalence toward schooling, especially for marginalized (e.g., lower track, lower income, and Black) students. The status quo is maintained as teachers feel they are more or less in control, accomplishing curricular goals, and popular with their students. This mix reflects varied and sometimes conflicting cultural ideas that are further complicated by ideologies that inform teachers' actions.

COMPETING IDEOLOGIES
IN A CONTRADICTORY CULTURE

Another reason why authority is difficult to pin down is the influence of competing ideologies shaped by contradictory commitments to individual freedom and community cohesion (Bellah, Madsen, Sulllivan, Swidler, & Tipton, 1985; Franklin, 1986; Page, 1991). Americans view authority as dangerous to individual rights yet also as necessary for a unified society. Ideological debates over authority began to grow in intensity in the late 1960s and early 1970s as a result of social, cultural, and political turmoil.

Christopher Hurn (1985) laid out the ideological camps promoting differing kinds of authority, which, as Metz (1978) showed, are linked to differing conceptions of education. He explained that, until the 1960s, teachers were expected to be traditional authority figures who fulfilled the role of *in loco parentis* and enjoyed wide discretion and scope in overseeing their charges. Although the days of absolute order in the classroom is a myth, society did not question the traditional legitimacy of teachers. A dramatic ideological shift occurred in the 1960s when the civil rights movement, women's liberation, protests against the Vietnam war, court cases supporting students' rights, and other calls to question authority facilitated the impact of liberal education reformers on schooling nationwide.

These progressive educators were heavily influenced by the philosophy of John Dewey (1899, 1916, 1938), who promoted a model of education premised on the belief that students become more engaged in meaningful learning if their individual interests and real life experiences are reflected in the curriculum. Concerned with both the individual and the society, he explained that educational growth and social progress are best fostered by practices that encourage moral and intellectual autonomy as well as joint inquiry. Dewey also argued that schools should create democratic communities. Progressive educators following Dewey denounced traditional authority relations in classrooms because they stifle individual growth; stymie democratic processes; and may be abusive and discriminatory, especially for students from poor and minority backgrounds (Hurn, 1985; Kohl, 1967; Silberman, 1970) Like Dewey, they have eschewed the enforcement of social control through overt disciplinary practices or the imposition of fixed dogmas. The progressive ideal is for classroom authority relations to be more democratic as teachers assume the role of "natural authorities" who offer guidance to students through their experience, wisdom, and care (Dewey, 1938). Many liberal educationists have focused on the importance of individual rights, which were supported by court decisions granting freedom of expression and due process to students (see Arum, 2003). Others have argued that educative authority at its best was an extension of a moral democratic community (Benne, 1938, 1970, 1986).

Radical reformers comprised another ideological camp. They argued that public schools, instead of being complicit in forms of social control and indoctrination that perpetuate social injustice, should promote curricula and relations that were liberating, to create a more just and humane society. Variations of these themes appear in writings of critical theorists, such as neo-Marxists, feminists, postmodernists, and other radical educational thinkers. Neo-Marxists in the 1970s equated traditional classroom authority with repressive domination and the reproduction of socioeconomic inequalities in a capitalist society. Bowles and Gintis (1976) claimed that there is a correspondence between hierarchical public school classroom relations and unequal divisions of labor in the workplace. Working-class students are relegated to lower track classes where foreman-like teachers socialize them into blue collar occupations. Middle-class students are placed in upper track classes where teachers essentially prepare them for high-status positions of authority. Bowles and Gintis argued for more egalitarian relations in which authority is continually questioned.

Paulo Freire's work (1970, 1998; Friere & Shor, 1987) with oppressed peasants in Brazil has been a major source of inspiration to critical educators in the United States. The crucial idea is that teachers empower students by diffusing authority in a manner that turns learning into a two-way process of knowledge construction rather than a one-way banking system of information depositing. Teachers and students educate each other as they work together to achieve social justice.

Feminists have produced extensions and revisions of critical theory about authority. Some believe teachers should facilitate consciousness raising to heighten awareness of and deconstruct patriarchal authority structures that sustain gender, racial, ethnic, class, and other social inequalities (Sarachild, 1975; Tetreault & Maher, 1994). Friedman (1985), Ellsworth (1989), and Luke (1996) have argued against critical and feminist pedagogies that encourage elimination of authority, stating that, for women, giving up authority feeds into sexist notions of what is feminine. They encourage women teachers to reclaim their professional authority while simultaneously challenging patriarchal positions of power. Noddings (1992) promoted an ethic of care by which teachers develop trusting relationships with students over years of working with them, sharing learning experiences, and having dialogue. Control should be relaxed so that students can exercise some choice over what they want to learn, and the development of caring people and communities should be at the center of education.

Postmodernism, poststructuralism, and other "post-" paradigmatic movements began to infiltrate educational scholarship in the 1990s. Many adherents embrace Foucault's (1977, 1979, 1980) contention that individual thought and action and human relations are circumscribed by discourses that normalize domination through authority relations and knowledge. (Here, authority is seen as part of a system of coercive, if not overt, power.) Lather (1991) encouraged teachers to implement pedagogies that combine critical reflection with practice, which is called *praxis*. This involves an analysis and deconstruction of classroom authority. The reconstituted relations that emerge between classroom participants are participatory, dialogic, and pluralistic; antihierarchical; and conducive to the decentering of typically unquestioned power and knowledge.

Although radical perspectives, which emphasize consciousness-raising and egalitarianism, are intellectually and morally tantalizing, interest in them has been largely limited to scholars and graduate students. Critical scholarship has not had much impact on K–12 public school reform or—for that matter, everyday classroom authority relations. When radical recommendations are applied, it is usually in college classes taught by professors who have the autonomy and favorable conditions to try out pedagogical alternatives (Ellsworth, 1989; Shor, 1996). At the same time, the cultural value placed on equality has encouraged a desire for classroom structures and relations that appear to be egalitarian (Pace, 2003b; Page, 1991).[2]

---

[2]Egalitarianism is a factor in anti-intellectualism (see Hofstadter, 1963) and is examined in Pace's (2003a, 2003b, 2003c) and Page's (1987, 1991) work.

Hurn (1985) pointed out how ideological debates inadvertently interfered with empirical sociological investigations of authority during the late 1970s and early 1980s. According to Hurn, this gap in research was filled by conservative educational thinkers such as Adelson (1981), Ravitch (1985), and Wynne (1981). They blamed increased deviance and lowered achievement in U.S. high schools, documented in the National Commission on Excellence in Education's alarming 1983 report, *A Nation at Risk*, on schools' abdication of authority. Hurn contended that, in actuality, as a result of ideological debates and the societal transformations of the 1960s, the moral order of schools became uncertain. Disagreement over what should constitute curriculum, pedagogy, and relations between adults and youth weakened school community and increased student detachment.

Although Hurn (1985) offered an illuminating and fascinating analysis of historical influences on school authority, he did not discuss the most dominant ideology in U.S. schools: social efficiency. This ideology emerged in the 1920s from the principles of scientific management and encouraged modeling schools after factories (Callahan, 1962; Kliebard, 1986, 1992). Teachers were expected to exercise impersonal forms of bureaucratic authority to achieve outcomes through the enforcement of practices that were based on the rational values of industrialization, such as efficiency and standardization. Students were expected to obey in exchange for credentials, much the same way as workers earn their wages.

The social efficiency model prevailed until the 1960s, when experiments with progressive education became popular. It regained its dominance in the 1980s in reaction to nationwide concern over educational outcomes, especially in high schools. Critical scholars such as Linda McNeil (1981, 1986) have written about the effects of increased bureaucratic control in schools, which include the undermining of teachers' professional legitimacy and the disengagement of students in response to a curriculum stripped of depth, controversy, and individuality. In the last several years, the social efficiency model has had a growing impact. Politicians and policymakers at the federal, state, and local levels of government proposed reforms intended to improve student achievement through accountability measures tied to standardized testing. Enthusiasm for these reforms grew in major political parties and eventually led to the passage of the No Child Left Behind Law of 2001. This law reinforces bureaucratic (legal–rational) forms of authority, in which students, teachers, and administrators are held accountable for test scores through positive and negative sanctions.

Giroux (1986, 1988) has critiqued both conservative and critical thinkers and asserted that the debate over the relationship between schooling and authority indicates a retreat from democracy:

Conservatives celebrate authority, linking it to popular expressions of everyday life, but in doing so they express and support reactionary and undemocratic interests. On the other hand, radical educators tend to equate authority with forms of domination or the loss of freedom and consequently fail to develop a conceptual category for constructing a programmatic language of hope and struggle. . . . Liberals, in general, provide the most dialectical view of authority but fail to apply it in a concrete way so as to interrogate the dynamics of domination and freedom as they are expressed within the asymmetrical relations of power and privilege that characterize various aspects of school life. (1988, pp. 78–79)

Giroux (1988) puts forth a vision of "emancipatory authority" that "expresses a democratic conception of collective life . . . embodied in an ethic of solidarity, social transformation, and an imaginative vision of citizenship" (p. 72). Schools are places where teachers are engaged in "critical, intellectual practice related to the issues, problems, concerns, and experiences of everyday life" and students learn and engage in collective struggle for economic, political, and social justice (p. 89).

Giroux (1988) pointed out that, although seductive in its appeal to ideals, scholarship on authority largely based on ideology does not acknowledge the complexities of everyday life in schools; neither does it guide K–12 teachers in improving their practice. Although ideological writings may not be based on empirical investigations or grounded in sound theoretical conceptions of authority, they do highlight the striking diversity of interpretations people have of what authority means, how it should be practiced, and whether or how it ought to be resisted.

AUTHORITY IS DYNAMIC, CONFLICTUAL, AND NEGOTIATED

Universal Tensions

Social scientists studying life in schools from the 1930s to the 1970s make clear the contradictory structural tensions that make classroom authority a phenomenon that, ironically, is difficult to control. The differing interests of youth culture and adult culture, compulsory school attendance, and the unequal status of teachers and students necessitates social control and simultaneously generates conflict, including challenges to authority (Bidwell, 1970; Jackson, 1968; Waller, 1932/1961). Waller (1932/1961) characterized the school as a "despotism in a state of perilous equilibrium" (p. 10), meaning that an entrenched hierarchy of authority and power exists in a precarious balance with the ever-present potential for rebellion from within and pressures from without.

Studies of the sociology of schooling make fundamental generalizations about classroom authority. For example, paradoxically, teachers must fulfill responsibilities that both create and threaten authority; for example, they must both maintain order and foster students' engagement in learning. These "twin tasks" (Metz, 1978) often are in conflict. Jackson (1968) observed that teachers are children's "first boss" as they socialize them to complete assigned work, curb their movements, and follow rules. Bidwell (1970) and Dreeben (1968) have explained that teachers must evaluate, discipline, and keep students on task and at the same time win students' emotional attachment and keep them happy in order to gain cooperation and pursue educational goals. It is important to note that there are developmental influences on authority relations. Children seeking the approval of adults are characterized by their docility (Henry, 1963) and "institutional innocence" (Metz, 1978), whereas adolescents are more "sophisticated clients," often questioning adult authority and likely to band with their peers in opposition to the teacher when conflict arises (Bidwell, 1970). So, tensions over authority increase with older students, who are more concerned than younger ones with gaining power, peer acceptance, and status. Just as teachers size up their students, adolescents become adept at "sussing out the teacher"—figuring out who the teacher is both professionally and personally, and what minor acts of rebellion will be tolerated or not (Delamont, 1983, p. 100). (In some cultures, the peer group is especially key at all ages; see D'Amato, 1993.)

Studies of high schools conducted in the wake of *A Nation at Risk* explain teachers' management of these classic tensions as winning the cooperation of adolescent students through "bargains," "treaties," "compromises," and other forms of exchange (Powell et al., 1985; Sedlak et al., 1986; Sizer, 1984). Good behavior is gained by doling out good grades, treating students as friendly equals, and minimizing demands (Sedlak et al., 1986, p. 106). The analyses in these studies postulate that because schools have become so large, diverse, and consumer oriented, and because U.S. society has become increasingly egalitarian as well as individualistic, teachers are pressured to accommodate individual needs and wants in order to remain popular (Cusick, 1983). Inhospitable conditions, such as school size, fragmentation, and bureaucratization make it extremely difficult for teachers to be professional experts; minimizing demands of students and of themselves is a way to cope (Sizer, 1984).

These classic high school studies contribute to the understanding that classroom relations are negotiations between teachers and students that may devolve into tactics for peaceable coexistence at the cost of serious involvement in education. Yet they lack explicit discussion of authority, suggesting that it no longer exists and has been replaced by exchange. An important exception is Grant's (1988) study of a desegregated high school, in which he applied sociological theory to explain the dilemmas faced by a school experiencing racial conflict, a weakening of its moral order, and an undermining of teachers' legitimacy. He described the effects of rampant individualism in which education in a particular school becomes bureaucratic and legalistic and erodes in moral character but then reconstructs itself through dialogue among teachers about the intellectual and moral purposes of public schooling in a democratic society. Grant's narrative is compelling; however, his work blurs the lines among advocacy, journalism, and ethnography.

Another issue with many studies, even when they do analyze relations through the lens of authority, is their universal versus particularistic approach to analysis, which omits discussion of specific schools and their communities. Along with Metz (1978) and Swidler (1979), both Grant (1988) and Lightfoot (1983) have shown that the nested contexts of schooling—including the school's particular ethos—are crucial in shaping teachers' legitimacy and the quality of classroom relations. Authority must be understood by examining up close the intricacies of classroom relations, in particular settings with distinctive cultures, taking into account the complex set of interacting variables that shape these relations.

AUTHORITY IS VARIABLE AND SHAPED BY MULTIPLE, INTERACTING CONTEXTUAL FACTORS

Sociocultural Identities and Differing Perspectives on Schooling

Teachers' authority relations with students are influenced by sociocultural factors that play out within, yet extend well beyond, the classroom. There is a wealth of qualitative research on the experiences of students representing groups that historically have been marginalized from mainstream (White, middle-class, male-dominated) schooling. A major purpose of this work is to explain underachievement and resistance among certain groups, including African Americans, Latinos, Hawaiians, Native Americans, and students from low-income families. We find that the implication of much of this research is that these issues are related to problems of authority due to racial and/or socioeconomic inequality, cultural conflicts and/or misunderstandings between teachers and students, and/or the school system's lack of legitimacy for subordinated groups. Researchers contributing to this line of inquiry usually concentrate on social class, ethnicity, or race.

Studies focused on social class and influenced by neo-Marxist theory argue that resistance of low-income students expresses a rejection of middle-class values and cynicism about what schooling in a capitalist society has to offer them (Anyon, 1983; Brantlinger, 1993; MacLeod, 1987; Stinchcombe, 1964; Willis, 1977). It is ironic that opposition to school authority has long-term consequences for students' life chances. Paul Willis's (1977) classic study described how working-class "lads" in England purposefully undermined classroom and school authority, created their own subculture, and unwittingly contributed to the foreclosure of their own socioeconomic mobility by cutting themselves off from middle-class opportunities.

John Ogbu's (1974, 1978, 1987, 1991) work, which has spearheaded many studies, focuses on race and links it to social class. Ogbu posited that Black students and other members of "involuntary minority groups" forced to become part of American society through slavery or conquest often oppose schooling in reaction to the perceived disparity between the upward mobility promised by American schooling and lack of occupational success due to job ceilings. According to Ogbu (1987, 1991, 2003), many Black students, in response to a long history of racism, have developed a collective oppositional identity and adopted coping strategies that have fostered a "low-effort syndrome." Fordham and Ogbu (1986) asserted that Black students have internalized a collective Black identity, which they express by resisting conventional classroom norms, including those related to authority relations. They see compliance to these norms as "acting White" and therefore a betrayal of Black culture and familial values. Fordham's (1996) later analysis importantly identifies marked ambivalence toward schooling among Black students, because they and their parents may perceive school achievement as a necessary step toward success; this is consistent with the findings of Metz (1978) and Pace (chap. 4, this volume).

Several researchers have based their analyses on Ogbu's central ideas but have argued that his classification of "voluntary" and "involuntary minorities" is simplistic, encourages stereotypes, and is unsupported by adequate empirical data (Trueba, 1988). For example, Lee's (1996) research breaks open the "model minority" stereotype that assumes that Asian American students—"voluntary minorities" in Ogbu's model—are "successful in school because they work hard and come from cultures that believe in the value of education" (p. 52) by uncovering differing orientations among groups typically lumped together. And Suarez-Orozco and Suarez-Orozco (1995) showed that an analysis of students' orientations requires attention to immigrant status and change over time. They found that confidence in formal education as the path to social mobility and a sense of moral responsibility to be academically successful is strong for Mexican and first-generation Mexican American youth but decreases for second- and third-generation students. The deflation of achievement motivation seems to correspond to experiences with racism and unrealized aspirations in the United States, as well as to the influence of ambivalence toward authority and schooling among youth native to the United States.

Other research, spanning 40 years, has investigated teachers' complicity in the reproduction of socioeconomic and racial inequalities (see Irvine, 1990; Leacock, 1969; Lipman, 1998; Rist, 1970). Research has shown that in classrooms composed largely of students from low-income and, often, Black or Latino families, teachers tend to operate on the *deficit model,* which blames low achievement on problems located in students' families and home cultures. With the view that students are less capable, they emphasize rigid control and use a routinized curriculum, which is accompanied by lowered academic expectations and restricted opportunities for learning. Anyon (1983), in a study of fifth-grade classes in different schools, found that teachers in a working-class school were socializing students to accept lower status roles in the stratified workforce of capitalist society. Rather than be passive absorbers of these lessons, students actively rejected them. In her neo-Marxist analysis, Anyon referred to this phenomenon as a "*conflict* relationship with capital," in which teachers abused authority by being rigid and mean, and students fought back by misbehaving. She showed how authority relations and curricula differed in their subordination or empowerment of students across schools, depending on social class status.

Another explanation for authority problems is *cultural discontinuity,* a phenomenon that has been explored by educational anthropologists who trace classroom conflicts to misunderstandings over what constitutes culturally appropriate classroom roles, norms, and discourse (Ballenger, 1992; Delpit, 1995; Erickson, 1987; Heath, 1983; McDermott, 1977; Philips, 1982; Vogt, Jordan, & Tharp, 1993). The teachers in these studies typically represent White, middle-class, mainstream society and unknowingly communicate in ways that may actually undermine authority. Delpit (1995) and Heath (1983) have revealed that liberal White teachers, who may be trying to diminish the power difference between themselves and students to create a more democratic tone, tend to be indirect in their commands, whereas Black children expect adults to authoritatively assert their expectations. Heath (1983) showed how not only communication but also the physical and temporal structure of elementary school classrooms are based on cultural assumptions not shared by many students, which may lead to apparent disobedience. Vogt et al. (1993) presented the case of improved relations due to the use of culturally relevant practices, such as co-educational, multiage group work, in the Kamehameha Early Education Program with native Hawaiian students. They juxtaposed this success with a case of damaged relations when these same practices were applied with Navajo students, because of the conflicts with Navajo culture.

Erickson (1986) stated that authority is a political relationship involving persuasion and power. Conflicts are especially volatile, and undermine legitimacy and the ability to persuade, when teachers impose the power of mainstream culture and imply that it is superior to the home cultures of students (Erickson, 1987; Fordham, 1996). An example is continual insistence on the use of standardized English and prohibition of other languages and dialects. Valenzuela's (1999) concept of "subtractive schooling" is based on an investigation of the negative impact of cultural domination combined with teachers' low expectations and lack of caring for Mexican American youth, which led to profound alienation and opposition—not to education, but to schooling. Valenzuela's theoretical model explains how schools' assimilation practices take away essential resources, such as language and cultural norms and values that constitute students' social capital, or supportive social networks. Structures such as tracking contribute to relegation of students to lower status and constraints on their educational opportunities. Teachers do not understand Mexican conceptions of education. Valenzuela argued that school personnel perceive Mexican American students as defiant or apathetic, but these students are actually searching for caring relationships with teachers as a basis for engagement in learning. The school is failing them, as it closes off motivation and opportunities for academic achievement.

Investigations of the influence of students' sociocultural identities on their orientations toward schooling and on discriminatory approaches and structures in schools have shed much light on factors that influence authority relations in classrooms with historically marginalized students. There are, however, several issues raised by much of this research. First, there has been an emphasis on resistance so that the highly negotiable nature of classroom authority relations and the ambivalence that is so prevalent among students has often been slighted or ignored. A welcome addition is more recent research that examines attachment to schooling among students from marginalized groups (see Hemmings, 1996; O'Connor, 1997). More studies are needed that examine racial and socioeconomic privilege as influences on classroom authority. Another issue is that discussions sometimes conflate race, class, and ethnicity and conclude with group generalizations that diminish variation and complexity while reinforcing stereotyping. Many studies address one aspect of identity to the exclusion of others, even though intersections among race, class, and gender as well as other factors matter greatly. It is important to note that student groups express elements of both consent and resistance to the dominant school order (McCarthy, 1990). Davidson (1996) found that high school students enacted identities that were fluid, changing from one context to another, and shaped by school structures such as tracking, disciplinary policies, and teachers and other school personnel. Students were constantly veering between normalizing discourses and identities that caused them to be in opposition to, in harmony with, and/or in constructive play with teachers' expectations, and teachers, for their part, were constantly trying to adapt to what students did. These findings speak to the dynamic complexity of authority.

Although these studies bear vital implications for authority, they most often do not explicitly address it; even when they do, it is undertheorized. The researchers tacitly speak to and even expand perspectives on the essential elements of legitimacy, consent, and the moral order, but they rarely bring conceptualizations of authority to bear in their work. Studies of classroom relations are needed that consider the multiple, interacting influences of sociocultural factors as well as of the classroom *and* that work from theoretically grounded conceptualizations of authority.

Curriculum, Tracking, School Culture, and Variations on the Moral Order

Authority is situated in the nested contexts of the school. Within the classroom, it shapes and is shaped by the enactment of *curriculum*, which is a translation of the school's moral order. Different subject matters are generally taught in different ways; for example, mathematics lessons are usually highly structured, with definitively right or wrong answers, as opposed to English lessons, which involve open-ended discussion and interpretation (Stodolsky, 1988). Because of curricular parameters, in the former, teachers tend to be more directive, and in the latter they tend to be more facilitative.

Another interrelated factor in classroom authority is *tracking:* the division of students into differentiated courses of study. Authority in lower track classes has often been described as especially problematic because of the students' oppositional attitudes toward schooling and teachers' negative attitudes toward these classes (Metz, 1978; Oakes, 1985; Page, 1991). Oakes's (1985) study indicated that difficulties may be exacerbated because of the disproportionately high representation of low-income and minority students in the lower tracks, which tends to trigger deficit model responses in teachers. Like Metz (1978), Oakes showed that teachers also have more intellectual goals for high-track classes and emphasize compliance with low-track classes, for which they have low academic expectations. Students respond in kind, with involvement and passivity, respectively. The control of knowledge may also evoke resistance as teachers' simplistic and rigid presentation of curriculum in low-track classes conflicts with students' knowledge (see Keddie, 1971).

Reba Page (1991) explained that the relationship between track level and classroom climate and relations depends on school values, attitudes toward tracking, and the significant role that teachers play in translating the school's moral order. For example, when a school is focused on high-achieving students and teachers are unclear about their role in lower track classes, the classroom atmosphere, including the exercise of authority, is marked by ambiguity. Depending on school context, lower track classes may be regimented or chaotic. These classes may also be understood as a caricature of regular classes in which teachers seem to flee from establishing authority based on legitimacy and moral purpose (Page, 1987). As Page (1991) showed, generalizing about tracking can obscure understanding its complexity. There is also a need to examine the variability of authority relationships within classrooms that are academically, as well as socioculturally, heterogeneous (see chap. 5, this volume.)

Studies point to the important role that school culture plays in the construction of authority (Grant, 1988; Lightfoot, 1983; Metz, 1978; Rutter, Maughan, Mortimore, & Ouston, 1979). In her study of six good high schools, Sara Lawrence Lightfoot (1983) examined the links between school ethos and faculty culture and authority. In all six schools, which range from public to private and from urban to suburban, there are clear standards for behavior, so a safe and orderly environment is maintained. These schools are strong communities, with a coherent set of values. Teachers are unafraid of and caring toward students, who are granted autonomy and adult status. In general, teachers are viewed as the "critical educational authorities; the ones who will guide the learning, growth, and development of students most closely" (Lightfoot, 1983, p. 334).

Other researchers have found a growing crisis of respect for authority, especially in poor urban schools (Devine, 1996; Hemmings, 2003; Plank, McDill, McPartland, & Jordan, 2001). In her study of seniors in two public urban high schools, Hemmings (2003) observed blatant expressions of disrespect among teachers and students, influenced by opposing discourses of mainstream respectability and streetwise reputation. A basic understanding of, and willingness to grapple with, the discourses and understandings that governed respect were missing from the consciousness of both teachers and administrators in these urban, socioculturally diverse environments. Hemmings (chap. 6, this volume) extends this analysis by comparing the very different moral orders of two schools in very different settings.

The Wider Community, Educational System, and American Culture

The surrounding community plays an important role in shaping authority in schools and classrooms (Grant, 1988; Metz, 1978; Schwartz, 1987). Schwartz's (1987) ethnography describes the moral cultures of communities that vary on the basis of location, social class, and ethnicity, and how these cultures influence authority. For example, in a cosmopolitan community—attached to the mainstream instrumental symbols of hierarchy, performance, and individualism—"youth are less receptive to communal forms of authority than their provincial counterparts" (Schwartz, 1987, p. 279). Adolescents feel great pressure to compete academically to achieve future success but lack examples of moral authority. Although schools as local institutions attempt to fit the culture of their communities (Schwartz, 1987), mainstream cosmopolitan values have greatly influenced the national educational climate.

Classroom authority relationships are influenced by the institution of schooling, where most decision making is beyond the control of teachers (Nyberg & Farber, 1986, p. 4). The exclusion of teachers from decisions about space, class size, scheduling, textbooks, budgets, testing, and many other conditions undercuts authority within the classroom. Another factor involves the larger values and purposes of schooling in American society during particular historical periods. In the early 1980s, Grant (1981) claimed that schools and society have become more legalistic and consumer oriented and less concerned with the quality of educational experiences and the integrity of intellectual and moral character. Fifteen years later, Labaree (1997) argued that social mobility for individuals has replaced two other traditional educational aims—development of democratic citizens and preparation of a stratified workforce—as the major goal of schooling. His assertion that schooling has subsequently become a private consumer good rather than a process that serves the public good suggests that the basis for authority has deteriorated. Critical scholars such as McNeil (2000) argue that the current emphasis on raising test scores has undermined more substantive educational purposes and the quality of classroom curricula and relationships. Public school teachers in the midst of No Child Left Behind reforms are feeling enormous pressure to link curriculum and teaching practices to test scores. McNeil and other critics of standards-based reform warn that teachers will be forced to teach in ways that essentially puts them into the role of production-line supervisors who make sure that students produce good test scores even if it means curtailing instruction that is more conducive for fostering intellectual growth (see chap. 2, this volume).

Schools in the United States are situated in a culture shaped by paradoxical commitments to community, egalitarianism, competition, and individual freedom (Bellah et al., 1985; Page, 1991). Individualism is especially central and contributes to Americans' general ambivalence toward authority. According to Bellah et al. (1985), "anything that would violate our right to think for ourselves, judge for ourselves, make our own decisions, live our lives as we see fit, is not only morally wrong, it is sacrilegious" (p. 142). People are expected to make their own judgments and decisions rather than go along with external controls. However, American culture is marked by individualism and conformity (Riesman, 1950), and U.S. politics in the past and present reveal Americans' attraction to strong authority figures who they believe will take care of them (Sennett, 1980).

The Teacher

Related perhaps to the search for strong authority figures, many assume that the most important factor in classroom authority is the teacher. Spady (1974) and Mitchell and Spady (1983) separated the four classic sources of legitimacy into two categories: (a) institutional and (b) personal. Traditional and bureaucratic legitimacy depend on the teacher's position within the school, whereas charisma and expertise are personal qualities of the teacher. Mitchell and Spady argue that, in contrast to power, authority is based on the ability of teachers to gain respect and trust and establish rapport by helping students develop feelings of worth, intimacy, security, and adequacy within the classroom (p. 1983, p. 30). Spady and Mitchell's (1979) contention about the importance of personal over positional legitimacy, although not substantiated by empirical investigation, has been supported by later scholars (Delpit, 1995; Grant, 1988). However, the term *personal* may be misleading, particularly when referring to professional expertise, which the authors describe as knowledge of subject matter and pedagogy. Indeed, Shulman's (1987) and Grossman's (1990) constructions of teacher knowledge carefully delineate the many professional categories and criteria that constitute expertise. Classroom authority and its various claims to legitimacy are rooted in the institution of schooling. Also, researchers have shown that when teachers largely rely on charismatic personality to create affective bonds needed to win cooperation, they may play the role of "buddy" (Henry, 1963) or "entertainer" (Pace, 2003b), and relations may slip from authority to influence.

In addition to the teacher's legitimacy, scholars as early as Willard Waller (1932/1961) have delineated other characteristics that influence authority:

> Age, social background, physical characteristics, dress, manners, manner, attitude toward students and subject matter, voice, expression of features, tempo of reactions, range of mental personality, and the nature of the organization of the personality (in which are included such factors as complexity, stability, etc.). (p. 212)

Hansen (1993) explained that teachers' styles (including gestures, body movements, facial expressions, and tones of voice) express moral standards that have an impact on students. From intensive observation in classrooms, he found that teachers adjusted their approach to students depending on the age group; for example, they were more directive with 9th graders than with 12th graders, but their everyday classroom habits remained consistent. He presented portraits of three teachers, showing how their styles convey moral expectations and foster particular kinds of relations with students.

While very different, all three cultivate "dispositions of commitment and involvement that help make it possible to take oneself, others and learning seriously" (Hansen, 1993, p. 417). Hansen argued, and we concur, that teachers' expressive style and its impact on classroom life is not often studied and merits further investigation.

Some studies illustrate how individual teachers adjust their approach—including curriculum—to foster more meaningful engagement of students from traditionally marginalized backgrounds (Dillon, 1989; Edelsky, 1983; Noblit, 1993). Oyler (1996) showed how a European American teacher from the suburbs dramatically changed her approach with poor, urban Mexican American, Puerto Rican, and African American first-graders by "sharing authority" with students. The teacher followed rather than controlled students' initiations in book discussions and other activities. Where these initiations would in many other cases have been treated as digressions from the educational agenda, they were encouraged as positive ways for children to help direct the process and content of lessons with their suggestions, questions, and contributions. Students were able to bring their knowledge to bear in ways that challenged the authority of texts and, occasionally, that of their teacher. Oyler contended that the sharing of authority, instead of undermining the teacher's authority, actually strengthened it.[3]

Metz (1978) concluded that the most important requirement for students' commitment to learning is that they see a purpose to it. Purposes may range from wanting to please a teacher to pursuing their intellectual interests, or students may trust teachers that their assignments will be valuable later on in life. For those students who do not see any purpose to schooling, teachers must build links between worthwhile goals and the values and interests of the students. The more skeptical students are, the more a developmental approach—with relatively open-ended goals, reciprocal teacher–student relationships, and motivating curricula and pedagogy—is needed to gain trust and cooperation. To be effective with this approach requires serious commitment and competence on the part of teachers. Other researchers also have discussed the important connection between intrinsically motivating curricula and pedagogy and students' consent to their teachers (D'Amato, 1993; Ladson-Billings, 1994). Metz (1978) also observed that conflicts between teachers and students over the nature

---

[3] Oyler's study presented—indeed, promoted—a progressive approach to authority with low-income students of color. However, her conclusions are limited in terms of generalizations because they are based on data gathered in a first grade classroom where children were developmentally predisposed to cooperate with adults. Additionally, Oyler's conceptualization of authority differs from sociological theory. In our view, authority is not a possession that can be shared. The teacher can welcome students' input and allow them some control, but first graders cannot claim legitimacy in the Weberian sense; neither would they be allowed to take charge without the teachers' backing.

of their relationships are not so much about different views of classroom authority but rather the perception on the part of students that teachers are defaulting on their obligation to establish a "relationship of *any* kind of authority" (p. 123). Students want teachers to take their education seriously and to treat them respectfully and fairly.

Implications for Future Research, Policy, and Practice

Understanding classroom authority as a social construction bears strong implications for future research, practice, and policy. First, we contend that many more theoretically grounded, ethnographic studies are needed to explore differing interpretations and enactments of classroom relationships, legitimacy, and the moral order of schooling. These studies should examine not only the mix of sociocultural and school-based factors that contribute to these variations but also forces on schooling that are undergoing dramatic changes, such as increasing sociocultural and linguistic diversity among students, standards-based reform, and attempts at privatization. Researchers should ask where is authority located within the local, state, and federal institutional contexts of schooling and how is it related to power within those contexts. Along with this, how is the definition of the teacher, and the teaching profession, changing, and how does this bear on classroom authority? New studies of classroom authority are vital in the face of forceful changes in our system of schooling and society, including what may be termed a current crisis of authority in the United States sparked by the September 11th terrorist attacks. In an attempt to reassure ourselves that authority exists, are we more accepting of coercion in the form of zero-tolerance policies, suppression of political dissent, and constraints on teaching and learning as well as on educational research?

Regarding practice, the construction of authority relations that promote students' learning and well-being requires teacher expertise as the strongest basis of legitimacy. Teachers who know their subject matter, are skilled pedagogues, believe in the potential of all learners, and are able to relate caringly and work well with students from different backgrounds are crucial. Teachers must also be clear about their purposes and their means of achieving them. Collegial and administrative support for teachers, and the ability and opportunity for teachers to reflect on their practice and continue to grow as professionals, are imperative.

However, these claims about research and practice contradict current policy. The trend has been to generate recommendations for reform on the basis of general impressions of teaching and learning rather than on research that carefully considers the intricacies of classroom relations (Metz, 2003). Simplistic, universal remedies that do not consider current realities, as well as complexity and context, are ill founded and can lead to undesired consequences, such as cheating on standardized tests. Even more serious is undermining of democratic principles and practices. Top-down pressures on teachers and students to raise test scores at all costs do not support teachers' professional legitimacy and curricula that are meaningful to students; thus, they undermine rather than support classroom authority. Standards-based reform—specifically, the No Child Left Behind legislation—has imposed federal control, which is distant, external, and centralized over educational structures, content, processes, and outcomes. The emphasis on accountability through sanctions imposed by the state indicates a shift from authority to coercion. The consequences of this and other changes for teachers' work and students' experiences of schooling, and for the system as a whole, must be critically examined.

We believe that educational policy must recognize that classroom relations are variable, negotiated by the participants, and shaped by many factors. It must support authority that serves the education of all students as well as the democratic values of justice, the common good, participation, and freedom to question. One of the primary purposes of schooling is to prepare educated democratic citizens who can think deeply and critically. If our policies do not support this, then our youth, the educational system, and our democratic society are endangered.

REFERENCES

Adelson, J. (1981, March). What happened to the schools. *Commentary*, 12–17.

Anyon, J. (1983). Social class and the hidden curriculum of work. In H. Giroux & D. Purpel (Eds.), *The hidden curriculum and moral education* (pp. 143–167). Berkeley, CA: McCutchan.

Arendt, H. (1977). *Between past and future.* New York: Penguin Books. (Original work published 1954)

Arum, R. (2003). *Judging school discipline: The crisis of moral authority.* Cambridge, MA: Harvard University Press.

Ballenger, C. (1992). Because you like us: The language of control. *Harvard Educational Review, 62,* 199–208.

Barnard, C. (1950). *The functions of the executive.* Cambridge, MA: Harvard University Press.

Bell, T. H. (1983). *A nation at risk: The imperative for educational reform.* Washington, DC: The Commission on Excellence in Education.

Bellah, R. N., Madsen, R., Sullivan, W. M., Swidler, A., & Tipton, S. M. (1985). *Habits of the heart: Individualism and commitment in American life.* New York: Harper & Row.

Benne, K. (1938). *A conception of authority: An introductory study.* New York: Teachers College Press.

Benne, K. (1970). Authority in education. *Harvard Educational Review, 40,* 385–410.

Benne, K. D. (1986). The locus of educational authority in today's world. *Teachers College Record, 88,* 15–21.

Bidwell, C. (1970). Students and schools: Some observations on client trust in client-serving organizations. In W. R. Rosengren & M. Lefton (Eds.) *Organizations and clients: Essays in the sociology of service* (pp. 37–70). Columbus, OH: Merrill.

Blau, P. (1974). *On the nature of organizations*. New York: Wiley.

Bowles, S., & Gintis, H. (1976). *Schooling in capitalist America: Educational reform and the contradictions of economic life*. New York: Basic Books.

Brantlinger, E. A. (1993). *The politics of social class in secondary school: Views of affluent and impoverished youth*. New York: Teachers College Press.

Callahan, R. (1962). *Education and the cult of efficiency: A study of the social forces that have shaped the administration of the public schools*. Chicago: University of Chicago Press.

Cusick, P. (1983). *The egalitarian ideal and the American high school: Studies of three schools*. New York: Longman.

D'Amato, J. (1993). Resistance and compliance in minority classrooms. In E. Jacob & C. Jordan (Eds.), *Minority education: Anthropological perspectives* (pp. 181–207). Norwood, NJ: Ablex.

Davidson, A. L. (1996). *Making and molding identity in schools: Student narratives on race, gender, and academic engagement*. Albany: State University of New York Press.

Delamont, S. (1983). *Interaction in the classroom* (2nd ed.). London: Methuen.

Delpit, L. (1995). *Other people's children: Cultural conflict in the classroom*. New York: New Press.

Devine, J. (1996). *Maximum security: The culture of violence in inner-city schools*. Chicago: University of Chicago Press.

Dewey, J. (1899). *The school and society*. Chicago: University of Chicago Press.

Dewey, J. (1916). *Democracy and education*. New York: Macmillan.

Dewey, J. (1938). *Experience and education*. New York: Macmillan.

Dillon, D. (1989). Showing them that I want them to learn and that I care about who they are: A microethnography of the social organization of a secondary low-track English-reading classroom. *American Educational Research Journal, 26*, 227–259.

Dreeben, R. (1968). *On what is learned in school*. Reading, MA: Addison-Wesley.

Durkheim, E. (1956). *Education and sociology*. New York: Free Press.

Durkheim, E. (1961). *Moral education: A study in the theory and application of the sociology of education*. New York: New Press.

Edelsky, C., Draper, K., & Smith, K. (1983). Hookin' em in at the start of school in a "whole language" classroom. *Anthropology & Education Quarterly, 14*, 257–281.

Ellsworth, E. (1989). Why doesn't this feel empowering? Working through the repressive myths of critical pedagogy. *Harvard Educational Review, 59*, 297–324.

Erickson, F. (1986). Qualitative methods in research on teaching. In M. C. Wittrock (Ed.), *Handbook of research on teaching* (pp. 119–161). New York: Macmillan.

Erickson, F. (1987). Transformation and school success: The politics and culture of educational achievement. *Anthropology & Education Quarterly, 18*, 335–355.

Fordham, S. (1996). *Blacked out: Dilemmas of race, identity and success at Capital High*. Chicago: University of Chicago Press.

Fordham, S., & Ogbu, J. U. (1986). Black students' school success: Coping with the "burden of acting White." *Urban Review, 18*, 176–206.

Foucault, M. (1977). The political function of the intellectual. *Radical Philosophy, 17*, 12–14.

Foucault, M. (1979). *Discipline and punishment*. New York: Vintage Books.

Foucault, M. (1980). *Power/knowledge: Selected interviews and other writings, 1972–1977*. New York: Pantheon.

Franklin, B. M. (1986). *Building the American community: The school curriculum and the search for social control*. London: Falmer.

Friedman, S. S. (1985). Authority in the feminist classroom: A contradiction in terms? In M. Culley & C. Portuges (Eds.), *Gendered subjects: The dynamics of feminist teaching* (pp. 203–208). London: Routledge & Kegan Paul.

Friedrich, C. (1958). Authority, reason, and discretion. In C. Friedrich (Ed.), *Authority* (pp. 28–48). Cambridge, MA: Harvard University Press.

Friere, P. (1970). *Pedagogy of the oppressed*. New York: Seabury.

Friere, P. (1998). Cultural action and conscientization. *Harvard Educational Review, 68,* 499–521.

Friere, P., & Shor, I. (1987). *A pedagogy for liberation.* London: Macmillan.

Giroux, H. A. (1986). Authority, intellectuals, and the politics of practical learning. *Teachers College Record, 88,* 22–40.

Giroux, H. A. (1988). *Schooling and the struggle for public life: Critical pedagogy in the modern age.* Minneapolis: University of Minnnesota Press.

Grant, G. (1981). The character of education and the education of character. *Daedalus, 110,* 135–150.

Grant, G. (1988). *The world we created at Hamilton High.* Cambridge, MA: Harvard University Press.

Grossman, P. L. (1990). *The making of a teacher: Teacher knowledge and teacher education.* New York: Teachers College Press.

Hansen, D. T. (1993). The moral importance of the teacher's style. *Journal of curriculum studies, 25,* 397–421.

Heath, S. B. (1983). *Ways with words: Language, life and work in communities and classrooms.* New York: Cambridge University Press.

Hemmings, A. (1996). Conflicting images? Being Black and a model high school student. *Anthropology & Education Quarterly 27,* 20–50.

Hemmings, A. (2003). Fighting for respect in urban high schools. *Teachers College Record, 105,* 416–437.

Hemmings, A. (forthcoming) Shifting images of model student blackness. In C. O'Connor & E. M. Horvat (Eds.), *Beyond acting White: Reassessing research on Black students and school success.* Lanham, MD: Rowman & Littlefield Publishers, Inc.

Henry, J. (1963). *Culture against man.* New York: Random House.

Hofstadter, R. (1963). *Anti-intellectualism in American life.* New York: Vintage.

Hurn, C. (1985). Changes in authority relationships in schools: 1960–1980. *Research in Sociology of Education and Socialization, 5,* 31–57.

Irvine, J. J. (1990). *Black students and school failure: Policies, practices, and prescriptions.* Westport, CT: Praeger.

Jackson, P. W. (1968). *Life in classrooms.* New York: Holt, Rinehart & Winston.

Keddie, N. (1971). Classroom knowledge. In M. F. D. Young (Ed.), *Knowledge and control: New directions for the sociology of education* (pp. 133–160). London: Collier-Macmillan.

Kliebard, H. (1986). *The struggle for the American curriculum: 1893–1958* (2nd ed.). New York: Routledge.

Kliebard, H. (1992). *Forging the American curriculum: Essays in curriculum history and theory.* New York: Routledge.

Kohl, H. (1967). *Thirty-six children.* New York: Signet.

Labaree, D. (1997). *How to succeed in school without really learning: The credentials race in American education.* New Haven, CT: Yale University Press.

Ladson-Billings, G. (1994). *The dreamkeepers: Successful teachers of African American children.* San Francisco: Jossey-Bass.

Lather, P. (1991). *Getting smart: Feminist research and pedagogy with/in the postmodern.* New York: Routledge.

Leacock, E. B. (1969). *Teaching and learning in city schools.* New York: Basic Books.

Lee, S. (1996). *Unraveling the "model minority" stereotype: Listening to Asian American youth.* New York: Teachers College Press.

Lightfoot, S. L. (1983). *The good high school: Portraits of character and culture.* New York: Basic Books.

Lipman, P. (1998). *Race, class, and power in school restructuring.* Albany: State University of New York Press.

Luke, C. (1996). Feminist pedagogy theory: Reflections on power and authority. *Educational Theory, 46,* 283–302.

MacLeod, J. (1987). *Ain't no makin' it: Aspirations and attainment in a low-income neighborhood.* Boulder, CO: Westview.

McCarthy, C. (1990). *Race and curriculum: Social inequality and the theory of politics of difference in contemporary research on schooling.* London: Falmer.

McDermott, R. P. (1977). Social relations as contexts for learning in school. *Harvard Educational Review, 47,* 198–246.

McNeil, L. (1981). Negotiating classroom knowledge: Beyond achievement and socialization. *Journal of Curriculum Studies, 13,* 313–328.

McNeil, L. M. (1986). *Contradictions of control: School structure and school knowledge.* New York: Routledge & Kegan Paul.

McNeil, L. M. (2000). *Contradictions of school reform: Educational costs of standardized testing.* New York: Routledge.

Metz, M. H. (1978). *Classrooms and corridors: The crisis of authority in desegregated secondary schools.* Berkeley: University of California Press.

Metz, M. H. (2003). *Different by design: The context and character of three magnet schools.* New York: Teachers College Press.

Mitchell, D., & Spady, W. (1983). Authority, power, and the legitimation of social control. *Educational Administrative Quarterly, 19*(1), 5–33.

Noblit, G. W. (1993). Power and caring. *American Educational Research Journal, 30,* 23–38.

No Child Left Behind Act of 2001. (2002). Pub.L. no. 107-110, §115 Stat. 1425.

Noddings, N. (1992). *The challenge to care in schools: An alternative approach to education.* New York: Teachers College Press.

Nyberg, D., & Farber, P. (Eds.). (1986). Authority in education. *Teachers College Record, 88,* 1–106.

Oakes, J. (1985). *Keeping track: How schools structure inequality.* New Haven, CT: Yale University Press.

O'Connor, C. (1997). Dispositions toward (collective) struggle and educational resilience in the inner city: A case analysis of six African-American high school students. *American Educational Research Journal 34,* 593–629.

Ogbu, J. U. (1974). *The next generation.* New York: Academic.

Ogbu, J. U. (1978). *Minority education and caste: The American system in cross-cultural perspective.* New York: Academic.

Ogbu, J. U. (1987). Variability in minority school performance: A problem in search of a solution. *Anthropology & Education Quarterly, 18,* 313–334.

Ogbu, J. U. (1991). Minority coping responses and school experience. *Journal of Psychohistory, 18,* 433–456.

Ogbu, J. U. (2003). *Black American students in an affluent suburb: A study of academic disengagement.* Mahwah, NJ: Lawrence Erlbaum Associates, Inc.

Oyler, C. (1996). *Making room for students: Sharing teacher authority in Room 104.* New York: Teachers College Press.

Pace, J. L. (1998). *Authority relationships in diverse high school classrooms.* Unpublished doctoral dissertation, Harvard University.

Pace, J. L. (2003a). Managing the dilemmas of professional and bureaucratic authority in a high school English class. *Sociology of Education, 76,* 37–52.

Pace, J. L. (2003b). Using ambiguity and entertainment to win compliance in a lower-level U.S. history class. *Journal of Curriculum Studies, 35,* 83–110.

Pace, J. L. (2003c). Revisiting classroom authority: Theory and ideology meet practice. *Teachers College Record, 105,* 1559–1585.

Page, R. (1987). Lower track classes at a college-preparatory high school: A caricature of educational encounters. In G. Spindler & L. Spindler (Eds.), *Interpretive ethnography of education: At home and abroad* (pp. 447–472). Hillsdale, NJ: Lawrence Erlbaum Associates, Inc.

Page, R. N. (1991). *Lower-track classrooms: A curricular and cultural perspective.* New York: Teachers College Press.

Parsons, T. (1964). Introduction. In M. Weber, *The theory of social and economic organization* (pp. 3–86). Translated by A. M. Henderson & T. Parsons. New York: Free Press. (Original work published 1925)

Philips, S. (1982). *The invisible culture: Communication in classrooms and community on the Warm Springs Indian Reservation.* New York: Longman.

Plank, S. B., McDill, E. L., McPartland, J., & Jordan, W. J. (2001). Situation and repertoire: Civility, incivility, cursing, and politeness in urban high schools. *Teachers College Record, 103,* 504–524.

Powell, A. E., Farrar, E., & Cohen, D. K. (1985). *The shopping mall high school: Winners and losers in the educational marketplace.* Boston: Houghton Mifflin.

Ravitch, D. (1985). *The schools we deserve.* New York: Basic Books.

Riesman, D. (1950). *The lonely crowd: A study of the changing American character.* New Haven, CT: Yale University Press.

Rist, R. (1970). Student social class and teacher expectations: The self-fulfilling prophecy in ghetto education. *Harvard Educational Review, 40,* 411–451.

Rutter, M., Maughan, B., Mortimore, P., & Ouston, J., with Smith, A. (1979). *Fifteen thousand hours.* Cambridge, MA: Harvard University Press.

Sarachild, K. (1975). Consciousness raising: A radical weapon. In K. Sarachild, C. Hanisch, F. Levine, B. Leon, & C. Price (Eds). *Feminist revolution* (pp. 144–150). New York: Random House.

Schwartz, G. (1987). *Beyond conformity or rebellion: Youth and authority in America.* Chicago: University of Chicago Press.

Sedlak, M., Wheeler, C., Pullin, D., & Cusick, P. (1986). *Selling students short: Classroom bargains and academic reform in the American high school.* New York: Teachers College Press.

Selznick, P. (1992). *The moral commonwealth: Social theory and the promise of community.* Berkeley: University of California Press.

Sennett, R. (1980). *Authority.* New York: Knopf.

Shor, I. (1996). *When students have power.* Chicago: University of Chicago Press.

Shulman, L. (1987). Knowledge and teaching: Foundations of the new reform. *Harvard Educational Review, 57,* 1–22.

Silberman, C. (1970). *Crisis in the classroom: The remaking of American education.* New York: Random House.

Sizer, T. R. (1984). *Horace's compromise: The dilemma of the American high school.* Boston: Houghton Mifflin.

Spady, W. (1974). The authority system of the school and student unrest: A theoretical explanation. In C. W. Gordon (Ed.), *Uses of the sociology of education* (pp. 36–77). Chicago: University of Chicago Press.

Spady, W., & Mitchell, D. (1979). Authority and the management of classroom activities. In D. Duke (Ed.), *Classroom management* (pp. 75–115). Chicago: University of Chicago Press.

Stinchcombe, A. (1964). *Rebellion in a high school.* Chicago: Quadrangle.

Stodolsky, S. (1988). *The subject matters: Classroom activity in math and social studies.* Chicago: University of Chicago Press.

Suárez-Orozco, C., & Suárez-Orozco, M. (1995). *Transformations: Migration, family life, and achievement motivation among Latino adolescents.* Stanford, CA: Stanford University Press.

Swidler, A. (1979). *Organization without authority: Dilemmas of social control in free schools.* Cambridge, MA: Harvard University Press.

Tetreault, M. K. T., & Maher, F. A. (1994). *The feminist classroom.* New York: Basic Books.

Trueba, H. (1988). Culturally based explanations of minority students' academic achievement. *Anthropology & Education Quarterly, 19,* 270–287.

Valenzuela, S. (1999). *Subtractive schooling: U.S.-Mexican youth and the politics of caring.* Albany: State University of New York Press.

Vogt, L., Jordan, C., & Tharp, R. (1993). Explaining school failure, producing schools success: Two cases. In E. Jacob & C. Jordan (Eds.), *Minority education: Anthropological perspectives* (pp. 53–65). Norwood, NJ: Ablex.

Waller, W. (1961). *The sociology of teaching.* New York: Wiley. (Original work published 1932)

Weber, M. (1964). *The theory of social and economic organization* (A. M. Henderson & T. Parsons, trans.). New York: Free Press. (Original work published 1925)

Willis, P. (1977). *Learning to labour: How working-class kids get working-class jobs.* Farnborough, England: Saxon House.

Wynne, E. (1981, Summer). What are the courts doing to our children? *The Public Interest,* 83–99.

Chapter 2

Authority, Culture, Context: Controlling the Production of Historical Knowledge in Elementary Classrooms

John S. Wills
University of California, Riverside

Throughout the 2002–2003 school year, I studied social studies education in one fourth-grade and two fifth-grade classrooms at one elementary school serving poor, primarily Latino, but also African American and White, students. My research documented the representation and narration of California and U.S. history in these classrooms. In particular, I was interested in understanding how these histories served as cultural tools or resources (Swidler, 1986, 2001; Wertsch, 1998; Wills, 1994, 1996, 2001, in press) for students in thinking about themselves and others as members of state and national communities. The three teachers, all White, were good teachers with many years of experience (over 20 years for both Mrs. Matthews and Mrs. Knight, who taught fifth grade, and over 10 years for Mrs. Thomas, who taught fourth grade) teaching in California schools and schools in other states (even, in Mrs. Knight's case, in other parts of the world). Although curriculum and instruction looked different in each of their classrooms, all three teachers sought to go beyond the simple transmission of historical information to their students. Mrs. Thomas worked to provide a history of California in which students could see themselves and one in which students often had to wrestle with ethical and moral issues. Mrs. Matthews's approach to U.S. history emphasized the development of students' critical thinking as they used history to think about contemporary U.S. society and current events. Mrs. Knight sought to build her students' understanding of historical figures and events, often using analogies and metaphors to narrate the past in ways that her students could grasp.

I did not conceive of this study as addressing issues of authority and control. However, it soon became apparent to me that understanding the production of historical knowledge in these teachers' classrooms and what they were able to achieve with their students necessitated understanding how the culture or moral climate of these classrooms and the academic engagement of students was shaped by the specific authority relations at Dusty Valley Elementary.[1] At the same time, understanding what these teachers were not able to achieve with their students in social studies meant situating this school and these classrooms within the context of high-stakes state-mandated testing in language arts and mathematics. At a good school (as I discuss later) such as Dusty Valley, the teachers and administrators were not preoccupied with the problem of maintaining order, a situation that often undermines the creation of rich learning environments in schools and classrooms (Gutierrez, Larson, & Kreuter, 1995; McNeil, 1986; Metz, 1978; Page, 1991). However, they were preoccupied with state testing in language arts and mathematics and the necessity that their students continue to show improvement on these annual examinations.

In classrooms, teachers did not struggle with their students; classrooms were orderly, and students conformed to teacher commands. The struggle for teachers was one of time, specifically, finding the time to educate their students in ways that they knew were best in social studies and science. Because of the focus on language arts and mathematics and the time and resources dedicated to these subject areas, because these were the subjects tested annually by the state, there was a constant lack of time for social studies and science education. In this situation, teachers faced the constant pressure to implement curricula and instruction that were quick and efficient rather than meaningful and authentic. For these three teachers, this manifested itself as a struggle between the efficient transmission of historical information through teacher lecture and a focus on student comprehension of curriculum content and alternative practices that placed students in the role of producer and user of knowledge. Put simply, the problem of social studies was to find the time to engage in lessons and activities in which student input was valued, validated, and incorporated into the historical knowledge that was constructed.

---

[1]All names of people and places are pseudonyms. In choosing appropriate pseudonyms for children and adults, I tried to assign pseudonyms that reflect the ethnic origins of original names. For example, an Edward would receive an Anglo pseudonym, whereas an Eduardo would receive a Latino pseudonym, even if both students were Latinos. Additionally, I have kept specific dates, demographic information, and other figures somewhat vague in particular instances to protect the anonymity of the adults and children at this elementary school.

In what follows, I illustrate this struggle by analyzing social studies lessons in Mrs. Knight's classroom. Mrs. Knight is firmly in control of curriculum, instruction, and students in her classroom. However, in the context of the culture and moral order (Metz, 1978; chap. 6, this volume) of Dusty Valley, this is a form of positive control (Noblit, 1993; Nystrand, 1997, p. 85). Mrs. Knight controls the process of knowledge production—who reads from the textbook, who gets to answer questions, who gets to participate in class discussions—but this serves to expand, rather than limit, the narration of historical events and the actual knowledge and understandings of history that are produced. Students are full participants—in fact, necessary participants—in the production of historical knowledge in Mrs. Knight's classroom, but not all of the time. When pressed for time (which is a constant problem but also fluid and variable), the enactment of social studies lessons is transformed in ways that circumscribe students' role in the production of knowledge and that privilege the transmission of information over the building of students' historical understanding. In a school where the culture, moral order, and authority relations between teachers and students support classrooms where students are engaged and where meaningful academic work occurs, the realization of these rich learning environments is constantly challenged by the demands of state testing by diminishing the time available for social studies (and science) education. These demands, in fact, have the potential to undermine the moral authority of teachers as opportunities for students to play a meaningful role in contributing to the production of knowledge are diminished, something I discuss in the conclusion of this chapter.

CONTEXT AND METHODOLOGY

During the 2002–2003 (August–June) school year, I conducted a qualitative case study of social studies curriculum and instruction in three classrooms at Dusty Valley Elementary, a Title I elementary school serving approximately 1,000 students located in a poor, rural community in the Inland Empire, an area in southern California encompassing Riverside and San Bernardino Counties. A little less than three quarters of the students at Dusty Valley were Latino, many recent arrivals to the United States or first-generation U.S. citizens. The remaining students were split almost equally between African American and White students. Over four-fifths of the students qualified for free or reduced-price lunches, and over one half of the students were English-language learners. The majority of teachers at Dusty Valley were White, although about one-fifth of the teachers were Latino, almost all teaching in the primary grades, and a few teachers were African American. The principal, Mr. Mendez, was Latino, and the assistant principal, Mr. Washington, was African American.

According to state-mandated testing in language arts and mathematics conducted by the California State Department of Education each spring, the results of which are used to rank schools throughout the state, Dusty Valley is a success story. The Academic Performance Index (API) is a system that ranks California public schools on the basis of student performance on standardized tests in language arts and mathematics. Mandated by the Public Schools Accountability Act of 1999, each school was given an API number as well as a target number for future improvement. Schools that demonstrated annual improvement were eligible for cash rewards, ranging from $5,000 to $25,000 for individual teachers at schools showing dramatic improvement in their 2000 API scores; the rewards were discontinued after the 1st year. Schools that failed to meet their annual target numbers for improvement must demonstrate improvement in subsequent years or face state sanctions.

A low-performing but improving school, Dusty Valley had an API in the low 400s (out of a possible 1,000, with a state target of 800 for all schools) when state testing began and was ranked 1 (on a scale of 1–10) compared with similar schools. The following year, the school's API increased enough to earn each teacher a cash reward from the state. Each year, Dusty Valley's students have performed well enough to exceed the target number for future improvement set by the state. During my study, Dusty Valley's API, for testing done in spring 2002, was in the mid 600s, and the school's ranking with regard to similar schools was a 10. Students again exceeded the improvement target set by the state in testing done in spring 2003, and Dusty Valley's API is quickly approaching 700. In comparison, schools in the Temecula Valley Unified School District, serving a community in southwestern Riverside County that is two thirds White and middle to upper income, began with APIs in the 700s and 800s, and almost all of their elementary schools have APIs in the 800s and state rankings of 9 or 10 based on testing conducted in spring 2003.

My investigation of social studies education was conducted in one fourth-grade classroom, where Mrs. Thomas taught California history to her students, and two fifth-grade classrooms, where Mrs. Matthews and Mrs. Knight taught U.S. history to their students. My research in these three classrooms involved regular observation and videotaping of social studies lessons, yielding 125 videotaped observations over the 10-month school year. These included virtually all the social studies lessons taught in Mrs. Matthews's and Mrs. Knight's classrooms and virtually all the social studies lessons except those during a unit on California geography in Mrs. Thomas's classroom. I conducted formal interviews with the principal, Mr. Mendez, and the three teachers, supplemented by regular informal conversations before and after classes, or during lunch, about the teaching and curriculum I was observing, their goals and objectives in social studies, and their thoughts on Dusty

Valley and its students. I also returned to Dusty Valley in the fall following my study to discuss my findings with these teachers, which also produced additional data as they talked about some of the new teachers who had been hired and whether they were appropriate teachers for Dusty Valley.

I conducted nine formal focus group interviews (three students per interview) with 16 fourth-grade students and 20 formal focus group interviews (three students per interview) with 50 fifth-grade students. In these interviews, students were asked to talk about what they were learning in social studies and about being a student at Dusty Valley. I collected a variety of student work (written essays, journal entries, digital photos of posters, models of Native American villages, and other artifacts that were displayed in these classrooms), and copies of curricular materials (textbooks, packets of information created by the teachers, historical fiction, and documentary and popular films shown to the students). Finally, I occasionally took the role of a participant—for example, serving as an aide in Mrs. Thomas's classroom—usually when I had time between observing a classroom and interviewing students, or working as a volunteer at one of the booths at the annual spring carnival.

SCHOOL CULTURE, THE MORAL ORDER, AND TEACHER AUTHORITY AT DUSTY VALLEY

Although there are various conceptions of authority in the education literature, Metz (1978) defined *authority* as a hierarchical relationship that serves the school's moral order, the educational values, norms, and purposes shared by administrators, teachers, and students. It is the moral order that provides legitimacy to authority relations, both for superordinates and subordinates:

> Authority is the right of a person in a specified role to give commands to which a person in another specified role has a duty to render obedience. This right and duty rests upon the superordinate's recognized status as the legitimate representative of a moral order to which both superordinate and subordinate owe allegiance. (Metz, 1978, p. 27)

As the literature on authority indicates, whether authority relations between teachers and students are clear and stable, or whether they are ambivalent, uncertain, and shifting, the character of the moral order that serves as the basis of these relationships can greatly influence the learning environments of classrooms, rendering them academically rich and purposeful or confusing caricatures of academic curriculum and instruction (McNeil, 1986; Metz, 1978; Pace, 2003c; Page, 1987, 1991; Swidler, 1979).

Hemmings (chap. 6, this volume) characterizes the moral order at one of the high schools she studied as dis/enabling care, describing teachers who cared about and for their students but provided them with a watered-down, academically impoverished curriculum and instruction. In contrast, the moral order at Dusty Valley could be characterized as one of enabling care, teachers who care about and for their students, enough to provide them with academically rich, even challenging, curriculum and instruction. Mr. Mendez captured this quite well when he described the struggle with parents during the first 2 years after Dusty Valley Elementary opened as they worked to establish high academic standards and expectations for all students:

> And I realized that our first thing, besides education was building relationships that were trustworthy. Uh, that took a long time. Fighting about, they had this much homework, we're gonna fight for that. They weren't used to that. They were used to, they cry loud enough they'll let us go, or we bicker we complain enough. No. We care to give you homework. We care to say your kids are not reading at grade level and we need to have them reading at grade level. So those were the battles. And, when they realized that the reason why we were, fighting that and battling that was for the betterment of their kids, they slowly began to see, they're not going away. (interview, May 8, 2003)

At Dusty Valley, the challenge was establishing a moral order (Metz, 1978) and gaining parents' and students' allegiance to this moral order. Because of a history of broken promises, the relations between parents and the school district were very poor, and Mr. Mendez spent his first 2 years at Dusty Valley building trust with parents and the local community. Eventually, parents came to see that Mr. Mendez and the teachers were invested in the academic growth and achievement of all their children and that this was not a temporary situation that would eventually be undone by the district, as in the past.[2] At the time of my study, families were purposely moving into the neighborhood from other parts of the district so their children could attend Dusty Valley Elementary.

The moral order of Dusty Valley, the shared belief that all children can learn, holding all children to the same academic standards and high expectations, and concern with the academic but also the social and moral development of children, was sustained by a school culture that Mr. Mendez characterized as the "culture of being positive." He explained during an interview that this included a shared understanding that "we're going to succeed, but together," an environment where caring teachers were "accepting of all kids," and the refusal to transform student poverty and other

---

[2]When Mr. Mendez came to Dusty Valley, he requested that he remain at least 5 years, rather than the 2 years intended by the district, and the district agreed to this, as well as granted him a significant degree of autonomy in running the school.

factors into excuses for failure. Dusty Valley was an overcrowded school when it opened in the mid-1990s as a collection of portable buildings on a site of less than 2 acres housing approximately 750 students.[3] Students were poor, and many did not speak English, and few students arrived at school with the resources or support to succeed academically. Mr. Mendez said that rather than complaining about the lack of resources or the challenges they faced in educating these students, he and the faculty realized that the small site enabled them to become "a close family," which included the children in their care: "We weren't saying, 'it's those parents, it's these kids, it's the discipline.' We were saying, 'They're our kids, what are we gonna do about it? What would we do in six and one-half hours?'" Administrators and teachers decided they would teach to the California content standards in all subject areas, holding all children responsible for learning the same curriculum and expecting all children to be academically successful.

Dusty Valley was successful in realizing this vision in large part because the core group of teachers who were present at Dusty Valley's opening remained. Mr. Mendez attributed this not only to a shared vision that all children can learn but also to the fact that these teachers, like Mr. Mendez, saw their work at Dusty Valley as a personal mission or calling. Although Dusty Valley is a public elementary school, virtually all of the teachers and administrators are devout Christians, although of a variety of denominations. What this provided Dusty Valley was a set of shared values, beliefs, and a perspective that informed how they thought about themselves as a family or community, the meaning of teaching and learning within this community, and their value of the children in their care. According to Mrs. Thomas, one of the participating teachers, Dusty Valley "works" as a school because, due to the teachers' and administrators' shared Christian beliefs, "kids are valued." Teachers and administrators share the belief that students "will be successful and we will help them be so," a positive attitude of "they will, they can, and see us do it." The culture and moral order of Dusty Valley Elementary is reminiscent of Catholic schools, for example, Valli's (1990) study of Central Catholic High School, where a strong school culture supported a shared set of meanings for teachers and students, a "curriculum-of-effort": Caring teachers will work for the academic success of all students, and students will work hard to succeed and meet the academic expectations of teachers.

Both observation and interview data confirmed that Dusty Valley is a place of high academic standards and expectations,[4] but these educational

---

[3] Today there is a permanent school, built on a site next to the original school, although Dusty Valley is still overcrowded, with approximately 1,000 students.

[4] This is evident not only in interviews with teachers and Mr. Mendez, and in the academic orientation of social studies lessons, but also in the everyday talk heard between teachers, administrators, and students at Dusty Valley. For example, in the morning announcements

goals are enveloped by notions of love, caring, and respect that shape the interactions between adults and children in classrooms and around the school. Mr. Mendez believes love is the "glue" that holds Dusty Valley together as a community—"the love to see a child, and to see their needs" (personal communication, May 8, 2003). The culture of being positive at Dusty Valley and the moral order of enabling care defines the traditional *in loco parentis* authority relations between teachers and students, based on the legitimate power of adults to control and command children, who are obligated to obey. The talk of teachers and administrators is filled with references to "family" and "our kids" when referring to Dusty Valley as a community. Authority is based on love and is distinct from authoritarianism. As Mr. Mendez told teachers at a fall staff meeting (as reported to me by Mrs. Thomas): "When I come into your room, I want to see the love. It is the love that gives you the authority to discipline. Without the love, it is simply obedience for obedience's sake. For all you new people, we are about love at this school."

Routine practices support this understanding of teacher–student relations as those of caring adults who are invested in the welfare of the children under their care, not only in their academic success but also in their development as good people. For example, the entire school gathers in the quad each morning to recite the Pledge of Allegiance, followed by the reciting of the "PeaceBuilder's Pledge," which provides a common behavioral and disciplinary code for teachers and students at Dusty Valley.[5] Although Mr. Mendez did not adopt the entire PeaceBuilder's Program for implementation at Dusty Valley, the pledge does serve as a common discourse for defining appropriate and inappropriate behavior for students. In addition, words of the week (e.g., *honesty, trustworthy, responsibility*) are oriented toward students' social and moral development, and teachers often have students incorporate these words into their writing. It is through these routine, daily practices that students are immersed in a caring environment, one

---

over the PA Mr. Mendez often talks about "when you go on to college," never "if you go on to college." This message has not been lost on students, who seem to have accepted this as a realistic future goal. For example, writing in essays about why they would remain drug free—as part of Drug Abuse Resistance Education Red Ribbon Week—over 60% of Mrs. Thomas' fourth-graders mentioned that taking drugs would prevent them from doing well in school and going on to college.

[5] The Pledge is: "I am a Peace Builder. I pledge to praise people. To give up putdowns. To seek wise people. To notice and speak up about hurts I have caused. And to right wrongs. I pledge to build peace at home, at school, and in my community every day." PeaceBuilders is a community-based program intended to change the climate of a school to make it more peaceful and safe, resulting in improved academic achievement, the development of positive social skills, and the building of character. Schools can purchase the PeaceBuilders Program, which includes training, materials, and other resources. The Web site is http://www.peacebuilders.com

that communicates the extent to which these adults value them as students and as children. The shared understanding of the legitimate authority of teachers over students at Dusty Valley was expressed by two students in Mrs. Knight's classroom, in response to an interview question I asked them about what makes students good citizens at Dusty Valley:

> *Linda:*   And uh, we really shouldn't disrespect our teachers since they, since probably preschool or until now they've been doing stuff for us and without them we wouldn't get an education. 'Cause really we shouldn't be disrespecting them.

> *Tamara:*   'Cause our teachers are kind of like our parents. They don't really like, we don't really live with them, but then they do take care for us they do help us get educated and be somebody in the future.

Dusty Valley Elementary has many of the elements that make for good schools, as laid out by Lightfoot (1983) in her study of six high schools. The social organization of Dusty Valley is based on clear and consistent authority relations, the traditional authority of loving and caring parents looking out for the best interests of the children in their care. These authority relations are reinforced by an explicit ideological vision that rejects a deficit model to explain and accept the academic failure of "at-risk" students (Lipman, 1998) in favor of a shared belief that all children can learn and that all children, with support, can achieve academic success. This moral order is academic as well as social and moral in its orientation, valuing the development of the whole child. Within the culture of being positive that characterizes Dusty Valley, students willingly consent to the commands of teachers and administrators, knowing that they are valued by these adults who love and care for them, much as parents care for their own children. As a result, teachers and students at Dusty Valley develop trusting relationships, relationships that make classrooms rich settings for academic engagement and learning (Nystrand, 1997).

MORAL AUTHORITY AND THE CONTROL OF KNOWLEDGE PRODUCTION IN MRS. KNIGHT'S CLASSROOM

Given the culture of being positive, the moral order of enabling care, and the traditional authority relations that characterize Dusty Valley Elementary, it is not surprising that curriculum and instruction in Mrs. Knight's classroom, and the other teachers' classrooms, looked quite different than in other studies in the educational literature. There were no "treaties" or "bargains" between teachers and students, where student compliance to teacher demands is ensured as long as teachers agree not to demand too much (Nystrand, 1997; Powell, Farrar, & Cohen, 1985; Sizer, 1984; see also Gutierrez et al., 1995, on "scripted pacts" between teachers and students). In fact, much like the Science, Engineering, and Technology magnet high school studied by McNeil (2000)—at least before state-mandated high-stakes testing in Texas was instituted—any "bargain" between Mrs. Knight and her students (like the other teachers and students at Dusty Valley) was a positive one that served educational purposes. Because Dusty Valley Elementary presented students with a supportive, caring environment rather than a coercive environment, there was no need for teachers to engage in defensive teaching, a means of attempting to shore up authority by tightly controlling the knowledge produced in classrooms (McNeil, 1986, 2000). Students were willing to work hard in Mrs. Knight's classroom because Mrs. Knight was truly interested in student learning and her students' academic success, and she validated and incorporated student contributions into the curriculum in use.

Although Mrs. Knight did not engage in defensive teaching, tightly controlling the knowledge produced in her classroom, she did tightly control the process of producing knowledge in her classroom. Mrs. Knight was in charge of her classroom, controlling students respectfully yet firmly and efficiently, often through the use of directives, a discourse style that expressed her personal power in her classroom (Delpit, 1995, p. 168). She held students to classroom rules—for example, raising one's hand and waiting to be called on before speaking out—and she was quick to discipline students who seriously violated these rules. She set the agenda for what students would learn, provided clear academic expectations for students (among students, it was widely known that "you have to work hard in Mrs. Knight's classroom"), and held students responsible for completing their work and not engaging in behaviors that prevented other students from completing their work.

In another context, Mrs. Knight might be considered authoritarian but for the fact that the control she exercised in her classroom was not simply in the service of behavioral goals but a means for creating an orderly learning environment that supported student participation and their engagement with subject matter content. Noblit's (1993) work is particularly useful in understanding Mrs. Knight's power—to control students, curriculum, and instruction in the process of knowledge production—as a form of positive control, as moral authority, as "power used in the moral service of others" (p. 35). Noblit argued for the necessity of distinguishing between *power,* which is often linked with oppression, and *moral authority,* which he defined as the "ethical use of power" (p. 24). Like Pam, the teacher Noblit observed, Mrs. Knight used her moral authority, as a teacher at a caring school focused on the academic success of all students, to create a structured and orderly environment in her classroom that controlled student participation in the process of producing historical knowledge but encouraged and valued student participation in that process.

The moral order of enabling care and the culture of being positive at Dusty Valley Elementary provided the foundation for teachers' moral authority, both inside and outside their classrooms, but the specific enactment and accomplishment of authority in the daily interactions between teachers and students varied from classroom to classroom. Quite simply, Mrs. Knight is not Mrs. Mathews; neither are either of them Mrs. Thomas. The moral climate of particular classrooms is inseparable from the moral order and culture of Dusty Valley and reflects the shared belief that all children can learn; norms of care, love, and respect; and a focus on the academic, social, and moral development of all students. However, the moral climate of a particular classroom is also shaped by a teacher's style (Hansen, 1993), which communicates moral messages to students regarding appropriate student conduct and the common purposes of teachers and students in classrooms. Mrs. Knight's style might aptly be described as "businesslike"—direct, to the point, focused on the task at hand, efficient and methodical—and students rather quickly learned to respond to this in kind. More often than not, students got down to business quickly and efficiently, knowing exactly what they were doing (reading, outlining, and discussing textbook content), what resources they needed to do it (textbook, paper, pencil), and how they should be (quiet, looking at Mrs. Knight at the front board, and ready to get to work).

Mrs. Knight's style also exhibited care and respect for her students and the subject matter, a key ingredient in the moral climate of her classroom and a necessary one for understanding how her classroom worked to support student learning. Mrs. Knight's care for her students (and their recognition of these feelings) was evident in the lighthearted exchanges that would often occur during lessons, her regular use of "please" and "thank you" in her talk, and her patient waiting for a student actively searching for an answer to a question or struggling to articulate a question of his or her own. It was also evident in her careful attention to her students' needs, reflected in the amount of time she spent listening to her students, her openness to their questions and comments, and her concern with whether they understood the historical events and ideas they were discussing. The depth and breadth of her students' understanding of history mattered to Mrs. Knight, and her students knew it mattered to her, and they responded by, at minimum, doing their work and, at most, asking questions, making comments, and being engaged in the outlining and discussion of history.

Mrs. Knight was both *in* authority in her classroom and *an* authority, the latter noting a teacher's expert knowledge in the subject areas she teaches (Buzzelli & Johnston, 2002). Mrs. Knight was a good social studies teacher with a good knowledge of U.S. history, something that was not lost on her students, who commented in interviews on how much history Mrs. Knight knew (sometimes adding "but not as much as you," assuming that being a professor I would know more history than Mrs. Knight). However, the notion of "expert knowledge" is not quite right in capturing how Mrs. Knight was an authority in the classroom. Key to understanding the moral climate of her classroom, at least during social studies lessons, was the clear respect she had for history, that the history of the United States was worthy of students' attention and effort to understand the past. Like Mr. Turner, one of the teachers Hansen (1993) observed, Mrs. Knight's practice demonstrated respect for both her students and the subject matter, respect that communicated a code of conduct for students during social studies that informed their substantive engagement in social studies lessons.

DOING SOCIAL STUDIES IN MRS. KNIGHT'S CLASSROOM

> I want them to say at the end and I hear some of them saying now, "I like social studies. I didn't like it in the beginning, but I do now." I guess that's what I want is for them not to go over there [the middle school] with a fear of what social studies or history is or, "oh this is a boring subject," but, "I like this, I can understand these people even though they happened a long time ago. I can understand what's going on." (Mrs. Knight, interview, May 2, 2003)

Mrs. Knight's approach to social studies might best be characterized as *methodical outlining,* an approach that involves generating an outline of the main points from the students' textbook, Houghton Mifflin's *America Will Be* (Armento, Nash, Slater, & Wixson, 1991), on the front board (which students copy down), coupled with discussion of the historical figures, events, and ideas being outlined. Other practices do occur in Mrs. Knight's classroom, for example, an occasional discussion not directly tied to a textbook chapter or lesson, student reports, and other projects. However, the mundane, daily practice of social studies typically means taking your seat, opening your textbook, and copying down the outline being generated on the front board (or, in the spring, on the overhead projector) as individual students are called on to read passages from the textbook.

If doing social studies consisted only of reading from the textbook and generating outline points to be remembered and regurgitated on chapter tests, the value of Mrs. Knight's curriculum and instruction would be questionable and might serve as a potent form of defensive teaching (McNeil, 1986, 2000) or the exercise of teacher power through the enforcement of the teachers' script (Gutierrez, Larson, & Kreuter, 1995; Gutierrez, Rymes,

& Larson, 1995). But methodical outlining also involved the discussion and elaboration of historical figures and events, an effort to provide knowledge of the past and build students' understanding of historical events and ideas. It was during these discussions that Mrs. Knight went beyond school knowledge to bring in her personal knowledge. For example, sharing stories and experiences from her grandfather's farm (which allowed a student, Tamara, to share similar information about her grandfather's farm in Mexico) helped students imagine and understand what life was like for White settlers establishing farms on the frontier. Or, talking about her time in Africa (both living there for a number of years as a girl and returning as an adult to teach there) and sharing pictures of the slave castles she visited helped students understand what it was like for captured Africans being shipped as slaves to the United States.

Equally significant in these discussions was the role of students as contributors to the production of knowledge as students' questions, comments, and insights shaped classroom representations of historical figures and events. As Metz (1978, p. 27) reminds us, authority is a relationship of roles, not of persons. Mrs. Knight's moral authority (in this sense, the ethical use of her power) to control curriculum, instruction, and students in her classroom—to control how they did social studies—defined specific roles for herself and her students in the knowledge production process. For students, their role was not only to diligently copy down the outline being generated on the front board but also to participate in the narration of history during class discussion by fulfilling the roles of authentic questioner and reflective commentator.

In Mrs. Knight's classroom, student questions were authentic in two ways. First, student questions often changed or modified the discussion (Nystrand, 1997, p. 38) as Mrs. Knight attempted to respond to students' questions by elaborating on points already made, frequently invoking analogies or metaphors to help students understand historical events or ideas. In this way, student questions were authentic in that they contributed to the building of shared understandings of the past in Mrs. Knight's classroom. Second, student questions were authentic in that they were "real questions," posed because students did not understand but wanted to understand, and they often reflected issues or concerns linked to students' lives outside of school. Student questions—about being pulled over for "driving while Black"; the use of the terms *Black, colored,* and *negro* to refer to African Americans; and surprise that Mexicans were considered "colored" in the past—were not concerned with doing school (Heath, 1978), a form of procedural display, but reflected real concerns of students and their substantive engagement in class discussions.

Because student questions were valued and utilized by Mrs. Knight—because Mrs. Knight cared for and valued her students—they shaped the discussion and remembering of the past in her classroom. If Mrs. Knight had simply moved from point to point on the outline with little discussion or elaboration, then the students (and Mrs. Knight) would be little more than chroniclers of history, generating a simple chronicle—a chronological listing of historical figures and events as they occurred in a sequence—and not a meaningful narrative of history (Cronon, 1992; White, 1973, 1978). However, Mrs. Knight was not interested in the simple transmission of historical information; social studies instruction was intended to transmit knowledge and build understanding of history among her students.

In what follows, I present an example of a typical social studies lesson to illustrate the roles played by Mrs. Knight and her students and how Mrs. Knight's moral authority translated into a form of positive control over the process of knowledge production that allowed for an active and meaningful student role in shaping accounts of history.

A Typical Social Studies Lesson

It is January 7, a Tuesday, and the first day back to school for students after winter break. Today they were beginning a new chapter, chapter 11, "War Breaks Out," in their social studies textbook, *America Will Be* (Armento et al., 1991). Lesson 1 is called "Forming a New Government." When I came in, they were finishing up a language arts lesson, specifically, working on vocabulary words (*oppose, Patriot, revolutionary, taxes, radical*) that fit nicely with the content they were covering in social studies. At 10:33 A.M., Mrs. Knight told her students to put their bookmarks in their language arts textbooks so they'll know where they are for next time. Then she told Linda, Rodney, and Enrique go to the back of the room to collect copies of the social studies textbook from the cart to pass out to the students sitting in their group of desks, although Linda and Rodney were already back at the cart before she said this. As the textbooks were being passed out, Mrs. Knight was beginning the chapter outline on the front board: "Forming a New Government (page 260)." Once the textbooks were passed out, students settled quickly, their textbooks open to page 260 and a piece of paper on their desks to copy the outline.

As was the usual routine when beginning a new chapter, Mrs. Knight told them to turn back one page to the two-page introduction to each chapter, which includes a timeline and a collection of photos, pictures, and documents, each with its own caption. Mrs. Knight read the italicized, introductory paragraph ("When the first shots of the Revolution were fired . . ."). She then called on individual students to read one of the captions (e.g., one under a picture of Abigail Adams, noting the role of women in the war), followed by Mrs. Knight offering some elaboration on what they have read or questioning students to confirm their understanding of the material.

After this, they proceeded to Lesson 1, and Mrs. Knight called on Tamara to read the introduction to the lesson, which concerned the British marching on Lexington and the farmers and shopkeepers who had gathered on the common to meet them. It was after reading and discussing this introduction that Mrs. Knight called on Tina to begin reading the first section, "The First Shot Is Fired." While Tina was reading, Mrs. Knight began the outline on the front board, and students were quietly copying these points down, with only a few students following along in their textbooks as Tina read. After two paragraphs, Mrs. Knight had Tina stop reading, and the following exchange occurred:

[1] *Mrs. Knight:*   OK. So we've got, the militia, who are people who are part-time soldiers. They're called the Minutemen because they could be ready in a minute. Obviously they're not jumping into uniforms or, uh, you know they're just taking what they have. They're ready to fight at a moment's notice. What are the soldiers looking for?

[2] *Male Student:*   For an inn? [Then four seconds of silence.]

[3] *Mrs. Knight:*   Very good Jennifer, you're looking in the book. Exactly where you're gonna find it. Soldiers are there, it's supposed to be a secret raid. They're supposed to be coming in secret. However, nobody was shocked, were they?

[4] *Male Student:*   No. [Student comes in, hands something to Mrs. Knight, who says "thank you" to the student. While this happens many of the students are looking in their textbooks.]

[5] *Mrs. Knight:*   The soldiers are looking for something. What are they looking for?

[6] *Male Student:*   [Comment I cannot hear.]

[7] *Mrs. Knight:*   Well, they don't expect anyone's gonna notice them, that's true. Yes?

[8] *Thomas:*   Weapons.

[9] *Mrs. Knight:*   They're looking for weapons. [Mrs. Knight adds this to the outline on the board: Soldiers were looking for hidden weapons. Students begin copying this point down.]

Usually, after a student is called on to read—almost always a student who had his or her hand up—Mrs. Knight would begin outlining the important points in the passage being read. Sometimes she would list all of the pertinent points while the student was reading, and then she would return to each point during discussion with her students. At other times, as in this case, Mrs. Knight would complete only a portion of the outline while the student was reading and then would add additional points as she discussed what had been read with her students. After Tina was done reading, Mrs. Knight began by briefly discussing the first point on the outline concerning the militia or Minutemen [1]. Mrs. Knight concluded these comments by asking a question about what Tina had just read, and this initiated the familiar Initiation Reply Evaluation (IRE) sequence, or recitation, that characterizes the structure of teacher–student talk in most classrooms (Drew & Heritage, 1992; Mehan, 1979a; see also Gutierrez, Larson, & Kreuter, 1995, and Nystrand, 1997, on "monologic" instruction). Mrs. Knight asked what the soldiers were looking for [1], a male student provided an incorrect answer [2], and then she praised Jennifer for looking in her textbook for the answer [3]. Another male student responded [6]; however, not with the answer Mrs. Knight was looking for, but then Thomas provided the correct answer, "weapons," [8] which Mrs. Knight confirmed "They're looking for weapons" [9] and then added this point to the outline on the front board.

Up to this point, the roles for teacher and students seem clear. Mrs. Knight was in control of the process of knowledge production, in the sense that she was either telling students what it was they needed to know or asked them "known information questions" (Mehan, 1979b) that required them to produce specific answers that reproduced the information in the textbook. Mrs. Knight controlled student participation in the lesson, calling on students who had their hands raised to select who would read passages in the textbook, or to answer her questions. Students who were not reading or answering questions were either quiet, listening to Mrs. Knight or their fellow students; copying down the outline points; or sitting quietly.[6]

---

[6]I do not want to paint a false picture of a "perfect" classroom where problems never occur. They do. Mrs. Knight at times raises her voice to quiet students. Students sometimes misbehave and need to be disciplined, from having a check mark put next to their name on the front board (enough marks lead to lunch detention), to being asked to leave the room to do their work in another teacher's classroom, to being sent to see Mr. Mendez. In these respects, this classroom is like any other. However, Mrs. Knight's disciplining of students, her authority to discipline students, is never called into question (nor did I ever observe this occurring in the other classrooms, and all three teachers confirmed this in interviews). Students get caught, and they take their punishment with little to no argument, even in one instance when a student was sent to Mr. Mendez's office knowing that his latest infraction would lead to his suspension from Dusty Valley. When he returned to Mrs. Knight's classroom he was his old self again, joking with Mrs. Knight and often participating in class discussions. Additionally, there is often a lot of movement in Mrs. Knight's classroom during lessons. Students are free to get up to sharpen pencils; place papers or assignments on Mrs. Knight's desk; or leave the room, after checking out, to use the bathroom. The climate in Mrs. Knight's classroom is not authoritarian, demanding strict obedience to rules and the rigid control of students' bodies

There were no control issues evident in this lesson, because the task they in which were engaged—outlining the content of the textbook lesson, which included answering questions posed by Mrs. Knight—was a legitimate, academic task to which students willingly conformed.

However, there is more to social studies instruction in Mrs. Knight's classroom, more to outlining, than the simple reproduction and transmission of historical knowledge located in the textbook. Mrs. Knight was interested in transmitting a body of historical knowledge to her students but, more than that, she was interested in helping students understand history; this is evident in the following exchange:

[10] *Mrs. Knight:*   After the colonists, threw the tea into the sea, at the Boston Tea Party, Britain came back and said, "We're not going to send ships into, um, to trade with you." OK? That was one. Two, nobody can have a gun.

[11] *Thomas:*   Why couldn't they?

[12] *Martin:*   Because they'd try to shoot.

[13] *Mrs. Knight:*   Because the soldiers, the British were now afraid. If you don't have a gun, who are you gonna hurt?

[14] *Many students, in unison:*   Nobody.

[15] *Mrs. Knight:*   If I'm a soldier and I have a gun and you don't have a gun I feel safer. Even if you have a stick. Or a rock.

[16] *Rodney:*   What if they have a pitchfork? [A couple of other students make brief comments here at the same time.]

[17] *Mrs. Knight:*   So, that was another thing they said is . . .

[18] *Jim:*   'Cause you have to reload your gun so it can hit you.

[19] *Mrs. Knight:*   No, no colonists, were to have guns. [Mrs. Knight adds this point to the outline on the board: "Colonists cannot have guns." Students begin copying this point down.]

[20] *Jim:*   Aw.

[21] *Mrs. Knight:*   Three, the third thing was, no group of colonists, could get together, for any particular reason. [Mrs. Knight is adding this point to the outline: "Colonists cannot meet in groups." Students begin copying this point down on their outlines.] You could meet, you

---

and movements, because students recognize her authority as teacher and their obligation to obey her commands. Although Mrs. Knight, like all teachers, must at times reassert her control over students and the situation, this is never problematic or challenged by students.

		know, two by two. But they didn't want any group of you meeting.
[22]	*Tamara:*	Why?
[23]	*Mrs. Knight:*	Because you might be planning a bad thing. You might be planning to fight against them. And so they said, "We don't want that."
[24]	*Thomas:*	But see, if the colonists they don't have guns, and the British were planning on another attack, the, the um colonists have no protection.
[25]	*Mrs. Knight:*	That's right. So the colonists said, "We'll hide our guns." And the soldiers were looking for, hidden weapons. Because they knew that they didn't have, all of the colonists' guns. And so they said, "Let's find them, we heard that there are guns hidden in," what is this Lexington or Concord? Lexington. So they went secretly to, find those guns.
[26]	*Nathaniel:*	Did they find them?
[27]	*Mrs. Knight:*	Instead, they found, a group of farmers who were waiting very anxiously or very, nervously, for them to come. What they realized when they met was, "We don't know what to do."
[28]	*Rodney:*	Hit 'em with their sticks.
[29]	*Linda:*	[has her hand raised]: Why didn't they just fight?
[30]	*Thomas:*	You could sneak up behind 'em and steal their gun.
[31]	*Tamara:*	Maybe they don't know how to work the gun.
[32]	*Rodney:*	Yes they did, they just didn't have any guns.
[33]	*Mrs. Knight:*	(chuckling): You know two hundred years later it sounds easy, but at that time, you know they're encountering soldiers and they're just a bunch of. You know it's kinda like if, if all of your dads got together to, fight against um, to fight against an army of soldiers.
[34]	*Martin:*	Ya we'd kill 'em [shouted out, a few students laugh in response to this]
[35]	*Mrs. Knight:*	Uh, that's kind of what they thought but, remember we're talking about, your uncle and your grandpa.
[36]	*Martin:*	They ain't goin'.
[37]	*Mrs. Knight:*	These you know the, fathers, your fathers your uncles your grandfathers, defending the town.
[38]	*Jim:*	Were the kids allowed to fight?
[39]	*Mrs. Knight:*	Well there was a sixteen-year-old.

[40] *Martin:*   We're talkin' about nine-year-olds and ten-year-olds using um um little BB guns.

[41] *Tamara:*   William Diamond [the sixteen-year-old drummer for the armed townsmen in Lexington, mentioned in the vignette that opens this lesson, which Tamara just read to the class].

[42] *Mrs. Knight:*   So, it's it's, you know it's just regular guys like your dads and your uncles and your grandfathers were out there and they're suddenly facing the soldiers. And realizing "whoa."

[43] *Nathaniel:*   They called them the redcoats.

[44] *Mrs. Knight:*   "We're not really sure what to do now."

[45] *Tamara:*   Well because Mrs. Knight . . .

[46] *Martin:*   My brother is in the army.

[47] *Mrs. Knight:*   OK so he could be a soldier and he'd have a better idea of what to do.

[48] *Tamara:*   'Cause Mrs. Knight they had to fight the redcoats and all.

[49] *Mrs. Knight:*   That's right. OK that takes us to two, the conflict begins. [The next subsection in this section of Lesson 1. Ernesto has his hand up and Mrs. Knight calls on him to read.]

After stating Point 2 on the outline, that colonists were not allowed to have guns, Thomas asked an authentic question, "Why couldn't they?" [11], leading Mrs. Knight to elaborate on this point. Similarly, after stating that groups of colonists were prohibited from getting together [21], Tamara asked an authentic question, "Why?" [22]. After answering Tamara's question Thomas drew an insightful conclusion that captured the situation the colonists found themselves in: "But see, if the colonists don't have guns, and the British were planning on another attack, the, the um colonists have no protection" [24]. Mrs. Knight followed up on Thomas's comment [25] and built on it, what Nystrand (1979) and others (Collins, 1982) refer to as *uptake,* agreeing with Thomas's assessment and then linking it back to the beginning of their discussion: What were the soldiers looking for?

Mrs. Knight and her students, working together, have transformed a simple point of fact about the British soldiers—they are looking for weapons the colonists might have hidden—into an understanding of the significance of that for the colonists and the perilous situation they will be in if the British find and seize their guns. Thomas's insightful comment was made possible by Mrs. Knight's control of the lesson, over the process of producing knowledge, which made the lesson orderly, manageable, and provided a role for active student participation. Students take this role seriously, knowing that Mrs. Knight values their questions and comments, because their questions and comments shape and contribute to the narration of history accomplished in these lessons.

After this, Nathaniel asked whether the British found the colonists' guns [26], and Mrs. Knight responded by characterizing the emotions and state of mind of the farmers who were waiting for the British soldiers to arrive [27]. What followed was a brief exchange among the students about what the colonists could have done, including a question from Linda, "Why didn't they just fight?" [29]. Mrs. Knight responded to Linda's question (Linda had her hand up) by drawing an analogy that she hoped would help students understand what the situation was like from the farmers' perspective 200 years ago [33], which she continued to develop in the ensuing discussion [35, 37, 42, 44]. These were "regular guys" like your fathers, grandfathers, and uncles, who were not soldiers and so unsure of what to do. This discussion also included another authentic student question from Jim about whether kids were allowed to fight [38], which was answered by Mrs. Knight [39] and Tamara [41], who referred back to the information in the textbook that she had read earlier. Finally, there was additional information provided by Nathaniel [43] and Tamara [48] confirming that the colonists were fighting the British, who were also called the Redcoats. Mrs. Knight acknowledged Tamara's comment [49]—but not Nathaniel's, because he simply called it out instead of raising his hand or directing it to Mrs. Knight, as Tamara did—before calling on Ernesto to read the next section in the textbook (who had his hand up).

Whose knowledge is this? Who does this knowledge belong to? It is evident in the preceding excerpt that this knowledge belongs to the classroom, a product of the joint participation of Mrs. Knight and her students in the narration of this particular historical event. Mrs. Knight played a critical role in leading and directing the discussion, calling on some students and not others, acknowledging some student questions and comments, and not others. Not every student gained the floor. For example, Mrs. Knight ignored Martin's comments ([36], [40]), because he did not raise his hand and he directed his comments not at Mrs. Knight but rather at his fellow students, some of whom laugh at his remarks.[7] Neither were Martin's comments use-

---

[7]It is unclear whether Martin's comment, "They ain't goin'" [36], is a serious comment. Martin is African American, and so this may be a serious comment that, being Black, his father or grandfather would not be fighting with the colonists, who have enslaved them. However, the role of African Americans during the war, who fought on both the colonists' and British sides, is not discussed until the next lesson in this chapter, and so Martin has no knowledge of this. Although I did not ask Mrs. Knight, because this comment follows his previous comment [34], which was said to get a laugh from his fellow students (although Mrs. Knight did incorporate it into the discussion), I would assume that she interpreted it as a less-than-serious outburst.

ful in advancing the conversation, at least in terms of Mrs. Knight's effort to help her students understand that these were just "regular guys" facing off against professional soldiers. However, Martin's final comment [46] was directed at Mrs. Knight and "usable" in the sense that Mrs. Knight could make use of it within the topic at hand, and so she incorporated it into the conversation.

Whether to answer or acknowledge a student's question or comment is something Mrs. Knight is constantly weighing during the lesson. As she explained in an interview, some kids will be "grossly irrelevant" because they would like to stop writing, and she does not acknowledge these questions or comments. But when students ask authentic questions—and ask them appropriately, that is, with hand raised or prefaced with "Mrs. Knight"—she attempts to answer them: "You know it's worth talking about because they're, they're likely to remember it and to take it somewhere else and maybe spark other interests in other kids." When in doubt, Mrs. Knight often seems to assume that students are asking authentic questions, and she does her best to answer them.[8]

Methodical outlining is a structure for learning, or a participation structure (Schultz, Erickson, & Florio, 1982) that controls the production of historical knowledge by providing students and teacher specific roles and a clear task in this process. For students, this meant participating as questioners or commentators, once they had legitimately gained the floor by being acknowledged by Mrs. Knight, typically by following appropriate "rules of engagement" such as raising their hand and waiting to be called on. However, if students followed these rules, followed this process, they could ask questions or make comments on a wide range of issues or concerns. Sometimes this resulted in Mrs. Knight refusing to answer a question or engage a comment she deemed off topic—"we're not going to go there"—but students knew Mrs. Knight's classroom was a place where their active participation was welcomed and valued. Even at the end of the year, students continued to ask Mrs. Knight about anything and everything, even students who often asked off-topic questions but sometimes asked excellent on-topic questions. The fact that students continued asking questions throughout the year—even students whose questions were regularly deemed "off topic" by Mrs. Knight—speaks to the trusting relationship between Mrs. Knight and her students.

---

[8]For example, near the end of this lesson one boy asks if two soldiers fired their rifles at each other if instead of hitting each other the bullets could collide in midair (although he doesn't say "collide"). I wasn't sure if this was an irrelevant question, meant to get them off topic and thereby stop the lesson, or a relevant, 10- or 11-year-old boy question. Mrs. Knight (whatever her assessment of this question) acted as if it were an authentic question and directed students' attention to a picture of musket balls in their textbook to explain that the guns then were very different and much less accurate, and so that was unlikely to happen.

   The authentic questions of students, and the occasional insightful comment, such as Thomas's [24], play a significant role in the content, scope, and direction of the discussion and, ultimately, the narration of historical events, what was remembered and what was forgotten, what was emphasized or deemed unimportant. The production of narrative accounts of history, the elaboration and development of points about historical figures and events, is typically driven as much by authentic student questioning as by Mrs. Knight's presentation of specific outline points. Mrs. Knight attempts to assist her students in understanding the historical events they have read about by outlining the main points on the front board, then elaborating on these points to clarify potentially confusing aspects. Oftentimes, as in the preceding example, she uses analogy or metaphor in an attempt to help her students see the past in a way that makes it "sensible" and understandable. At the same time, she often relies on her students, through their questions and comments, to guide her to specific aspects of past events that need clarification and elaboration. In these interactions, Mrs. Knight's role as teacher and "knower of history" is complemented by the student role of thoughtful questioner of, and sometimes, insightful commentator on, history. Because Mrs. Knight's authority is unambiguous and unproblematic, she and her students are able to concentrate on academic endeavors rather than behavioral ones. This translates into a relaxed control of students and a firm yet positive control over the process through which knowledge and understanding of history is produced and utilized.

   Mrs. Knight's classroom is a place for the joint production of historical knowledge, because she, like the other teachers at Dusty Valley Elementary, believes in taking the time to listen to her students, because she values them as children. As Mrs. Thomas told me, in explaining that reading groups are "safe" places where students often share information about their personal lives,

> You know so we didn't read more than two pages but, you know if they needed to talk about something and it related to our story then I just let them do it (chuckles, then laughing), which is why we always get behind. But I think part, you know, that's part of my philosophy too. These are kids and they need to be valued. And if you're not gonna take the time to listen to them then why should they listen to you? (interview, May 3, 2003)

State Testing and the Production of Knowledge

In the preceding lesson excerpts, one can see how outlining and discussion are complementary aspects that make methodical outlining a structure for learning that meaningfully includes students in the knowledge production process. This is made possible by Mrs. Knight's positive control over the process of knowledge production, which provides meaningful roles for student participation, control that is made possible by her unambiguous moral authority over curriculum, instruction, and students in her classroom. However, at times state testing, which takes time away from social studies, controls the process of knowledge production. In these instances, Mrs. Knight is forced to decide between the lesser of two evils. She wonders whether she should quickly and efficiently cover the content so as to at least provide her students with some, albeit superficial, knowledge of historical figures and events or whether she should pursue the more time-consuming task of building her students' understanding of history, knowing that this will ultimately result in her students not being exposed to some historical figures and events that are part of the fifth-grade social studies content standards in California. This is a constant dilemma faced by teachers at Dusty Valley and, although covering the content is a sensible and understandable choice in these circumstances, it turns control over curriculum and instruction to the demands of state testing, undermining the rich learning environments made possible by the culture and moral order of Dusty Valley. This is evident in a hurried lesson in Mrs. Knight's classroom, in which she attempts to finish a five-page lesson in the textbook in one 40-min lesson, made all the more difficult by constant interruptions (two phone calls, a PA announcement about girls' basketball, and pens for the whiteboard that keep running out of ink).

On this day, they were outlining and discussing a lesson on everyday life in the United States following the end of the Revolutionary War. This was the final lesson in this chapter and the following day, a Friday, they were going on a field trip, and Mrs. Knight wanted to complete this lesson, and therefore this chapter, on this day. She was also attempting to keep up with the year plan she had made for social studies with Mrs. Matthews, a plan that ensured that they cover the material specified in the state content standards for history and social studies. What characterized this lesson—and other hurried lessons, as well as times in typical lessons that became hurried as they began to run out of time before recess—was the focus on outlining the material, and the failure of Mrs. Knight or her students to transition from this task to the joint narration of history. After outlining a section on changes in religion and the different religious groups in the new nation, they moved on to outline the different types of church services:

[1] *Mrs. Knight:*   OK types of church services. First one down here is going to be, in cities and towns [this is point E1 on the board: "E. Types of Church Services 1. In Cities and Towns a. quiet"]. People went to church, and it was, quiet. OK? In villages, which are very small towns, and farms, they had what were called, camp meetings [adding this to the outline as students copy

it down: "2. Villages, farms a. camp meetings." Also, Mrs. Knight switches pens because the one she was using has run out of ink]. And camp meetings were, loud. We had loud preaching, or loud sermons.

[2] *Rodney:* They had they had, loud voices.

[3] *Roberta:* Mrs. Knight is that an "eye" or a one?

[4] *Mrs. Knight:* It's a small one.

[5] *Male Student:* Please slow down.

[6] *Mrs. Knight:* Loud music. And, people were, excited. Lots of excitement. [Begins reading again] "The Baptists and Methodists had many of these camp meetings. The Baptists had a long history in America. One of the first Baptists was Roger Williams, who started the colony of Rhode Island in the sixteen thirties. The Methodists got started about a hundred years later. They followed the teachings of John Wesley, an English clergyman who preached in Georgia, which is down in the southern United States, in the seventeen thirties." So we have a long history, coming out of, camp meetings. [adding to the outline: "1. Loud preaching, loud music, excitement"] The Baptists did the camp, a lot of camp meetings, and they followed [finishing up point 1], who did it say they followed? [checks textbook] Roger Williams. [adding to outline: "b. Baptists followed Roger Williams"]. And we also have, Methodists. Who followed, John Wesley [adding to outline: "c. Methodists followed John Wesley"] And that takes us to, number two. [Mrs. Knight throws out the pen she was just using—out of ink—and picks up the orange one she had been using, which is not easy to see on the board. Then she erases the left side of the board. Students continue copying down what's on the right side of the board].

[7] *Tina:* Don't erase "c."

[8] *Nathaniel:* The same thing Mrs. Knight? Everyday Life? [he asks, because Mrs. Knight has left the large heading up, "Everyday Life in the Young Nation," and has just written "II. Growth of Free Black Community (330)," underneath it]

[9] *Mrs. Knight:* This is growth of the free Black community.

[10] *Nathaniel:* But it's still everyday life?

[11] *Mrs. Knight:* Yes. And this is divided into, three parts. We're gonna start with part one [begins writing point on board: "1. How Blacks Become Free"].

This was quite a contrast to the discussions that characterized most lessons in Mrs. Knight's classroom, including the lesson presented in the previous section. First, Mrs. Knight's voice dominated the classroom as she read from the textbook and articulated specific outline points as she wrote them on the front board. The students were silent, diligently copying down the outline points while Mrs. Knight read, talked, and wrote. Students did ask questions and made comments, but these were almost entirely about the outline itself and not the content of history ([3], [7], [8], [10]). Mrs. Knight and her students appeared to be stuck in the role of chroniclers, rather than narrators, of history, jointly producing (although Mrs. Knight clearly dominated the process) a simple chronological listing of historical figures and events as they occurred in a sequence set out in their social studies textbook. Mrs. Knight was intent on reading the entire lesson in the textbook and translating this information into an outline for her students, and her students were focused on copying down the outline on the front board quickly and correctly.

Mrs. Knight, who values and pursues her students' understanding of the past and works to build that understanding in her lessons, was undermined by her own efficiency. Because she was reading from the textbook and not calling on her students to read from the textbook, she was able to generate many of the outline points in a short amount of time, and her students had to work hard to keep up with her ("please slow down" [5]). In typical lessons, Mrs. Knight added outline points while students were reading from the textbook and during class discussions, where Mrs. Knight and her students jointly narrated the past. In these lessons the production of the outline was spread out, and students had time to copy outline points both while other students were reading from the textbook and while Mrs. Knight was producing a narrative account that meaningfully tied the outline points together, which included students as thoughtful questioners and commentators.

In this lesson, and in other lessons when time to do social studies was short, students were so busy trying to keep up with Mrs. Knight's production of the outline that they had little opportunity to play the crucial role they had in these lessons in jointly producing meaningful narratives of historical events with Mrs. Knight. It is not that the role of thoughtful learners who ask authentic questions or make insightful comments was no longer available to students in this hurried lesson.[9] However, because of the fast

---

[9] In fact, near the end of this lesson one student does ask an authentic question, the only break in outlining during this entire lesson. Roberta asked Mrs. Knight why their textbook called African Americans "Black" rather than "colored," which led Martin to ask about the use of the term *Negro*. Although the ensuing discussion was very brief, Mrs. Knight noted that in

pace of this lesson, the accessibility of that role was severely circumscribed ("Do I think about the past, or do I accurately copy down the outline points before recess?"), and for Mrs. Knight, her desire to assist her students in gaining knowledge and understanding of the past and the value she places on student questions and comments has not changed. However, she must face the dilemma of covering the content or falling behind, and she opted for covering the content as the lesser of two evils. This circumscribed not only the students' role in knowledge production but also her own role, as she became a chronicler, but not a narrator, of history.[10] Both the roles of chronicler and narrator are legitimate and necessary roles in doing social studies in Mrs. Knight's classroom, but the availability and accessibility of the narrator role can become severely circumscribed for both Mrs. Knight and her students when they are pressed for time.

This was not an easy day for students, who copied down a tremendous amount of material in a short amount of time. But there were no complaints, and students were diligently copying down the material, even moving around the room to get a better view of the front board (as they often did) or standing at their desks to look over the heads of the students seated in front of them so they could see the bottom of the board. The focus continued to be on the production of the outline, with students asking questions clarifying what point they were on, asking Mrs. Knight to move the board so they could see better, or one student proudly showing Mrs. Knight the two pages of outline notes he had taken. Although outlining was especially rigorous today, it was a legitimate task in Mrs. Knight's classroom, and there was no challenge in regard to Mrs. Knight's right to ask them to do this. However, that is understandable, not only given the culture and moral order of Dusty Valley that supports Mrs. Knight's moral authority over the children in her charge but also because it is evident to her students that she sincerely cares about them and values their questions, comments, and ideas. Although there was little discussion in this lesson, there normally is room for such discussion in social studies,[11] and that preserves the legitimacy of

the past if you weren't "lily white" you were considered colored, leading Nathaniel to ask, "if you were a Mexican you were colored too?", which Mrs. Knight confirmed. Although this discussion was not expansive, it was significant and important in reaffirming the value and availability of the student role as thoughtful and engaged learners in Mrs. Knight's classroom.

[10] And, in fact, Mrs. Knight was not willing to accept the lesser of two evils. After this lesson I noted how hurried it seemed, and she agreed and noted that she would have to return to this material the following week, and she did.

[11] It is important to understand how social studies instruction is different in Mrs. Knight's classroom, in terms of time, than Mrs. Matthews's or Mrs. Thomas's classrooms. Because social studies instruction is very important to Mrs. Knight, and she believes it is very important for her students, she made more room for social studies by eliminating physical education for the entire school year. Mrs. Matthews and Mrs. Thomas were not willing to do this, and Mrs. Knight acknowledged that this was particularly difficult for her students. However, because of this Mrs. Knight got very close to completing the social studies curriculum, as laid out by state

Mrs. Knight's authority and control over students in this lesson, even as Mrs. Knight, her students, and curriculum and instruction are being controlled by the demands of state testing.

STATE TESTING AND THE MORAL ORDER OF DUSTY VALLEY

The culture of being positive, the moral order of enabling care, and traditional authority relations between teachers and students at Dusty Valley Elementary promoted the creation of rich learning environments in classrooms. Classrooms were characterized by trusting relationships between teachers and students; they were places of academic engagement where teachers used their authority to control the process of knowledge production, a form of positive control that expanded rather than limited the content of historical knowledge and understandings that could be generated. In Mrs. Knight's classroom, students were active participants in the process of knowledge production, fulfilling roles as questioners and commentators that enabled Mrs. Knight and her students to go beyond the mere chronicling of history to create meaningful narratives of historical figures, events, and ideas. The moral climate of Mrs. Knight's classroom encouraged students to ask about anything and everything, and their questions and comments, coupled with Mrs. Knight's own efforts to narrate the past in ways that would be sensible and understandable for her students, shaped the direction, scope, and content of the historical narratives accomplished in her classroom.

Dusty Valley Elementary was, and is, a good school, but its ability to provide a rich educational experience to students in all subject areas is seriously challenged by high-stakes state-mandated testing in language arts and mathematics. This is manifested as a lack of time for social studies (and science) education, and teachers found themselves in a bind that forced them to choose between practices that efficiently transmitted content knowledge to students versus practices that developed students' understanding of history and included them as active, meaningful participants in the narration of history. As was evident in the excerpts from two lessons in Mrs. Knight's classroom, social studies instruction is often authentic and meaningful, embodying the kind of dialogic instruction (Nystrand, 1997) in which student questions and comments shape the character and content of the knowledge produced. In hurried lessons, student accessibility to more active and participatory roles is circumscribed, resulting in monologic

standards, whereas both Mrs. Matthews and Mrs. Thomas finished the year without addressing large portions of U.S. and California history. Nonetheless, even Mrs. Knight was often pressed for time, leading to hurried lessons in social studies.

instruction or recitation (Drew & Heritage, 1992; Mehan, 1979a; Nystrand, 1997) in which the teacher's voice dominates and the focus is on reproducing textbook content. The threat of state-mandated testing is the potential to transform the classrooms at Dusty Valley into spaces where recitation is the norm and authentic, meaningful conversations between teachers and students are squeezed out as time and resources are devoted to language arts and mathematics instruction.

More important, I would argue that the demands of state testing also pose a threat to the very factors that make Dusty Valley Elementary a good school. Authority depends on, and is constituted by, the character of the interactions between teachers and students in classrooms. Students consent to teacher commands because they know teachers care about them and value them, and they know this because they experience this every day in lessons, where teachers listen to their questions and comments; make space for their voices in the curriculum; and incorporate their knowledge, ideas, and concerns into the knowledge production process.

Authority is not a possession that Mrs. Knight simply has but an interactional accomplishment, a relationship made and remade daily through the interactions between Mrs. Knight and her students (Macbeth, 1991; Pace, 2003a, 2003b, 2003c). The students consented to participate in what for them was a somewhat grueling exercise in outlining, a lesson that may have been academic in its orientation but provided few opportunities for their authentic participation, because their relationship with Mrs. Knight is based on what happens in most lessons. Students know that Mrs. Knight values their questions and comments, values them because they have an active voice and a meaningful role in narrating history in her classroom most of the time, even if there was little time for such participation in this particular lesson.

However, state-mandated testing in language arts and mathematics, by squeezing the time available for meaningful practice in social studies, threatens to undermine classroom (and school) authority relationships by removing opportunities for sustaining, enacting, and reenacting these trusting relationships. Students know they are valued because their questions, comments, and opinions are valued, and that is made possible by a structure for learning, methodical outlining, that provides a meaningful role for their participation in the process of knowledge production. To the extent that state testing makes that role less accessible to students—not because teachers no longer value the children in their care but because there is little time to demonstrate this in lessons—the trusting relationships between teachers and students will become less real and more difficult to sustain or even establish. It is in these ways that high-stakes state-mandated testing is not simply a threat to social studies (and science) education but presents a potential threat to the culture and moral order that makes Dusty Valley Elementary a successful school.

REFERENCES

Armento, B. J., Nash, G. B., Salter, C. L., & Wixson, K. K. (1991). *America will be*. Boston: Houghton Mifflin.

Buzzelli, C., & Johnston, B. (2002). *The moral dimensions of teaching: Language, power, and culture in classroom interactions*. New York: RoutledgeFalmer.

California Legislature. (1999). *Public schools accountability act of 1999*. Available: www.cde.ca .gov/ta/ac/pa/index.asp

Collins, J. (1982). Discourse style, classroom interaction and differential treatment. *Journal of Reading Behavior, 14*, 429–437.

Cronon, W. (1992). A place for stories: Nature, history, and narrative. *Journal of American History, 78*(4), 1347–1376.

Delpit, L. (1995). *Other people's children: Cultural conflict in the classroom*. New York: New Press.

Drew, P., & Heritage, J. (1992). *Talk at work: Interaction in institutional settings*. Cambridge, England: Cambridge University Press.

Gutierrez, K., Larson, J., & Kreuter, B. (1995). Cultural tensions in the scripted classroom: The value of the subjugated perspective. *Urban Education, 29*, 410–442.

Gutierrez, K., Rymes, B., & Larson, J. (1995). Script, counterscript, and underlife in the classroom: James Brown versus *Brown v. Board of Education*. *Harvard Educational Review, 65*, 445–471.

Hansen, D. T. (1993). The moral importance of the teacher's style. *Journal of Curriculum Studies, 25*, 397–421.

Heath, S. B. (1978). Teacher talk: Language in the classroom. *Language in Education: Theory and Practice, 1*, 1–30.

Lightfoot, S. L. (1983). *The good high school: Portraits of character and culture*. New York: Basic Books.

Lipman, P. (1998). *Race, class, and power in school restructuring*. Albany: State University of New York Press.

Macbeth, D. (1991). Teacher authority as practical action. *Linguistics and Education, 3*, 281–313.

McNeil, L. M. (1986). *Contradictions of control: School knowledge and school structure*. New York: Routledge & Kegan Paul.

McNeil, L. M. (2000). *Contradictions of school reform: Educational costs of standardized testing*. New York: Routledge.

Mehan, H. (1979a). *Learning lessons*. Cambridge, MA: Harvard University Press.

Mehan, H. (1979b). "What time is it, Denise?": Asking known information questions in classroom discourse. *Theory Into Practice, 18*, 285–294.

Metz, M. H. (1978). *Classrooms and corridors: The crisis of authority in desegregated secondary schools*. Berkeley: University of California Press.

Noblit, G. (1993). Power and caring. *American Educational Research Journal, 30*, 23–38.

Nystrand, M. (1997). *Opening dialogue: Understanding the dynamics of language and learning in the English classroom*. New York: Teachers College Press.

Pace, J. L. (2003a). Managing the dilemmas of professional and bureaucratic authority in a high school English class. *Sociology of Education, 76*, 37–52.

Pace, J. L. (2003b). Revisiting classroom authority: Theory and ideology meet practice. *Teachers College Record, 105*(8), 1559–1585.

Pace, J. L. (2003c). Using ambiguity and entertainment to win compliance in a lower level U.S. history class. *Journal of Curriculum Studies, 35*, 83–110.

Page, R. (1987). Lower-track classes at a college-preparatory high school: A caricature of educational encounters. In G. Spindler & L. Spindler (Eds.), *Interpretive ethnography of education: At home and abroad* (pp. 447–472). Hillsdale, NJ: Lawrence Erlbaum Associates, Inc.

Page, R. N. (1991). *Lower-track classrooms: A curricular and cultural perspective.* New York: Teachers College Press.

Powell, A. G., Farrar, E., & Cohen, D. K. (1985). *The shopping mall high school: Winners and losers in the educational marketplace.* Boston: Houghton Mifflin.

Shultz, J., Erickson, F., & Florio, S. (1982). Where's the floor? Aspects of the cultural organization of social relationships in communication at home and in school. In P. Gilmore & A. Glatthorn (Eds.), *Children in and out of school: Ethnography and education* (pp. 88–123). Washington, DC: Center for Applied Linguistics.

Sizer, T. R. (1984). *Horace's compromise: The dilemma of the American high school.* Boston: Houghton Mifflin.

Swidler, A. (1979). *Organization without authority: Dilemmas of social control in free schools.* Cambridge, MA: Harvard University Press.

Swidler, A. (1986). Culture in action: symbols and strategies. *American Sociological Review, 51,* 273–286.

Swidler, A. (2001). *Talk of love: How culture matters.* Chicago: University of Chicago Press.

Valli, L. (1990). A curriculum of effort: Tracking students in a Catholic high school. In R. Page & L. Valli (Eds.), *Curriculum differentiation: Interpretive studies in U.S. secondary schools* (pp. 45–65). Albany: State University of New York Press.

Wertsch, J. V. (1998). *Mind as action.* New York: Oxford University Press.

White, H. (1973). *Metahistory: The historical imagination in nineteenth-century Europe.* Baltimore: Johns Hopkins University Press.

White, H. (1978). *Tropics of discourse: Essays in cultural criticism.* Baltimore: Johns Hopkins University Press.

Wills, J. (1994). Popular culture, curriculum, and historical representation: The situation of Native Americans in American history and the perpetuation of stereotypes. *Journal of Narrative and Life History, 4,* 277–294.

Wills, J. (1996). Who needs multicultural education?: White students, U.S. history and the construction of a usable past. *Anthropology and Education Quarterly, 27,* 365–389.

Wills, J. (2001). Missing in interaction: Diversity, narrative, and critical multicultural social studies. *Theory and Research in Social Education, 29,* 43–64.

Wills, J. (2005). "Some people even died": Martin Luther King, Jr., the civil rights movement, and the politics of remembrance in elementary classrooms. *International Journal of Qualitative Studies in Education, 18*(1), 109–131.

Chapter 3

Playing With Pedagogical Authority

James Mullooly
California State University, Fresno

Hervé Varenne
Columbia University

Pedagogical authority is a crucial intermediary step in Bourdieu and Passeron's (1970/1977) model for the reproduction of any educational system. We agree with placing authority at the center of what educational researchers should consider, but we do this with a major caveat: Authority must not be approached as the property of a position or person that others must accept. It is a property of an interaction, constituted by the active work of all involved, regardless of the position they may display. We argue this point by looking carefully at two brief moments when four students and a teacher joke without disrupting the flow of the lesson. We place these moments within the lesson in which they occurred and within the history of the school as it was made to articulate with at least three major movements in the United States relating to religion, poverty, and pedagogy. Our main focus remains on the continuing attempt to understand major features of American schooling, particularly the asymmetries between teachers and students, in a fashion that fully acknowledges the work that all involved must continually perform for the overall cultural form to persist across generations of students. Our specific focus is to explore the place of play in work that constitutes particular forms of asymmetries.

In Bourdieu and Passeron's (1970/1977) model, *pedagogical authority* is an aspect of the work of *inculcation*—a word we take as synonymous with other words, such as *socialization* and *enculturation*, if not *teaching* or *education*.

If it "lasts long enough," this work "produces a durable training, i.e. an habitus" (Bourdieu & Passeron, 1970/1977, p. 31). Through this argumentation, Bourdieu and Passeron appear to conceive of authority as the property of an agency ("agent or institution") in a relation of pedagogic communication. We understand this to mean that, in a classroom such as the one on which we report, the teacher is constructed by the theory as having authority over students. Conversely, the students are constructed as having the property of not seeing in full truth that which produces the asymmetry. Authority, in this model, is something that some have and others do not have. Through this argumentation, Bourdieu and Passeron gave further life to a long line of investigation in political science, sociology, and education.

Authority remains of pressing interest to many educational researchers, wherever they stand on any of the ideological divides about the proper ordering of schools. In these debates, authority further becomes the practices of those who have it. This stance opens the way to considerations of the value of effectiveness of various versions of these practices. As summarized by Pace (2003a, 2003b), who is building on the work of Metz (1978) and others, "authority relationships . . . involve . . . strategies . . . to enforce and soften the demands of schooling" (Pace, 2003a, pp. 38–39). There are different ways of exercising authority, and they can have different impacts on school atmospheres and students' learning. More radical authors, including Bourdieu and Passeron, treat authority as radically tied to the overall structuring of contemporary societies and thus probably not subject to local reform at the school or class level. We even suspect that they would consider the more enlightened forms of authority the more symbolically violent, because they are more likely to be successful in hiding themselves. Regardless of whether one hopes that the practice of authority can be reformed, the main concern of all these models remains what students are learning (or what is inculcated into them). By focusing on authority as something that is done to students, much of what students actually do is discounted. Similarly discounted is what teachers do in relation to those in authority over them (administrators and the like), as well as the regulators and politicians who may have authority over those—and so on, in a long chain of asymmetries.

For ourselves, we are attempting to contribute to the development of an alternative line of investigation where authority is approached as an aspect of the active structuring of particular kinds of scenes. In such scenes, *all* participants work together to produce a peculiar asymmetry in which *some* people are identified as having the authority of explicitly (in the case of school classes) starting and ending the class, organizing its various moments, or labeling the other participants, among many other responsibilities. Identifying types of "exercising authority" and types of "accepting authority," or worrying about the states of mind of those who appear to do either, is not our concern. Our concern is with the work all people involved do—including those who call on, say, teachers to "start" a class and thereby impose on them an authority some of them may wish they were not given.

Observers may find it difficult to notice this work. In the routine of caricatural lessons, teachers pass out tests, and students take them. The work of authority may be even further hidden in seminar-like lessons where students appear to lead. In all classrooms and schools, however, there are moments when what may have been settled must be reconstituted. At these moments, what is at stake—or, to index our main theme, at play—may be revealed in the acts of all. These moments can involve direct challenges and can be quite dramatic if they escalate to any kind of violence. They can be pathetic. They can also be playful.

Our focus here is on moments of play. We chose this focus for a variety of reasons. First, mutually constituting authority can be fun and perhaps even pleasurable. At the very least, it can be made fun of. After all, the "know-it-all" is a stock comic character in the American imagination. Second, theoretically stressing the reality that people do play with authority grants the participants forms of practical awareness that a focus on *habitus* can make invisible. After all, it is much easier not to blame the victims of authority if one has brought out their work against it—even when it was unsuccessful. Third, and most important, a focus on play emphasizes the indeterminacy in the experience of school authority patterns. No teacher can enter a classroom without worrying that what should happen will not happen. Authority cannot be assumed; it must be reconstructed, moment to moment, in shifting contexts. The teacher–student asymmetry is a potentiality: How it will reveal itself at any particular time must be taken as radically indeterminate. There is no way to predict what will happen in a classroom even if one knows what is at play.

We are not sure how this approach to authority will help reformers design new regulations or curricula about what a teacher may or should do with students. We err on the side of caution: Researchers must come up with more inclusive theories before they enter the reform fray with the special authority that they can claim.[1]

PLAYING WITH AUTHORITY AND PLAY IN THE SOCIAL SCIENCES AND EDUCATION

This is not the place for a full review of work on authority, or play, or their role in education. At this moment we just wish to point out the traditions from which we distinguish ourselves and the traditions on which we build.

---

[1] This is not to belittle personal involvement but to warn against the temptation to make too much of one's expertise as a tool to push ideological agendas.

In educational research, authority is often discussed in terms of *moral order,* or the effectiveness of various types of authority patterns for student success. This is an interesting issue that other chapters in this volume address. Many in this tradition are comfortable with Bourdieu's (1972) *habitus* and are mostly concerned with making the process either more humane or more efficient and, it is hoped, both. This is good as far as it goes, but it does not address our fundamental question: How are these patterns actually produced in everyday life?

Our concerns are closer to the concern of the extensive work that has been produced in the sociology of medical settings (Davis-Floyd & Sargent, 1997; Fisher & Todd, 1986; Heath, 1986; Jordan, 1992). Like ours, much of this work proceeds through detailed analysis of interactions where another form of authority is routinely implicated: the authority to diagnose and prescribe. Much of this work uses words such as *negotiation, contestation,* and *resistance.* These words also appear extensively in educational research starting at least with Willis's (1977) classic *Learning to Labor* and continuing in the work of Giroux and others. There is a parallel development in anthropology including a concern with the "weapons of the weak" (Scott, 1985). This has been criticized as possibly masking the impossibility, in most of the cases, of winning significant battles against the dominant patterns. This can lead to turns toward notions of hegemony (Apple, 1996; Giroux, 1983; Williams, 1977) that can easily collapse back into the assumption of misunderstanding and internalization that vitiates, for us, Bourdieu's (1972) theory of *habitus.*

Worrying about the production of dominance is something that we must all do, but worrying about the fate of those who are dominated can move us away from understanding the social processes at work. Hervé Varenne has made this argument elsewhere, and this chapter is an expansion of discussions of the complexity of what can happen in the detail of school-relevant interaction—in classrooms, choirs, and families (Dore & McDermott, 1982; Varenne & McDermott, 1998). This chapter is a companion piece to the case when some students' laughter is interpreted as confirmatory proof that they were failing students (Rizzo-Tolk & Varenne, 1992). It also takes the analysis further by directly addressing students' laughter and play as a theoretical problem that can shed more light on various issues related to cultural dominance, including authority.

We mention only two main theoretical conversations to locate our stance. First, we take seriously Bateson's (1955) famous question: How do we know that play is play? Bateson's concern with the message "this is play" can be taken as a simple technical question for theories of communication, but it is in fact a profoundly challenging one: How do we know that anything in human interaction is what all participants appear to be sure it is? How do we know that a particular question is an authoritative question while another is not? Note the ambiguity of the *we* in this sentence: Does it refer to observers or to analysts? Does it refer to participants? These questions are fundamental to all work in conversation analysis and ethnomethodology. Most relevant to this chapter from this tradition is Sacks's (1974/1989) article on joking.

Our work is also located within another conversation that has had much less impact so far on educational research. The anthropologist James Boon (1999) recently challenged us to consider the "extra-Vagance" of human culture in which nothing is what it is for good—either in the long run (thus cultural "diversity") or in the short run (down to face-to-face moments in the everyday life of everyday classrooms.). Unlike analyses that may include a reference to class clowning as one form of resistance, the radical playfulness that Boon proposed is fundamental to cultural production. It moves analysts to face uncertainty, their own as well as that of those they observe. What did I just see? What am I going to do with it? What will happen to me if what I just did is taken in this or that way? Of course, analysts have the luxury of editing their statements many times before publication. In everyday life, timeframes are so short as to preclude what is never quite a rationalistic process of strategizing. In life, and even after editing, one will always be caught in a web where even probabilities as to what generally happens next are not helpful. In these ways Boon brought together what is most powerful in Lévi-Strauss's (1962/1966) opus, particularly his understanding of collective imagination as a form of *bricolage* and what is most powerful in Geertz's (1973) interpretative approaches, particularly his writings about "deep play."

AN OCCASION FOR CLASSROOM PLAY

In this chapter we are trying to understand two moments of classroom play as historically located joint practices of all participants and draw some consequences of this stance. In both, the students take something from the teacher's immediate performance and elaborate on it. In one case the students respond to the teacher in a way that directly acknowledges what she asks them to do ("say 'yes'") and do something related: Some of the students do not say "yes"; instead, they say "sí" and "oui oui." In the other case, the elaboration culminates in a gestural "f—— you" gesture performed in full view of the teacher. In both cases the students laugh and the teacher proceeds as if both elaborations fully fitted within the lesson—which they did, on that day. The authority is not a property of the teacher so much as what all had to take into account as they achieve at least two other things: a lesson and a joke.

In the body of this chapter we show in detail how both cases involve all five participants (the four students and the teacher); how both cases directly fit within the structuring of jokes as well as classrooms; and how the students use features of the immediate situation, some of which can be understood only in terms of the history of the school. The school, however, must not be treated as the "cause" of whatever may have happened; instead, it is what made whatever happened possible. With this in mind, we summarize some of the broad features of this school. Note that we do not present these features so much as properties of the school but rather as moments in the evolution of a long conversation that produced various kinds of schools in the United States, including one particular kind of religious, Catholic schools: the Jesuit school. Jesuit schools have a long history of transformation, and they come in many different shapes. The one where Mullooly (2003) conducted his research[2] is the recent product of reformers searching for better ways to serve recent immigrants into the United States—in this case, predominantly immigrants from Mexico into a small midwestern city where they now occupy the position once occupied by various immigrants from Europe and particularly from Ireland.

"Loyola Middle School" was established 1993. One founding document states that "The school makes an 11-year commitment to its students," through middle school, high school, and college. This is more than rhetorical flourish. It is a guide to a particular form of single-minded practice. For example, a few years after its inception, when Loyola's first graduates were enrolled in elite high schools, a problem emerged: A few of its graduates

---

[2]The full context for this case study can be found in Mullooly's (2003) doctoral dissertation. This study involved year-long (1998–1999), daily participant observation in the school and its summer camp along with data collection strategies that included note taking, interviewing, systematic observations, and videotaping of many activities (Mullooly, 2003). Mullooly spent the following 2 years (1999–2001) as a part-time teacher and ethnographer as well, which made it possible to confirm many of the hypotheses generated in the 1st year of the study. This particular school has been very successful in its goal of placing these boys into locally defined elite, competitive high schools and well-rated colleges. Its graduates complete high school at a rate of 90%, compared to a 53% national rate and a 42% high school completion rate within the city of the school (for Hispanics; Greene, 2001; Greene & Winters, 2002). There are similarly impressive results regarding college participation and completion. Given these results, the primary objective of Mullooly's dissertation was to analyze the social–interactional work involved in constructing and maintaining students of this school as successful from a variety of angles. The findings indicate that, contrary to the belief that it is difficult to bring about success in students who are likely to fail (based on economic and ethnic disadvantages), it is quite easy to have them succeed if they attend a small, well-endowed school, staffed by very dedicated members. These findings do not imply, however, that social reproduction can be done away with all together. Mullooly's dissertation includes descriptions of this "work of maintaining successful students" as indexed in talk during staff meetings (that was found to either accentuate or ignore depictions of student behavior as "bad"), during group activities at the school's 6-week summer camp (where student failures at public speaking moments were considered successes because of the positive responses they received), and during classroom moments (where students' unwillingness to follow interactional guidelines was ignored by the teacher to the benefit of completing a successful lesson).

were dropping out. In response, the principal at the time assigned himself to the newly created position of Director of Graduates, whose sole purpose was to help these students stay in high school. The school itself, as a set of policies and not-quite-routinized practices, is thus not a stable entity but rather a temporary answer to an analysis of conditions in terms of available resources. As of 1999, the ethnographic present for this study, the school remains small and local: Students must live in the neighborhood of the school, one of the most poverty stricken in the city.[3] Most of the staff work long hours during the school day and return for evening study hall, and some attend the summer camp, for pay that is less than 80% of a public school teacher's base salary in that town. This decade of work by many different kinds of people has produced something altogether unique.

Whatever one may think of the decision of these adults to work within the confines of this school, Loyola is not simply the product of an unfolding Catholic *habitus*. It is a very deliberate construction by a staff of certified teachers who attend professional conferences on topics ranging from bilingual education to Catholic education in general. One principal is a curriculum specialist with a PhD in education and 20 years of experience in public schools. Nothing much that transpires in Loyola happens without much talk—talk that often focused on what is going wrong.

The one instance of this kind of talk that is most relevant to this chapter is a set of long conversations that led to the abandonment of earlier pedagogies and the introduction of a scripted teaching methodology—Direct Instruction—that was presented as a cutting-edge method and implemented against the opinion of some on the staff. Direct Instruction is a patented method that builds on the research in experimental instruction of Bereiter and Englemann (1966) at the University of Illinois. Since its inception, Direct Instruction has been quite controversial among educationists. Adams and Englemann (1996) provided a comprehensive description of Direct Instruction, and Heshusius (1991) and Allington and Woodside-Jiron (1999) made well-reasoned critiques of it. Most debates about it have indexed a long-standing dilemma recently raised by Wong Fillmore and Meyer (1992) regarding the purpose of schooling. If assimilation is the goal, then the finite, inflexible set of facts that are to be mastered in Direct Instruction will readily accommodate. If, though, the goal of education involves a

---

[3]Specifically, there are 49 boys in the school, and all are of Central or South American descent (45 from Mexico, 2 from the Dominican Republic, and 1 each from Puerto Rico and Bolivia). They all have some facility in both English and Spanish. Forty-four of the 49 are from families officially classified as below the poverty line. These boys' peers attend public schools with low graduation rates and an even lower rate of college attendance. There are 14 full-time members of the teaching and administrative staff, plus several part-time volunteer teachers. This produces a student–teacher ratio of 1:7, allowing for small, flexible classes. This staff is mostly White and prosperous or on career tracks that all but ensure future prosperity. Some of this teaching staff had little to no teaching experience.

celebration of tolerance and cultural pluralism, then Direct Instruction is a less effective means. Heshusius echoed this sentiment through claims that Direct Instruction's entire epistemological framework dubiously considers some things as essential content while disregarding more holistic perspectives founded on contemporary teaching theory. One implication of Direct Instruction, whether intended or not, is "that teachers' expectations for students are too low and that too many teachers are not competent enough to be able to deliver an effective curriculum without careful guidance or even complete scripting" (Hamann, 1999, p. 54).

At Loyola, Direct Instruction swept through the school with great speed. A new principal advocated for them, and his support had a legitimizing effect: The founders of the school had delegated some of their authority to him to do just such things as implement curricula. Within 1 year, scripted methodologies replaced existing curriculum in most language arts classes (writing, reading, comprehension) and the science classes. Although some staff questioned its rote, dry style, most accepted it initially. Their acceptance was based on ignorance or hope (that it may help improve the students' abilities) and on its expedient appeal (in that it was sold to the staff as a short-term program).

Most important for our case are the body movements that are an integral part of this pedagogy: the up-and-down movements of the forearm that it prescribed for teachers offered a hook for a kind of visual joking that, after the fact, must seem inevitable.

Before we focus on the class and the jokes, we need to address briefly whether everything that we saw at Loyola could be explained as a simple product of it being a Catholic school. There is a long literature on Catholic schools in the United States and a continuing search for the set of features that make them successful for the children of immigrants on the kinds of measures that make many public schools "failures." For at least 30 years, much research has shown that Catholic school students generally outperform their public school counterparts (Coleman, Greeley, & Hoffer, 1985; Gamoran, 1992; Neal, 1997; Polite, 1992; Sander, 1996), graduate high school in higher percentages (Evans & Schwab, 1995), and go on to college more frequently (Falsey & Heyns, 1984; Hodgkins & Morrison, 1971). The success of Catholic education is most pronounced for students who are disadvantaged by low socioeconomic status and ethnic minority status (Bryk, Lee & Holland, 1993; Polite, 1992). The reasons for this success remain controversial. Whether the main feature is school atmosphere, discipline, moral order, family involvement, or creaming (i.e., selecting only the better students), the argumentation proceeds from the kind of social science we resist: the kind where behavioral "outcomes" are produced by independent "variables"—however numerous the variables or complex the analysis of their statistical relationships. Catholic schools, in any event, have come, and continue to come, in many different shapes, from the classical cases of the schools for Irish immigrants run by severe nuns trying to control 50 poor boys or girls, to the cases of the schools for elites for which the Jesuits are best known. In recent years, Catholic schools have served predominantly non-Catholic students and, as in the case at Loyola, there is little emphasis left on doctrinal or ritual matters. The dominant concerns of the senior staff are how to design a school that uses the latest pedagogies and curricula. Loyola is not the kind of school caricatured by Powers (1975) in his instant classic *Do Black Patent-Leather Shoes Really Reflect Up?*

Mullooly (2003) argued elsewhere that, if we were to speculate as to why almost all students at Loyola enter locally acknowledged elite high schools and then move on to college, we would not focus on its success with inculcating school knowledge into the students. We would focus instead on the continuing work of the staff to disregard various evidence that the students were not learning and convincing the high schools to do the same. In the long run it may be the case that the students did learn in a possibly more humanistic sense than is possible in schools where tests and assessments are used to send students onto different tracks. Tests, assessments, and evidence of "bad" behavior rarely made a radical difference in the life of the Loyola boys lucky enough to have been chosen. The case on which we now focus is but one of the many observed instances when forms of behavior that in other schools may have had serious consequences were in fact actively ignored by the adults observing them.

Class, Authority, Joking

Classic ethnographies of classrooms have abundantly demonstrated the complexity of the work of all involved. We are directly building on these ethnographies. The classroom we discuss is another token of the types that have now been abundantly discussed in the literature on American schools (McDermott, Gospodinoff, & Aron, 1978; Mehan, 1979; Metz, 1978; Page, 1991; Tobin, Wu, & Davidson, 1989; Varenne, 1983). It is, of course, unique, but this uniqueness is precisely produced by the participants playing close attention to well-described features of American schooling. We are particularly interested here in all that has been written about the authority of teachers to ask questions and evaluate answers. To clarify this, and then move on to the analysis of the actual jokes, we must summarize briefly what is known about the social organization of classroom lessons and joking. We emphasize in particular what allows for these two types of scenes to be performed jointly. This has a formal element: How do the participants mesh the requirements of both lesson and joking so that each can proceed to their end? It also has a more political element because the jokes are about the lesson and its peculiarities. The jokes could be taken as improvised political cartoons that provided instant comments about what was going on—including, perhaps, an investigation of how far the students could go before the teacher intervened.

In many ways, Direct Instruction is an unwitting caricature of the lesson as modeled in Mehan's (1979) classic analysis. Mehan described the lesson as a sequence composed of three basic steps requiring a minimum of two actors: (a) an Initiation (e.g., a teacher's question), (b) a Response (e.g., a student's attempt at answering the question) and (c) an Evaluation (e.g., the teacher's judgment of the student's answer). In many pedagogies there are many different ways to actually perform any of the steps, and many more than two persons can be involved. In Direct Instruction, however, each of the three steps are fully elaborated in gesture as well as words, and they are scripted to occur again and again at a rapid rate. The proponents of Direct Instruction are very serious about the needs for unwavering specificity. Everyone else can see the potentiality for comedy. Still, Direct Instruction itself is but one way of doing what remains one of the most powerful moments in the cultures of the school: the moment of evaluation through which, it is hoped, ever more inculcation is to take place.

We are particularly concerned here with the possibilities for further elaborations of the basic sequence—the elaborations that Direct Instruction precisely attempts to prevent. Mehan (1979) was aware that, in regular classrooms, any one of the three basic steps in a lessons could be elided when the completion of an earlier sequence (or the start of a new sequence) could count as the first or last step of the next (e.g., a new question to a second student can signal to the first that the answer was satisfactory). Others have shown that much can happen within the sequence itself, including a lot that is not part of the sequence. This is particularly visible in certain settings—for example, at home, when several tasks have to be performed simultaneously. It is possible, for example, for a set of people to do homework, snack, watch television, and discuss the events of the day. It is only observers who can become confused until they notice how participants dance from one task to the other by, among other things, using the off-times from one sequence to perform their role in another.[4] We approach joking about pedagogy as a form of this kind of multitasking. In our case, however, the students are not really performing a task unrelated to the lesson that

---

[4]For example, in one instance of homework while watching television, close analysis showed that each of the participants (mother in the role of teacher and daughter in the role of student) moved in and out of the homework task to watch the screen in such a way as not to disrupt the homework by sequencing their watching with the moments when homework tasks did not require their immediate involvement: when the mother looked for a question to ask, the daughter looked at the screen, and when the daughter searched for the answer, the mother looked at the screen. McDermott and Webber (1998) continued this kind of investigation in their discussion of the "organization of certain activities in concert with other activities" (p. 323).

is co-occurring. Instead, they do exactly what Direct Instruction is not supposed to allow: They elaborate on what was being presented as they stray from the content to be inculcated.

A brief musical example may introduce the simple version of what we have in mind here. The kind of play with pedagogical authority we are attempting to account for here is a kind of elaboration[5] on a theme or melody. This works all the better when the elaboration is demonstratably linked to a property of the theme but adds something that will appear both novel and obvious. In Bill Moyers's (1990) famous documentary on the history of "Amazing Grace" in the American religious imagination, Jesse Norman, the famous opera singer, talks about the technical aspects of one of the many elaborations that have made the "same" hymn so "different" at different times and for different groups in the United States:

> Even the melody has changed a little bit. When I sing it, I try to sing it as it was published about 1900, but the melody itself has had some variations as well. The way it was written we have [Norman sings an example of the original melody]. All of that is really quite straight, but I think by the time, in the '60s, when Judy Collins was doing it, it took on an even more kind of lyrical quality. [Norman sings an example of the original melody with the Collins elaborations.] All of these lovely moving notes in between the original melody.

Joking within a lesson, like adding judiciously placed notes within a melody, is not only possible, it is a fundamental a property of all human interaction, and we must pay attention.

Before we proceed, we must note that joking is itself a complex social practice, a joint accomplishment that must proceed through a series of steps that Sacks's (1974/1989) work has helped model: Preface, Telling and, Response.[6] According to Sacks, words (and, we would add, gestures) are used to create an interactional field for a joke to be told (Preface). The joke is then told (Telling). Finally, there is some sort of reaction from the audience (Response). For example,

Preface   A: Have you ever heard the one about the chicken?
             B: No

---

[5] The term *ornamentation* may be more apropos historically, but its current connotation is more indicative of standard melodic formulas or performance styles (e.g., *arpeggio*). Prior to approximately 1800, ornaments were considered melodic embellishments (Apel & Danial, 1960).

[6] Although Sacks generally modeled the Telling part of a joke as performed by only one person, there is no reason why this telling might not be distributed across several participants, as happened here. Similarly, Sacks did not mention that a joke might not be scripted and that it might be a subsequent, although his model does allow for the kind of distributed elaboration we document here.

Telling   A: Why did the chicken cross the road?
             B: I don't know; why?
             A: To get to the other side.
Response   B: (Laughter.)

Although laughter is a common response, it is also possible to have the felt absence of laughter (often accompanied by a grimace or a smirk) indicative of a Response consisting of an evaluation of the joke as inappropriate or of poor quality. In other words, a joke, like a lesson, is also a political field within which authority and power patterns are activated around issues of direct relevance (is the joke genuinely funny?) and also of indirect relevance (what might be the implications for a subaltern not to laugh at the failed joke of a superior?).

We now turn to the four students and their teacher who, together, improvised joking elaborations on a lesson theme. The performance elicited only brief and ambiguous smiles on the teacher's face as she continued with the scripted lesson as if nothing was happening.

THE SETTING, THE PARTICIPANTS, AND THE JOKES

Four students of the eighth-grade class of 1999 and Danielle, their homeroom teacher, comprised one of the reading groups of this third-period reading class. The students had been together in such classes for the previous 2.5 years. They are the upper group in their class in term of their reading scores. The teacher had been at Loyola and with these students (as the reading and eighth-grade homeroom teacher) for 6 months, since the start of the school year. The scenes we briefly sketch for this chapter are part of a longer videotaped record of the introduction of Direct Instruction in this classroom. The teacher herself had expressed some dissatisfaction with the method to the staff and the researcher. Eventually, however, she had to accept that it would have to be used. Whether the students sensed this reluctance fully or not, and even though they had next to no knowledge of Direct Instruction prior to this period, they immediately found ways of expressing dislike. Taping of another classroom of students at the same time revealed similar responses.

We start with a brief overview of the whole lesson. The half-hour tape was transcribed and roughly coded for what we present as elaborations on the initiation–response–elaboration model. This initial coding helped us gain a quick sense of the overall organization of the lesson. We mention it here mostly to indicate that the joking in which we are interested is not at all a rare occurrence. We do not want to suggest that this code might be valid

FIG. 3.1.   Default position.

for correlative purposes in other kinds of investigation. The coding task was simplified by the very organization of Direct Instruction that includes specific definitions for the kind of talk that is to fit within the lesson. Most of the elaborations were verbal and could be heard by the teacher and researcher. Others were matters of postural shift away from the default positioning. These were visible to the teacher as they occurred right in front of her (see Fig. 3.1). Instances of inaudible talk between the students were also coded as an elaboration. The elaborations themselves were coded as either jokes; complaints; other kinds of small talk, inappropriate questions, and banter. Table 3.1 gives a sense of the frequency of these elaborations and their frequency throughout the lesson. We do not analyze frequency

TABLE 3.1
Elaborations on the Lesson

Time	Jokes	Complaints about Direct Instruction	Student Small Talk	Inappropriate Questions	Banter/ Competition
9:51–9:57	4 method 2 other	2	3	3	0
9:58–10:04	1 other	2	2	0	1
10:05–10:11	2 method 3 other	1	0	1	0
10:12–10:18	1 method	4	0	1	1
10:19–10:27	2 other	0	4	1	1
Total: 36 min.	7 method 8 other	9	9	6	3

issues but the sheer volume of these elaborations should be noted: 42 instances in 36 minutes.

We now look in detail at two of the jokes. The first operates mostly in the world of gestures. The second is a multilingual play on a direct request to say "Yes." The two jokes follow each other within a span of 30 seconds.[7] They are the first after the marked start of the lesson. The students had shifted from a "waiting for the teacher" to a "listening to the teacher" positioning. Danielle is now standing and fronting the four students who are sitting in one line, two to a desk. All hold this positioning for most of the lesson. This default positioning is shown in Figure 3.1.

Danielle started the lesson with "This is designed for reading" (9:53:14). The transcript included in the Appendix starts a few seconds later, at 9:53:29, with Danielle (the teacher) explaining the significant role arm gestures and hand signals have for the Direct Instruction she is introducing. She is demonstrating the gestures and telling the students what their responses will have to be. She has stated the general rule: *"This means listen* [9:53:39—Danielle's left hand faces the ceiling and her palm faces the students] . . . *this means talk* [9:53:40—Danielle's arm is outstretched, hand pointing at the students and palm facing to her right]." Every 5 seconds or so she calls to check that the students are with her; *"OK?"* There is an audible response once, but in each case Danielle proceeds. During one 30-second interval, Danielle moves her forearm several times in an up and down motion and a student responded with a *F—— you* joking gesture. The interval is dissected in Table 3.2 and pictured in Figures 3.2 and 3.3.

At 9:53:50, one student (Gerardo) asks for a general explanation (*"but why these hand signals?"*) while gesturing with his arms in a kind of dancing motion. By itself, this is already an elaboration of, if not a challenge to, the lesson. But there is more. It is as if Gerardo had a humorous phrase on the tip of his tongue (or a humorous gesture on the tip of his fingers). Christian picks up on one possibility and performs a full "F—— you" gesture by putting his left hand on his right extended elbow and then raising his hand while closing his hand. This completes what is now, in Sacks's (1974/1989) term, a full Telling. This makes Gerardo's gesture, retrospectively, a Preface. The Response comes in the form of laughter and an exchanged glance between Gerardo and Christian. Danielle, the teacher, (or the other two students) cannot help having "seen" the joke that was performed immediately in front of them. The absence of an acknowledgment must be taken as a performance. Looking at a transcript of the "F—— you" joke (see Fig. 3.2) and the accompanying frame grab, it is clear that much of the information

---

[7] The Appendix contains the transcript of the full minute within which the two jokes are embedded. The transcription conventions are those used and justified by Varenne (1992).

FIG. 3.2. "F—— you" joking gesture.

TABLE 3.2
The "F—— You" Joke

	Time			
Speaker	*9:53:53*	*9:53:54*	*9:53:55*	*9:53:56*
Danielle	~ when I put down like this	~We're all going to say	yes.	~ ok?~ When I put my hand
Gerardo	[arms moving across each other rapidly/glancing over at Christian]	[smiles]	[laughs]	
Christian		["F—— You" gesture, i.e., while holding the left arm horizontally in front of his chest, rapidly thrusting his right arm vertically upward, perpendicular to his left arm]	[laughs]	
Victor			[smiles]	
Edgar				

FIG. 3.3.   "Oui oui" joke.

needed to maintain the field is dependent on gestures, proximal location, and orientations of the participants (Birdwhistell, 1970; Scheflen, 1973). It is also evident that she did not note the students' performance as requiring the full performance of a discipline sequence. Danielle is actively ignoring some of what is happening in front of her.

Danielle continues reading the script of the method introduction where the first "pretend" lesson is scripted out for the teacher and students to perform. She reads and performs the gestures for various elicitations of "yes," first in unison and then individually. The students have just done a chorused "Yes" (9:54:10) and Danielle proceeds to point at the first student who had just been told to say "Yes" and proceeds to say "Sí" (9:54:14).

The teacher's initiation, in the form of a gesture expecting a routine response (e.g., "Yes"), is not accomplished until the fourth student (Edgar) is asked. Although all of the students are Spanish/English bilingual, their utilization of Spanish ("Sí") cannot be construed as a linguistic error. Furthermore, the participants' reliance on some kind of French (a language none speaks) and the general laughter that immediately follows the "*Oui oui*"—including laughter in the voice of Danielle as she proceeds down to the last student—places this sequence in the world of a multiperson joke, initiated by Victor's "*Sí*," told by Christian's repetition, completed by Gerardo's multilingual punch line: "Oui oui!" What we have here is the improvisation of an altogether original joke occurring in the midst of other activities and so sequenced as not to require a breaking of the other frames: "Sí" and "Oui" are functionally equivalent to "Yes," but they are also significantly different from the habitual and authoritatively required answer. They open the possibility for laughter—and disruption. After all, the teacher could have started a redirection routine ("Victor, say 'Yes'") or completed the sequence with a general reprimand ("You kids will never succeed if you cannot follow directions"). We do not know why she did this (or why the students joked). We have no information about her state of mind at that moment and do not trust what she might have said about what she did had we interviewed her later.[8]

MAKING CULTURE IN PLAY

It is said that it is just a mark of good teaching not to pick on every occasion of student elaboration. As McDermott and his colleagues have shown, a focus on who is to read next can lead to altogether baroque elaborations of possibilities for contestation and can produce an occasion when very little reading is actually done (McDermott & Aron, 1978; McDermott et al., 1978; McDermott & Tylbor, 1983). Danielle did not pick up any of the 40 such elaborations, and the lesson in the basic processes of Direct Instruction was completed—the students could be treated as having learned and all could move on to the next task.

We understand the temptation to label the students, the teacher, and even the school in terms of properties that would then be the proximate "cause" for the detail of the events. It may be that Danielle was a particularly good teacher (or completely unaware of her surroundings, or scared to challenge boys from a different background from hers). It may be that the students had already learned so much in the school that they were indeed properly to be identified as successes. It may be that the school, perhaps because it is a Catholic school, and a particularly enlightened one at that, is likely to produce good teachers and good students. It may then be that the joking is akin to safe political commentary in the style of a cartoon or caricature that stresses the property of an event but will not, by itself, have much impact.

All this is plausible, and we could offer interview data from the administrators, teachers, and students in the school that would further develop these possibilities. To do so would, however, distract our attention from what was actually done to what can be said about what was done. We consider it important to remain focused on what was actually done. Specifically, at every moment within the lesson/joking sequences the teacher was exercising the authority delegated to her (she asked questions prescribed to her by those in authority over her); students were acknowledging it (they answered the questions) and were commenting (by asking probing

---

[8] Mullooly conducted many interviews about the school with most participants but the data from these are less about everyday practices than about "what can be said about one's teaching to outsider interviewers."

questions about the prescribed questions, by gesturing and laughing); and the teacher was ignoring these comments (she continued to ask prescribed questions without breaking rhythm).

Most important, all involved were doing all this in real time, without recourse to planning or editing of what was to be done or what had been done and, equally important, without access to each others' motivations or feelings. We, as observers, must recognize that we are in the same situation: We cannot either claim access to internal motivation or feeling; we, as authoritative educational researchers, must particularly fear the consequences of an evaluative identification not only for those whose handling of school tasks we approve but, more fatefully, for those which, and possibly only by implication, of which we disapprove.

It is essential to our method that cultural analysis of charged human interaction remains with what is available to all at the time and not postulate that what happens must be the product of something that is in fact not directly available, for example, the *habitus* of students. Bourdieu (1970/1977) has now encouraged at least one generation of educational researchers to base their work on the sense that, if students like those at Loyola do whatever it is they do in such a way that they do not disrupt the school or their successful (failing) careers, it must be because of various properties. There are optimistic versions of this that stress parents teaching their children how to do school; schools of education developing new curricula and pedagogies to prepare teachers to be particularly sensitive to student needs, languages, and ways of doing; or researchers identifying the properties of settings more likely to produce the needed schools and teachers. There is also a pessimistic version which, with Bourdieu and Passeron (1977/1990), emphasizes the violence that is being made to all who do not recognize in their explicit speech and actions that the pedagogical authority they accept is in fact a tool of the forces that enslave them and make the process legitimate.

We hope we have developed the demonstration that there are other ways of accounting for what people do, particularly when what they do can, in some situations, hurt them. We do not have to say that teachers and students at Loyola do not understand what they are doing because of internalized cultural habits that they have stopped being aware of. Culture is not quite like water for the fish—something that they are not likely to notice.[9] Culture is about the transformation of experience for future experience. It is in this spirit that we looked at Loyola and its classrooms as settings for the production of new performances, rather than for the reproduction of old patterns.

---

[9] This is the analogy proposed by Kluckhohn (1949, p. 11) to introduce one theory of culture that was becoming dominant in American anthropology.

It is precisely not that we are discounting the various asymmetries that do exist among administrators (who impose pedagogies on teachers), teachers (who use the pedagogy on students), and the students who are under some threat of being expelled (like teachers are threatened to lose their jobs, and the administrators of seeing their school close). Nothing of what we saw would make sense if we, as analysts, refused to acknowledge what all participants did acknowledge. Once they had become participants, there was no way to build personal lives outside the authority patterns. There was little choice possible here for any of the participants—and certainly not for the students whose parents had sent them there with, we suspect, continuing threat about having to attend the public schools their neighbors were attending. We do not even want to discount the asymmetry that the school was producing among the Mexican immigrants of the city. We are almost sure that the school could have selected any of the children in whom it was interested and achieve with them what it was achieving with those we met during this research, but we are sure that it could not have achieved this for *all* of them. There is room for only some of the children coming of age in 2000 to become the leaders of the Mexican American community in 2050.

This recognition of delegated pedagogical authority as a moment in the production of a particular social order cannot, however, lead to the assumption that, in the details of their lives, those who are caught within this order are determined either through their habits or direct coercion. They are not free to radically discount their surroundings, but they can make many different things with it precisely because these surroundings are, in terms Bourdieu and Passeron (1977/1990) borrowed from classic cultural theory, *arbitrary*. But this arbitrariness is not to be taken as fate; instead, it arises because human beings, everywhere and always, play with their surroundings, sometimes for temporary fun and sometimes with unexpected results which, given particular circumstances, can produce what will then be identified as change. The joking exchanges we present here probably mostly belong to the first kind of play: They are fun, they alleviate boredom, and they do not threaten order. However, they also were what might have made this lesson "different" from any other; what might make this generation of students different from earlier generations; and what might make this American, religious, Catholic, Jesuit school for immigrants not quite the same as any other that might have similar characteristics.

Loyola has already changed since this study was conducted. We offer this case not as a case of stasis (this is what these boys were and what the school was) but rather a case of the process that makes change inevitable. After all, what is most dangerous in Bourdieu and Passeron's (1977/1990) work is the title: "*Re*-production." Social systems do not reproduce. Social systems keep being produced in particular contexts that participants must acknowledge even as they play—open new kinds of schools, adopt new pedagogies, make fun with arm movements. Some of this was "deep play," particularly for the founders of the school, who staked their professional reputation, if not their religious faith, on the school being acknowledged by their peers as a success. It was deep play for the parents. Education, inscribed as a continually reformed set of immensely complex regulations about proper schooling, may even be extremely deep play for all the political figures who have bet that "it is only through education that a proper democracy can be built." None of this can be done automatically if only because someone will continually remind those who have stopped thinking that nothing is settled for good. A new child is born, a cartoon gets printed, a new regulation is proposed, and everything is up for grabs again.

Varenne and McDermott (1995) argued that all such play, particularly when it gets inscribed in major institutions, can be quite dangerous for many, and thus play with pedagogical authority can be quite pathetic, as it was for McDermott's Rosa: Even as she succeeded in "not getting caught not knowing how to read," she moved out of regular classrooms into the realms of urban special education at a time when this was a euphemism for final failure. By contrast, Gerardo and his friends' story in this chapter is anything but pathetic: They laughed when they could have been bored, and still ended up in high school and college. What is important to us here, however, is that both stories are about moments of extra-Vagance that will be shown to be ubiquitous in the classrooms of all schools. Once researchers begin to notice such intricate interweaving of high and low, of formal and informal, of lesson and lesson play (or elaboration), much can be gained—and we may even have some fun on the way to greater theoretical sophistication! And so we end with Boon's (1999) extra-Vagant introduction of extra-Vagance:

> Acts of extra-Vagance abound in human rituals and interpreting them, lucid languages and translating them, and multimedia and transposing them; engaging such acts can help unsettle cozy dogmas, complicate critical clichés, and reshuffle scholarly and popular prejudices. (p. xv)

REFERENCES

Adams, G. L., & Engelmann, S. (1996). *Research on direct instruction: 25 years beyond DISTAR.* Seattle, WA: Educational Achievement Systems.

Allington, R., & Woodside-Jiron H. (1999). The politics of literacy teaching: How "research" shaped educational policy. *Educational Researcher, 28*(8), 4–13.

Apel, W., & Danial, R. (1960). *The Harvard brief dictionary of music.* New York: Washington Square.

Apple, M. W. (1996). *Cultural politics and education.* New York: Teachers College Press.

Bateson, G. (1955). The message "This is play." In B. Schaffner (Ed.), *Group processes: Transactions of the second conference* (pp. 145–242). New York: Josiah Macy, Jr. Foundation.

Bereiter, C., & Engelmann, S. (1966). *Teaching disadvantaged children in preschool.* Engelwood Cliffs, NJ: Prentice Hall.

Birdwhistell, R. (1970). *Kinesics and context: Essays on body motion communication.* Philadelphia: University of Pennsylvania Press.

Boon, J. (1999). *Verging on extra-Vagance: Anthropology, history, religion, literature, arts . . . showbiz.* Princeton, NJ: Princeton University Press.

Bourdieu, P. (1972). *Outline of a theory of practice.* Cambridge, England: Cambridge University Press.

Bourdieu, P., & Passeron, J. C. (1990). *Reproduction in education, society and culture.* London: Sage. (Original work published 1977)

Bryk, A., Lee, V., & Holland, P. (1993). *Catholic schools and the common good.* Cambridge, MA: Harvard University Press.

Coleman, J., Greeley, A., & Hoffer, T. (1985). Achievement growth in public and Catholic schools. *Sociology of Education, 58,* 74–97.

Davis-Floyd, R., & Sargent, C. (Eds.). (1997). *Childbirth and authoritative knowledge.* Berkeley: University of California Press.

Dore, J., & McDermott, R. P. (1982). Linguistic indeterminacy and social context in utterance interpretation. *Language, 58,* 374–398.

Evans, W., & Schwab, R. (1995). Finishing high school and starting college: Do Catholic schools make a difference? *Quarterly Journal of Economics, 110,* 941–974.

Falsey, B., & Heyns, B. (1984). The college channel: Private and public schools reconsidered. *Sociology of Education, 57,* 111–112.

Fisher, S., & Todd, T. (1986). *Discourse and institutional authority: Medicine, education and law.* Norwood, NJ: Ablex.

Gamoran, A. (1992). The variable effects of high school tracking. *American Sociological Review, 57,* 812–828.

Geertz, C. (1973). *The interpretation of cultures.* New York: Basic Books.

Giroux, H. A. (1983). Theories of reproduction and resistance in the new sociology of education: A critical analysis. *Harvard Education Review, 53,* 257–293.

Greene, J. (2001, November). *High school graduation rates in the United States.* Retrieved March 25, 2002, from http://www.manhattan-institute.org

Greene, J., & Winters, M. (2002). Public school graduation rates in the United States. *Civic Report, 31.* Retrieved January 12, 2003, from http://www.manhattan-institute.org/html/cr_31.htm

Hamann, E. (1999). *Georgia Project: A binational attempt to reinvent a school district in response to Latino newcomers.* Unpublished doctoral dissertation, University of Pennsylvania.

Heath, C. (1986). Body movement and speech in medical interaction. New York: Cambridge University Press.

Heshusius, L. (1991). Curriculum-based assessment and direct instruction: Critical reflections on fundamental assumptions. *Exceptional Children, 57,* 315–328.

Hodgkins, B., & Morrison, J. (1971). The effectiveness of Catholic education: A comparative analysis. *Sociology of Education, 44,* 119–131.

Jordan, B. (1992). *Technology and social interaction: Notes on the achievement of authoritative knowledge in complex settings.* Palo Alto, CA: Institute for Research and Learning.

Kluckhohn, C. (1949). *Mirror for man.* New York: McGraw-Hill.

Lévi-Strauss, C. (1966). *The savage mind.* Chicago: University of Chicago Press. (Original work published 1962)

McDermott, R. P., & Aron, J. (1978). Pirandello in the classroom. In M. Reynolds (Ed.), *The futures of education* (pp. 41–64). Reston, VA: Council for Exceptional Children.

McDermott, R. P., Gospodinoff, K., & Aron, J. (1978). Criteria for an ethnographically adequate description of concerted activities and their contexts. *Semiotica, 24,* 245–275.

McDermott, R. P., & Tylbor, H. (1983). On the necessity of collusion in conversation. *Text, 3,* 277–297.

McDermott, R. P., & Varenne, H. (1995). Culture as disability. *Anthropology and Education Quarterly, 26,* 324–348.

McDermott, R. P., & Webber, V. (1998). When is math or science? In J. Greeno & S. Goldman (Eds.), *Thinking practices in mathematics and science learning* (pp. 321–339). Mahwah, NJ: Lawrence Erlbaum Associates, Inc.

Mehan, H. (1979). *Learning lessons.* Cambridge, MA: Harvard University Press.

Metz, M. (1978). *Classrooms and corridors: The crises of authority in desegregated secondary schools.* Berkeley: University of California Press.

Moyers, B. (Writer). (1990). Amazing grace. [Television series episode]. In PBS Home Video, *The Bill Moyers show.* Beverly Hills, CA: Newbridge Communications.

Mullooly, J. (2003). *Work, play and consequences: What counts in a successful middle school.* Unpublished doctoral dissertation, Columbia University.

Neal, D. (1997). The effects of Catholic secondary schooling on educational achievement. *Journal of Labor Economics, 15,* 98–123.

Pace, J. L. (2003a). Managing the dilemmas of professional and bureaucratic authority in a high school English class. *Sociology of Education, 76,* 37–52.

Pace, J. L. (2003b). Using ambiguity and entertainment to win compliance in a lower-level U.S. history class. *Journal of Curriculum Studies, 35,* 83–110.

Page, R. N. (1991). *Lower-track classrooms: A curricular and cultural perspective.* New York: Teachers College Press.

Polite, V. (1992). Getting the job done well: African American students and Catholic schools. *Journal of Negro Education, 6,* 211–222.

Powers, J. (1975). *Do black patent-leather shoes really reflect up?: A fictionalized memoir.* Chicago: Regnery.

Rizzo-Tolk, R., & Varenne, H. (1992). Joint action on the wild side of Manhattan: The power of the cultural center on an educational alternative. *Anthropology and Education Quarterly, 23,* 221–249.

Sacks, H. (1989). An analysis of the course of a joke's telling in conversation. In R. Bauman & J. Sherzer (Eds.), *Explorations in the ethnography of speaking* (2nd ed., pp. 337–353). Cambridge, England: Cambridge University Press. (Original work published 1974)

Sander, W. (1996). Catholic grade schools and academic achievement. *Journal of Human Resources, 31,* 540–548.

Scheflen, A. (1973). *Communicational structure: Analysis of a psychotherapy transaction.* Bloomington: Indiana University Press.

Scott, J. (1985). *Weapons of the weak: Everyday forms of peasant resistance.* New Haven, CT: Yale University Press.

Tobin, J., Wu, D., & Davidson, D. (1989). *Preschool in three cultures: Japan, China, and the United States.* New Haven, CT: Yale University Press.

Varenne, H. (1983). *American school language: Culturally patterned conflicts in a suburban high school.* New York: Irvington.

Varenne, H. (1992). *Ambiguous harmony.* Norwood, NJ: Ablex.

Varenne, H., & McDermott, R. (1998). *Successful failure: The school America builds.* Boulder, CO: Westview.

Williams, R. (1977). *Marxism and literature.* New York: Oxford University Press.

Willis, P. (1977). *Learning to labor.* New York: Teachers College Press.

Wong Fillmore, L., & Meyer, L. (1992). The curriculum and linguistic minorities. In P. Jackson (Ed.) *The handbook of research on curriculum* (pp. 626–658). New York: Macmillan.

APPENDIX

Time	Danielle	Gerardo	Christian	Victor	Edgar	seconds
9:53:29	So remember when my hand is like this	~~	~~	~~	~~	1
9:53:30	You need to be looking at	~~	~~	~~	~~	2
9:53:31	Me	~~	~~	~~	~~	3
9:53:32	And paying attention	~~	~~	~~	~~	4
9:53:33	ok?~	~yeah				5
9:53:34	If I ask you a question ~	~~	~~	~~	~~	6
9:53:35	~when it's your turn to	~~	~~	~~	~~	7
9:53:36	answer	~~	~~	~~	~~	8
9:53:37	I'll point to you like this	~~	~~	~~	~~	9
9:53:38	~ ok?	~~	~~	~~	~~	10
9:53:39	This means listen ~	~~	~~	~~	~~	11
9:53:40	this means talk ~	~~	~~	~~	~~	12
9:53:41	When I point down	~~	~~	~~	~~	13
9:53:42	and in the middle of your two tables ~	~~	~~	~~	~~	14
9:53:43	it means that you're	~~	~~	~~	~~	15
9:53:44	all going to answer together~	~~	~~	~~	~~	16
9:53:45	~ok?	~~	~~	~~	~~	17
9:53:46	If I'm going to have one	~~	~~	~~	~~	18
9:53:47	person answer	~~	~~	~~	~~	19
9:53:48	I'll point just at you ~	~~	~~	~~	~~	20
9:53:49	~right?	~~	~~	~~	~~	21
9:53:50	~~	Oh XX XX but why	~~	~~	~~	22
9:53:51	So when I put my when I put my	why these	~~	~~	~~	23
9:53:52	hand down~	signals?~	~~	~~	~~	24
9:53:53	~ when I put down like this~		~~	~~	~~	25
9:53:54	We're all going to say	~~		~~	~~	26
9:53:55	yes.	Laughter	Laughter	Laughter	Laughter	27
9:53:56	~ ok?~ When I put my hand	Laughter	Laughter	Laughter	Laughter	28

(continued)

Time	Danielle	Gerardo	Christian	Victor	Edgar	seconds
9:53:57	down like this just	~~	~~	~~	~~	29
9:53:58	at Victor he's going to say	~~	~~	~~	~~	30
9:53:59	Yes~ Just at Christian~	~~	~~	~~	~~	31
9:54:00	He will say yes	~~	~~	~~	~~	32
9:54:01	Just at you~	XX	~~	~~	~~	33
9:54:02	you will say yes	~~	~~	~~	~~	34
9:54:03	And just at Edgar~	~~	~~	~~	~~	35
9:54:04	He will say yes~	~~	~~	~~	~Why do we have to say yes?~	36
9:54:05	Ok ready~ on the count of	~~	~~	~~		37
9:54:06	three~	~~	~~	~~	~~	38
9:54:07	I'm going to put my hand down~ we're all	~~	~~	~~	~~	39
9:54:08	Going to say yes~	~~	~~	~~	~~	40
9:54:09	One two three	~~	~~	~~	~~	41
9:54:10		Yes	Yes	Yes	Yes	42
9:54:11	Ok ~	~~	~~	~~	~~	43
9:54:12	Victor~	~~	~~	~ sí	~~	45
9:54:13	Carlos~	~~	~~	~~	~~	46
9:54:14	~~	~~	sí	~~	~~	47
9:54:15	Greg~	~~	~~	~~	~~	48
9:54:16	~~	oui oui	~~	~~	~~	49
9:54:17	Laugh	laugh	laugh	laugh	laugh	50
9:54:18	And Edgar	laugh	laugh	laugh	laugh	51
9:54:19	Ok ~	~~	~~	~~	Yes	52
9:54:20	please wait	~~	~~	~~	~~	53
9:54:21	For the hand to come down	~~	~~	~~	~~	54
9:54:22	As specially if it's a	~~	~~	~~	~~	55
9:54:23	Problem~ ok?	~~	~~	~~	~~	56
9:54:24	because uhm I will give you	~~	~~	~~	~~	57
9:54:25	two or three seconds to	~~	~~	~~	~~	58
9:54:26	think of an answer~	~~	~~	~~	~~	59

Saving (and Losing) Face, Race, and Authority: Strategies of Action in a Ninth-Grade English Class

Judith L. Pace
University of San Francisco

> *It is truly amazing; they'll do whatever you ask them to do. It's a model class;*
> *I genuinely love that class.* —Ms. Goodman,[1] 3/14/97
>
> *They appear to be doing what I'm asking them to do. But when it came time*
> *to do the grades they were incredibly, decidedly lower than mid-year. I find that*
> *just incredibly discouraging, because it's clear what they're expected to do and*
> *what I believe will help them be smarter, better, more effective individuals, and*
> *they just sort of thumb their noses at it and just don't do it.*
> —Ms. Goodman, 4/15/97

Throughout the spring semester of 1997, I studied a ninth-grade English class as part of a larger research project on classroom authority and academic involvement. Within the first several weeks of observing Ms. Goodman's "Perspectives in Literature" class, I saw how perplexed and frustrated the teacher became as her feelings of success at winning students' consent and promoting their academic engagement turned into a sense of failure as she realized these same students were not meeting her expectations. She had spoken during our first interview about how pleased she was with students'

---

[1] All names of people and places have been changed to protect anonymity.

"incredible growth" as they appeared to be taking more responsibility for completing assigned work without too much prompting. A month later, in our second interview, my question about goals for learning sparked a long, emotional response about poor grades and students' lack of willingness to fulfill her demands. Ms. Goodman believed her efforts had actually helped students to succeed, but her calculation of the report card grades revealed that students had not been doing their assignments. She reinterpreted the engagement she perceived as "a semblance that they're doing what they're supposed to but they're really not." The semblance, she went on to explain, was "really good learned behavior about what it means to be, what it looks like to be a student."

Ms. Goodman was a White teacher quite dedicated to promoting the academic success of Black youth.[2] When telling me about how excited she was about the class's dramatic improvement since first semester, she noted "three African American girls," Malaika, Justine, and Doreen, as "fabulous" and "absolutely amazing" since they had enrolled in a "self-esteem class," aimed at raising achievement.[3] Later on, she spoke about six students, five of whom were Black, who were not meeting her expectations. She referred again to the three girls, this time with disappointment: "I was so excited 'cause they were so gung-ho and they were really turning things around . . . I think I misread it." Ms. Goodman said with frustrated resignation: "They just don't read. Period. [T]hose girls do not read." The teacher understood the problem as "a kind of a modus operandi that they just can't seem to break out of" and as resistance[4]— " 'I'm not gonna do it.' "

As my study progressed, it became evident that students' actions demonstrated ambivalence, which was shaped in part by Ms. Goodman's approach to authority. In this chapter I explain the teacher's approach using Swidler's (1986, 2001) sociocultural concept of *strategies of action*. Culture in this view is a toolkit of symbolically meaningful resources that are varied and even contradictory. Individuals select from these options, based on their own culturally shaped competencies, habits, and styles, to construct strategies of action, or patterned ways of being. Faced with the inherently contradictory demands of having to gain students' voluntary cooperation within the coercive structures of schooling, teachers use symbolic actions, such as using grades as incentive as well as evaluation, to accomplish what they need

---

[2] I use the term *Black* to include people from other countries besides the United States (see Nieto, 1996). Additionally, although adults at this school site used the term *African American*, students of African descent tended to identify themselves as Black.

[3] The teacher's characterization of the class points to the theory that Black students underachieve because they have self-esteem problems and that raising self-esteem will foster higher achievement.

[4] My use of the term *resistance* represents the teacher's perception of student behavior and its more general, common-sense connotation rather than the conceptualization theorized by Giroux (1983).

to do. They construct and improvise on culturally influenced strategies to respond to ongoing and immediate situations with their students.

Ms. Goodman's patterned approach to authority combined face-saving politeness, establishment of boundaries, and other strategies intended to simultaneously control and engage students. This pattern fueled and dissipated tensions in three key areas: (a) completion of assignments in the school's meritocratic system, (b) student participation and teacher-imposed boundaries, and (c) success or failure with challenging curricula. It indicated the teacher's own ambivalence towards her involvement with students and curriculum. The approach was met with a mixture of assent and resistance most visible among individual Black student underachievers as they negotiated the cultural context of Hillsdale High.

CONTEXT AND METHODOLOGY

Hillsdale High's Moral Order

In a metropolitan school setting I call *Hillsdale High School* (HHS), I studied both higher and lower level classes taught by Ms. Goodman and a social studies teacher to investigate how authority was negotiated and interpreted by teachers and students. Hillsdale High School appealed to a diverse clientele because of the quality and range of academic and extracurricular opportunities, permissive yet safe atmosphere, good rapport between staff and students, and competitive ethos. Almost 85% of the graduates in 1996 planned to attend 4-year colleges or universities, and 16 were National Merit finalists. The faculty had a reputation as well-educated, intellectually oriented, and accomplished professionals able to relate successfully with adolescents. They enjoyed professional autonomy and collegial relationships.[5]

Salient features of the moral order of HHS were in line with Mathews's (1998) characterization of elite public schools as embracing "a national culture that worships high test scores, good grades, and placement in fine colleges" (p. 5). This preoccupation with producing competitive college applicants interferes with reforms directed at lower performing and less motivated students because impressive records of college admission serve as a rationalization for maintaining the status quo. Ambitious parents advocating for their children's happiness and success influence school personnel to serve their children through tracking arrangements and provision of good grades. Less motivated students whose parents do not wield power, or who are segregated from high-achieving students through the tracking system,

---

[5]Metz (1978); Rutter, Maughan, Mortimore, and Ouston (1980); and Lightfoot (1983) have argued that school culture has a major influence on authority.

are not productively challenged. The system reinforces inequality because the school's prestige and parental support depend on getting privileged students into the best colleges.

Like other privileged schools in cosmopolitan communities, competitive values prevailed at HHS (Schwartz, 1987). Many teachers and students emphasized good grades, higher track placement, and college admission to secure access to economic and social success. According to common lore resonant with research on high schools (Cusick, 1983; Grant, 1988; Hurn, 1985), increasing demographic diversity as well as progressive trends in education during the 1970s contributed to a shift in the school's ethos from a clear focus on elite, traditional academic excellence toward egalitarianism and accommodation of diverse orientations, creating an uncertain moral order. In the late 1990s, the high school's student population of 1,700 was 70% White, 14% Asian, 11% Black, and 5% Latino. Within these categories, more than 30 languages and 60 nations were represented. Half of the Black students were bussed from the inner city through a voluntary integration program (VIP). The prevailing view was that the quality of education at HHS depended to a large extent on track level. According to research on tracking, the meaning of a class's level is relative to other levels in a particular school (Oakes, Gamoran, & Page, 1992; Page, 1991). Although all courses in the main academic program were college preparatory, administrators, teachers, and students at HHS said that in most of the lower level classes (those not designated as Honors or Advanced Placement [AP]) classes, students posed behavioral, motivational, and academic challenges, and teachers compromised their expectations and standards for them. As a result of democratizing the placement process over the last few years, more students signed up for Honors courses to enhance their transcripts, which contributed to smaller enrollments and lowered status of Standard classes.

As is typical of U.S. secondary schools, a disproportionately large number of students in lower level classes were Black (Lipman, 1998; Metz, 1978; Oakes, 1985). African American[6] student underachievement was a topic of discussion in the superintendent's speech to faculty at the beginning of the 1996–1997 school year. The district had an African American Achievement Committee, and a group of high school faculty met periodically to discuss race-related issues, including low numbers of African American students in higher track classes. I did not, however, see signs of these activities during my study. By talking with faculty, I learned about the African American achievement class and tutoring for VIP students. However, closing the achievement gap was not visible as a schoolwide priority; instead, as was revealed during the course of my data collection, it was a more particular concern of individual teachers such as Ms. Goodman.

---

[6]Here, *African American* represents the faculty's use of that term to discuss Black students.

Data Collection and Dilemmas of Representation

During my fieldwork in the 1997 spring semester, I observed Ms. Goodman's "Perspectives in Literature" class two or three times per week, totaling over 30 observations. Observations were documented through field notes and, occasionally, through transcriptions of audiotaped lessons. I held four hour-long interviews with the teacher, supplemented by informal conversations, and two 30- to 60-minute individual interviews with each of four students from the class. I conducted informal interviews with other teachers, students, and administrators in the school; gathered classroom-, school-, and district-related documents (including class lists, assignments, syllabi, tests, course catalogues, and school newspapers); and did participant observation in various places in and around the school building, including the hallways, cafeteria, and staff rooms. I thus collected rich, abundant data on classroom authority and pertinent factors within its social contexts.

The direction of this case study was shaped by Ms. Goodman's, my own, and the nation's preoccupation with the achievement gap between Black and White students (Fordham, 1996; Johnston & Viadero, 2000; Nieto, 1996; Ogbu, 1978, 2003; Pollock, 2001). As a young White teacher of early adolescents in the 1980s, I noticed a disproportionate representation of middle-class Black students in special education classes and disparities in achievement between Black and White students in other classroom settings. Ms. Goodman's "Perspectives in Literature" class was of special interest to me because of her clearly articulated struggle with getting students to complete their work to be academically successful and her particular concern with Black students. This signaled an opportunity to learn about factors related to authority relationships that might contribute to underachievement of Black students in a privileged setting.

Probing underachievement among Black students in a classroom case study presents dilemmas regarding representation of data. First is the risk of reinforcing the cultural construction of the phenomenon. Discussions of the achievement gap between different racial groups in U.S. schools abound in both research and practice, but often reflect taken-for-granted assumptions about its existence (Pollock, 2001). By analyzing underachievement, I as a researcher might inadvertently re-create it as a culturally constructed category (Varenne & McDermott, 1997). Additionally, generalizing about all Black students in the class as a separate group is impossible because of numerous intragroup differences and intergroup similarities. Rather than determining causes of underachievement among Black students, I attempt here to reveal classroom dynamics that generate both consent and resistance to the agenda of schooling.

A second dilemma is criticism of the teacher. I do not want to contribute to a large body of literature that blames teachers for the problems of schooling and society. At the same time, I am obligated to report accurately what I learned (Hammersley & Atkinson, 1995). The point of this study is not to focus on the individual qualities of a particular teacher. Instead, I try to show cultural and institutional influences on teachers' actions as they face difficulties inherent in their work. My assumption is that all teachers have blind spots (Spindler & Spindler, 1982) and, although distressing, it is vital to examine how they tie into the "knot" of Black students' academic failure (L. Powell, 1997, p. 3).

A third dilemma is my identity as a White researcher. Despite my open desire to learn about race, I assume that being White influenced interviews with Black participants and my collection and interpretation of data (Lipman, 1998; Price, 2000). My analysis has evolved over time, aided by feedback from researchers with different racial identities. The complexity of the case study lends itself to multiple interpretations, and I remain tentative particularly about the meaning of Black students' actions and experiences.

The ensuing presentation of data revolves around three sets of data that reveal key areas of tension for teacher and students. Such tensions expose the dynamics of authority that are usually hidden because they seem so ordinary and can be so subtle (Metz, 1978). The first set of data is the teacher's quotes presented at the beginning of the article and a short vignette. It points to the dilemma of using grades to get students to complete assignments. The second is a lesson that illustrates friction between student participation and the teacher's imposition of boundaries between home and school knowledge. The third episode reveals difficulty posed by a very challenging text and concerns about academic success or failure. Throughout, we see the teacher constructing strategies of action that blend pressure and politeness, which evokes a mix of cooperation and opposition and ultimately creates distance among teacher, students, and subject matter. Additionally, we see how classroom dynamics are situated within the contradictory moral order of a school that values egalitarianism and competition, representative of liberal schools that purport to be the "great equalizer" but also serve the interests of dominant elites (Giroux, 1983, p. 258).

MS. GOODMAN'S CLASS: TENSIONS
WITHIN AUTHORITY RELATIONS

Ms. Goodman was White, middle aged, and native to the United States. Out of a total of 24 students, there were 16 female, 8 male, 11 White, 3 Asian, and 10 Black students. The number of Black students was unusually large given that 11% of the school's student body was Black. According to the teacher, 6 of the Black students were bussed from the inner city through

VIP and another also lived in the city but was admitted to HHS because her mother worked for the town of Hillsdale. Ms. Goodman told me 3 especially troublesome students had thankfully left the class, but it was still a demanding group with 8 students diagnosed with mild to moderate special needs on individualized educational plans.

The students presented an interesting mix of personalities, backgrounds, academic orientations, and social groupings. Ten vocal students, the most enthusiastic participants in class discussions and the most likely to make challenging remarks or jokes, had the closest rapport with the teacher. Seven were Black (1 from Jamaica, 6 from the United States) and 3 White (U.S. born). Based on what Ms. Goodman told me, most of these students often did not turn in assignments; more of the quiet students were doing the work and getting better grades. Ten quiet students included 3 of Asian descent (Indian, Chinese, and Thai), 2 Black (U.S. born), and 5 White students (1 from Russia, 4 from the United States). Four students, 1 Black (his parents were immigrants from Nigeria) and 3 White (born in the United States), took other subjects at the honors level and appeared uncomfortably silent in this diverse, lower status class.

In general, students showed up to class on time; followed the teacher's directives; and, some socializing notwithstanding, kept disruptions to a minimum. At the same time, between the teacher's animated style, the social energy of ninth graders, and the assertive personalities of some students, the classroom atmosphere was quite lively, in contrast to the "flat" character of many high school classes (Goodlad, 1984).

The academic and sociocultural heterogeneity of the class was complicated by its paradoxical track-level status. All courses in the regular academic program at HHS were considered college preparatory. Previous debates had resulted in an idiosyncratic "leveling"[7] system that differed across grade levels and departments. While terms such as Basic, Standard, Honors, and AP were typically used, courses were labeled in the school catalogue with numbers. "Perspectives in Literature" was a Level 2 freshman English course that Ms. Goodman regarded as lower track. Yet the curriculum was influenced by standards for the Level 1 course and included challenging texts such as *Antigone* and *Julius Caesar.*

Ms. Goodman in her instructional approach emphasized basic skills; assigned short stories, novels, and plays; and conducted reading, discussion, and writing activities. During the third quarter Ms. Goodman had students choose one of two books to read independently at home. This was accompanied by a series of journal assignments for homework and a final test on the book. The class worked on autobiographical narratives and descriptive writing. They read Shakespeare's *Julius Caesar* and finished the

---

[7] The term *leveling* was used as a euphemism for tracking.

year with a unit on poetry. Ms. Goodman regularly designated class time and homework for vocabulary and grammar.

When I asked the teacher about her goals for students' learning, she told me that for any freshman class she had "very specific goals for writing, reading, group interaction, homework, adjusting to high school." Her "big goals are that I want to see as the year goes on that they are more independent learners, that they've bought in, that their grades you would think should be pretty consistent, when they realize expectations are getting higher they should work a little bit harder." Ms. Goodman thus focused on producing high school students who completed assigned tasks and whose success was measured by grades.

Unlike White liberal teachers discussed in other research, Ms. Goodman seemed comfortable asserting direct control in her management of the class (Delpit, 1988; Obidah & Teel, 2001). With a loud, clear voice, she ran a tight ship, expecting on-time attendance; assigning seats; maximizing time on task; using established routines; and asserting standards for classroom behavior, such as prohibition of food and drink. She defined herself as more controlling and teacher centered than other faculty and believed her style was well suited to Level 2 freshman classes. At the same time, Ms. Goodman was personable, upbeat, and solicitous, making small talk and joking with students while implicitly asserting that she was in charge. She smoothed over the antics of vocal individuals and set limits on off-task peer interactions while tolerating a small amount of distraction. She made it a point to give students individual attention and encouragement. Students in the class from different backgrounds described her as both more helpful and more imposing with her demands than other teachers at HHS. One Black student, Ali, complained Ms. Goodman was too intrusive, whereas teachers in his other, Honors-level classes, allowed students more freedom. Although Ms. Goodman also was controlling in the 10th/11th grade Honors U.S. Literature class I concurrently observed, she was more structured and solicitous with the younger, racially diverse, lower track group.

Ms. Goodman took a special interest in supporting Black achievement. On the basis of observations and interview data, she made a point of being attentive, encouraging, and friendly toward Black students. She successfully encouraged the participation of several Black students, most of whom were female, to the point where they had the strongest voices in class discussions. She also avoided conflict by letting the most vocal girls get away with occasional grumpiness or answering back, passing around cosmetics, and other unsanctioned activities.

Ms. Goodman told me that part of the reason why she liked this class so much was the large number of Black students and her simpatico with them. She maintained regular contact with the teacher of the African American achievement class and worked with colleagues on placing more

Black students in higher track classes. Her obvious interest in Black students' academic success made their refusal to complete assignments and consequential low grades especially troubling. She reassured herself in our interviews that the distribution of grades in the "Perspectives" class did not break down by race but indicated that underachievement among Black students was a problem.

Important to understanding Ms. Goodman's practice is that she had taught reading skills for most of her career and was forced to make a change due to budget cuts at HHS. Teaching reading is an entirely different and much more technical enterprise than teaching English. Ms. Goodman explained the required changes:

> When you're asked to teach English as opposed to reading there's a significant change. There's also a body of material you are expected to teach. A huge difference is moving from individualized instruction to group instruction, which is huge. For example something that I had virtually a) no experience in and b) no training in is running a discussion. I mean how would I even know how to do that. The expectation was that I would be the one who would do the training, either that or, they must have assumed that I knew how. Which of course I didn't, but flew by the seat of my pants (chuckle).

Ms. Goodman was aware of certain gaps in her expertise. These limited the range of resources available to construct authority. She relied on grades to motivate students, which fueled tensions in her approach to authority.

Tension Over Completion of Assignments in the School's Meritocratic System

In all high schools, students' completion of assignments is symbolic of academic engagement and consent to teachers' directives. It is treated as a moral good and rewarded with high grades, whereas not completing assignments is considered delinquent and punished with low grades. Grades are commonly identified as the main source of students' motivation to fulfill their obligations in high schools, especially elite ones (Labaree, 1997; Mathews, 1998; Pope, 2001). They are the most visible measure of academic achievement and the major vehicle for student competition in the stratified order of the school. Teachers' use of grades to motivate students is pervasive, but in a lower track class students are less likely to invest in the meritocratic system that supposedly offers all members "an equal chance to develop their abilities and rise in the social hierarchy" but that inevitably creates winners and losers (Spring, 1998, p. 8). Detachment from the system may be more pronounced for Black students who respond with performance anxiety, anger, and/or cynicism toward various forms of racism in schools and society (Fordham, 1996; Metz, 1978; Ogbu, 1987, 1991; Steele, 1992).

Malaika was one of the Black students who perplexed Ms. Goodman, because her enthusiastic participation in class conveyed engagement, and the teacher knew she was very bright and capable, yet she did not turn in assignments, which resulted in low grades. Malaika came from a middle-class Jamaican family who had immigrated to Hillsdale when she was in fourth grade. In our first interview, Malaika expressed her ambivalence toward the "Perspectives" class, saying she liked the class and the teacher, but the only book she enjoyed was Rosa Guy's *Friends,* because of its relevance to her life. Malaika repeated emphatically that she refused to read books she did not like. She also said she would not write journal entries even if she had done the reading, and she was cynical about Ms. Goodman's reason for assigning them: "I know she wants to see what we've read." She asserted, "If I don't see the point in something usually I won't do it." Malaika's comments point to the importance of intrinsic value in academic activities and resistance to control through grades.

In contrast with her opposition to the homework assignments, Malaika expressed positive feelings about the teacher. She appreciated that Ms. Goodman discussed various topics with the students, asked their opinions, and gave them choices in their writing. She said the teacher tried to make the class fun, was a nice person, and was fair in giving students a chance to make up work they had missed. She also said Ms. Goodman let students know how they were doing and compared her with less supportive teachers: "If you need to make up work she'll say, 'You can come work in my office and I'll help you on whatever you need help on.'"

But when I asked how much grades mattered to her, she replied, "It means a lot to my mother; to me, it makes me feel bad when I get a bad grade but it doesn't matter all that much to me because I don't take grading as, grading doesn't really show how much you know." When prompted with a question about whether she thought about what she would do after high school, she made an immediate association between college and grades. "Mhmm. I want to go to college and I know I can't go to college if I don't get better grades and I'm trying to bring up my grades." Malaika simultaneously acknowledged yet resisted the power of the meritocratic system's exchange of credentials for submission to the competitive structure embedded in the school's moral order (Willis, 1977). Her refusal to do homework seemed to indicate not that she was merely pretending to be a good student but that the teacher's efforts were not sufficient to generate the genuine, deep involvement in literature needed for outside reading to occur and that the pressure of grades may have provoked resistance to assignments.

On the other hand, when I asked Ms. Goodman what motivates students to do their work, she replied, "Grades. Really I think it's grades. . . . Y'know you'd love to think that you're motivating them because the material is so fascinating that they just can't wait to find out what happens at the end of *Julius Caesar* but I don't think that that's realistic." But she framed the moral import behind schoolwork and grades ambiguously, as is evident in the following vignette of a classroom exchange that occurred after she realized many students were not reading their books and doing the accompanying assignments. This vignette illustrates the tension between pressuring students to buy into the meritocratic system and acknowledging that they may not be willing to submit to it.

Ms. Goodman began class by reminding students that their second journal entry was due the next day. She told them that they "always have a choice . . . but to not do a journal entry leaves you with a poor grade." A couple of students walked in late, and the class was still somewhat restless until Ms. Goodman quieted students by telling them "OK, ladies and gentlemen here we go. Shh. Let's try to settle down and I will tell you what I think I'm right about."

Ms. Goodman proceeded to read through a list of students who had not turned in Journal Entry 1. She said in a stern voice, "Will it count as late—yes. It's your responsibility to get it into my possession. You have a choice; you may do or not do. You have a choice. This is the work designed to help you improve your skills; if you don't do it it's your problem." No one answered back, and she handed out a small slip of paper with the next journal assignment.

The next day, Malaika informed Ms. Goodman that she did not do the journal entry. She apologized, but her tone sounded unapologetic and slightly aggressive. Ms. Goodman responded by telling her that she needed to turn in a journal or a separate paper to get full credit. She informed everyone in the class that if they didn't give her their entry today she'd take it tomorrow. A student asked, "For how much credit?" Ms. Goodman said it would be worth 10 points today and 5 tomorrow. She continued emphatically, "There's no excuse. This is March. You will be sophomores next year. Some have asked to go up a level. I was very clear on your homework. If you don't do it that's a choice you've made, but there are consequences."

The teacher during the course of this exchange expressed defensive agitation over having to threaten students with bad grades, as if she knew that such a tack has limited impact and creates a negative tone. She proceeded nevertheless, not knowing what else to do. In anticipation of students' refusal to obey, she ambiguously framed the situation as a moral obligation; an individual choice; and, finally, as a threat. The threat consisted not only of poor grades but also of continued low-track status in the school's meritocratic hierarchy. The long-term "consequences"—failure in high school and beyond—were ambiguously implied. The teacher tried to get students to take responsibility by identifying missing work as their "problem." The meaning of this judgmental term also was ambiguous but communicated that her commands were legitimate and not to be questioned, while students were guilty of not fulfilling their obligations. Although loaded with moral meanings, the teacher's message also divorced homework from intrinsic educational value and conveyed that the main reason for reading and writing was to get credit and compete for success. This accidental undermining of educational purposes weakened the teacher's authority relationship with the students and set up a potential power struggle. Students did not directly contest Ms. Goodman's warning, but Malaika's assertion about not doing her work, and another student's bargaining tactics, suggested opposition.

Although she saw grades as a primary motivator, Ms. Goodman was actually conflicted about using them because of the negative influence they could have on students' feelings about their performance and attitude toward the class. In the second interview, after discussing her disappointment over students' grades she said:

> You know, for their self-esteem, I think I've done a good job of not making them constantly conscious of how they're doing on their grades and that in fact, I don't think that that's a bad thing. I think that positive attitude, they seem happy to be there; they don't seem stressed. And I think that's a good environment for learning. The fact that they haven't bought in and aren't doing the reading and don't have the good grades to go along with it well I'm sorry about that. But I'm not sorry—I don't want to have grim faces, a tension-filled room; I would prefer what appears to be this happy productive engaged room.

She continued, "On the other hand somebody could say, 'But look what you've got here. Look at your results—this kid hasn't read a damn thing. You should be keeping her after school, you should be sending her to detention, you should be'—y'know?" The teacher clearly expressed a common dilemma between pushing students to meet expectations versus lowering expectations to keep the peace. The press for positive relations and face-saving is paramount yet often in conflict with authority (Pace, 2003a, 2003b; A. Powell, Farrarr, & Cohen, 1985; Sedlak, Wheeler, Pullin, & Cusick, 1986; Waller, 1932/1961). Perhaps her focus on the maintenance of "what appears to be this happy productive engaged room" interfered with paying closer attention to missing homework and contributed to her surprise at low report card grades. Observations following these classroom events confirmed that Ms. Goodman's main strategy to persuade students to do their work was to refer to tests, homework credit, and grades rather than convey the desirability of learning, while softening this pressure, as is described shortly, with polite talk.

Tensions Between Student Participation and Boundaries

In addition to grading, teachers inevitably confront the classic tension between two fundamental educational goals that are interdependent and in conflict: (a) engaging students and (b) keeping order (Metz, 1978; Page,

1987, 1990, 1991; Waller, 1932/1961). Some teachers try to ensure control by continually occupying students with worksheets and other private, routine assignments. This is especially the case in lower track classrooms (Metz, 1978; Page, 1991). But when a daily diet of routine work does not sit well with the mixed abilities of the students or the orientation of the English department, the dilemma becomes how to balance student participation with boundaries on that participation to preserve control.

The lesson described in this section illustrates how this tension was managed by Ms. Goodman through an inherently contradictory strategy of action that combined positive politeness intended to encourage student participation with the establishment of boundaries meant to control teacher–student relations and classroom discourse. Sociolinguistic theory defines *politeness* as linguistic strategies used to save face or another person's public self-image (Brown & Levinson, 1987; Goffman, 1967, p. 5) and to foster harmonious relations and/or persuasion. There are positive and negative aspects of saving face. Positive face depends on the approval and empathy of others; negative face relies on freedom from imposition.

Cazden (1988) applied Brown and Levinson's (1987) politeness theory to the classroom and showed that teachers' everyday discourse is filled with redressive linguistic strategies that offset their inevitably constant face-threatening acts, especially acts related to evaluation of students and commands. Language that indicates warmth, friendliness, and caring enhances positive face, whereas language that suggests choice or minimizes demands is used to save negative face. "We will work together on this assignment" is an example of positive politeness, with its suggestion of inclusiveness. "Could you do me a favor, please, and shut off the light?" expresses negative politeness through making a request rather than a command and implies the teacher's indebtedness to the student.[8]

Although politeness is a universal sociolinguistic phenomenon, particular uses of politeness are influenced by culture. In liberal schools, it is used to create the appearance of egalitarian relationships between adults and youth. Polite talk neutralizes, and thereby facilitates, classroom interactions by making the assertion of authority palatable (Page, 1991). For example, teachers may use language that implies openness and intimacy but exert control through regulation of discourse (Mehan, 1979; Nystrand, 1997) and establishment of boundaries between safe and controversial topics (Boler, 1999; McNeil, 1981; Page, 1991; Simon, 2001). If disagreements arise, they are resolved quickly and subtly, so that "conflict between teacher and students is concealed but the teacher's point of view prevails" (Page, 1991, p. 71).

---

[8]Delpit (1988) and Heath (1983) have discussed the problems that occur when White middle-class teachers veil their commands and young Black children therefore do not take them seriously, because they are accustomed to more direct expression of authority in their homes and communities.

An excerpt from Philip Roth's *Portnoy's Complaint* can be seen as a refracted mirror of this case study, as it deals with a struggle over authority between a father, who represents obedience to tradition, and his son, who stands for rebellion and individual freedom. Ms. Goodman expressed contradictory cultural orientations to authority in a notably paradoxical approach to the excerpt, which was presented as a story titled "Father and Son" (without mention of its source). She took a progressive stance by sympathizing with the son and criticizing the father, yet she invoked traditional authority as she quelled students' attempts to construct their own interpretations. She seemed determined to get students to arrive at the "correct" interpretation and to steer them away from topics she was not prepared to discuss.

Ms. Goodman started the lesson with the statement: "You might not see the connection with anything in your life. That's OK. You'll get credit for reading and answering the questions." She reinforced her point: "This can offset not handing in the homework." Ms. Goodman introduced the text as a family argument in which a father struggles with his son over observing Jewish traditions. Once students started reading, the class was silent and apparently very absorbed. As they finished reading and began the accompanying handout, some of them became restless. Ms. Goodman tried to focus students on their work with what sounded like a social invitation: "How about in another two or three minutes we'll chit-chat?" Despite the emotional and moral provocation of the piece, she framed class discussion as a casual, light conversation rather than a search for deeper meaning.

The teacher began the discussion with an open-ended appeal: "Talk to me about the story." Then she switched gears by directing students to the first question on the handout, which asked what emotions were felt by the characters. Ms. Goodman enthusiastically called on raised hands: "Heather, Heather! Talk to us." Heather talked about anger and sadness. Ms. Goodman gave a quick affirmation and kept things moving: "Good! Someone else." Ben said there was fear. Ms. Goodman asked who showed fear, and Ben said everyone did, especially the father. Malaika volunteered that the father feared his children wouldn't learn about their culture. Without responding, the teacher moved on to the next student.

Dennis said another emotion was confusion, and clarified that Alex didn't know the importance of his religion, referring back to Malaika's point. Ms. Goodman asked, "What is he really reacting to? Do you know the term 'generation gap'?" She explained it, and asked rhetorically, "Does this story reflect that process?"

The next person Ms. Goodman called on went back to religion. Ms. Goodman implored: "Let's not open up the floor to where religion fits in one's life. I don't want to open that can of worms; that's a very different discussion. Is the father making a good convincing argument? Is the father respectful of the son?" Will picked up on her lead and drew the "correct" conclusion that the story was not about religion at all. Ms. Goodman nodded and said, "Right. Good."

The teacher called on Malaika, who had wanted to speak earlier: "Malaika—did you lose your train of thought? Is it a respectful argument?" Malaika said it was a good argument; the son should know about his background and heritage. Once again, Ms. Goodman avoided the perspective Malaika and Dennis had persistently raised and pushed her point: "Is that a nice way for a father to talk to a son?" Finally, Trudy articulated the lesson Ms. Goodman was trying to get across: "The son would change his mind if the father talked to him differently." The teacher said, "Exactly."

Malaika tried again, this time by connecting her personal experience to the text. She shared that she got into arguments with her mother about how to dress for church. Picking up on her friend Malaika's comment, Justine said that her mother wanted her to dress up for church, but the Reverend said that God doesn't care what you wear, as long as you come to church. Ms. Goodman repeated that this story could be about anything, not just religion. She asked whether everyone had written down the homework assignment; reminded them about tomorrow's quiz; and told them to hand back the story, the questions, and their answers as they left.

Paradoxical enactments of authority and the tensions they evoked were evident in the discussion. On one hand, Ms. Goodman encouraged involvement using positive politeness by facilitating conversation with her warm, energetic tone when inviting students to "talk to me about the story." Students responded enthusiastically in kind, and the teacher affirmed their answers. But when students expressed views different from hers, Ms. Goodman dismissed them, suggesting their job was to provide specific, correct answers sought by the teacher. Essentially, Ms. Goodman enacted a typical initiation–response–evaluation recitation structure, which gave her control over the form and content of the discussion. Rather than engaging in open dialogue with students, she narrowed the direction of the discussion and determined which conversational paths were legitimate in order to conclude with specific points. The teacher's interpretation of the text seemed to advocate for a liberal understanding of authority relations. Her focus on the form authority takes—specifically, the need for politeness—paralleled her efforts to make her approach to the discussion seem democratic. However, the teacher's criticism of the traditional authority figure ironically contradicted her simultaneous enactment of this role, which assumed that ultimate knowledge and control rest with the teacher.

Amidst the confusion created by a shift in tone from encouragement of free expression to teacher control, some students (from different races) figured out what the teacher wanted and supplied answers sought by her. Three Black students—Malaika, Justine, and Dennis—tried to connect the story to their own experience and in so doing contested her agenda. They seemed to view knowledge as something they could appropriate and make personally meaningful, as they created a bridge that crossed racial, cultural, religious, and generational lines in their identifications with the Jewish father. Malaika, Justine, and Dennis's comments pointed to respect for the substance of the commands made by an elder—preserving religious traditions—rather than polite communication between parent and child. Ms. Goodman's dismissive response, and the main point she tried to transmit about the importance of form over substance, can be seen as implicitly devaluing the knowledge students brought from their home communities to the class and imposing White middle-class values.[9] Her approach ran counter to research findings that teachers' successful engagement of students involves forging connections between the curriculum and the child and between the culture of school and students' home culture (see, e.g., Davidson, 1996; Dewey, 1902; Erickson, 1986; Heath, 1983; Ladson-Billings, 1994). It also diminished the literacy capacities of three Black students, two of whom she complained refused to read.[10]

What culturally shaped knowledge explains the teacher's rigid construction of boundaries between school knowledge and the knowledge students brought? One factor was a concern with maintaining control and keeping students focused on "academics." Ms. Goodman described her style as "very teacher centered" and "controlling." She wanted students to find the work meaningful, but she was "not interested" in talking with students about nonacademic topics: "I don't think that's what my role in here is. I think my role is to try and offer something in the way of written material, print . . ." She said, "I can't stand free-wheeling discussions about life," and referred to another class: "They started to talk about really random things this (story) reminded them of, and the next thing you knew there were really idiotic connections made that I would not want to promote." She implied that inviting students to share their interests and experiences was risky, because it would detract from an academic focus. To make the class productive, she controlled the discourse so it stayed centered on her treatment of the text and steered it away from students' personal associations to the material.

Ms. Goodman was not unusual in drawing boundaries to control knowledge (see McNeil, 1981, 1986) during class discussion. Classroom lessons often neglect the essential, moral questions that lie at the heart of literature, history, and so on (Simon, 2001). Many teachers avoid moral deliberation because they have not been taught its importance or how to facilitate it, they are pressured to cover a huge curriculum (high-stakes testing was not a factor for Ms. Goodman at the time; today it would be), and they fear losing control. Avoidance of intellectually and morally complex topics is

---

[9]Delpit (1995) addressed these issues in her book *Other People's Children.*

[10]Gilmore (1983) showed that teachers' low assessment of Black children's literacy capacities is narrow, rigid, and inaccurate.

especially true in lower track classes, in which control is top priority (Oakes, 1985; Page, 1991). Additionally, many teachers unwittingly marginalize the knowledge students of color bring from their home communities (Davidson, 1996; Valenzuela, 1999).

A second factor was a view of classroom roles and relationships. Although she claimed to be providing a "personal connection with the teacher," which was important to students, Ms. Goodman defined this as knowing them well as students, encouraging them to achieve, and being available to help with schoolwork. She told me, "I don't want to be a counselor. I don't want to be a social worker. I just want to be their English teacher." Ms. Goodman avoided learning about students' lives outside of school with the assumption that if they had problems at home she was not qualified to get involved.

To address the tension between student participation and control, the teacher both elicited involvement through positive politeness yet constrained it by constructing boundaries that created distance, both between teacher and students and between the class and subject matter. Paradoxically, in this mini-unit on personal narratives, Ms. Goodman stressed the importance of revealing "personal significance"—that the stories they had read had a special "meaning" or "importance," and the narratives students were assigned to write must have this as well. Because of the emphasis on order, class discussion of "Father and Son" lost its potential to scaffold students' writing and promote personal involvement in literature.

Tensions Over Success or Failure With Challenging Curriculum

A third area of tension in the teacher's authority relationships with Black students involved the issue of academic success or failure. Black students' withdrawal from schooling has been explained by social psychologists (Howard & Hammond, 1985; Steele, 1992) as stemming from performance anxiety generated by internalized racist stereotypes of intellectual inferiority. Many interpret this anxiety as low self-esteem; this interpretation is commonly linked with the belief that underachievement also stems from cultural deprivation (Lipman, 1998). In a review of theories that explain educational inequality, McCarthy (1990) concluded that although liberal educators do not believe in innate inferiority of certain groups, they do "'blame the victim'" by attributing school failure to lack of access to cultural and intellectual resources in students' homes (p. 35). While advocating for equality, these educators often are oblivious to the ways in which success and failure are reproduced in schools. They assume the validity of meritocracy and related structures of schooling such as grades, tests, and tracking (Varenne & McDermott, 1997), while avoiding meaningful talk about race, and treating Black people as guests rather than integrated community members (Chalmers, 1997; Tatum, 1997). These norms may exacerbate Black students' performance anxiety and/or alienation from school, as indicated by the following vignette.

The lesson that Ms. Goodman taught on this occasion revealed volatile classroom dynamics due to uncertainty regarding students' academic success or failure with a challenging text. The teacher's strategy of action in persuading students to attend to the lesson both exacerbated and smoothed over these dynamics as she used politeness, pressure, and boundary setting. When the literature was accessible, as in the preceding vignette, Ms. Goodman judged that students did not require excessive demands or face-saving. But when the assigned text posed significant difficulty to many students' understanding, and to the teacher's ability to make it comprehensible, the level of politeness, pressure, and ensuing conflict rose dramatically.

The class had started reading *Julius Caesar* aloud the day before, and the homework included five questions on Act I, Scene I. Ms. Goodman told me she had trepidations about *Julius Caesar* because she believed students would find it difficult and unenjoyable. She also said the homework was too hard for them. Given this challenging situation, how did she attempt to get them to review the first scene with her so that they could gain some understanding and set a foundation for the rest of the play?

Ms. Goodman called attention with a cheerful, loud greeting: "Good morning, everybody." She immediately took charge: "Take off your sunglasses (to one student). Take out your copy of *Julius Caesar* and these little questions, and whatever you *were* able to do." Students were still quite noisy, chatting while they took out their papers. The teacher continued:

> Okay. We really need to settle down folks. Everybody needs a notebook. Let me tell you why. I'm gonna help you go over the questions. Those people who answered them with ease or with help or did what they could will help us all answer the questions. Next week, put those pictures away, next week, there will be a test on Act I. So as we go over these questions you need answers, even if you couldn't get them on your own. OK, so, lemme give you a minute or two to get out a notebook. Ben, notebook. Ali, notebook or paper where are you gonna put your notes?

After her greeting, Ms. Goodman issued direct commands that established her role as teacher, their role as students, and the task before them. Yet with negative politeness she minimized the assignment ("little questions") and subtly expressed doubts about students' ability as she tried to lessen anxiety about the homework ("whatever you *were* able to do"). This suggested she was comfortable creating boundaries that promoted control but worried about the imposition created by a demanding assignment for lower track students. She reassured students that they would all get the answers to the homework questions and then provided the reason why this was important.

Hypothetically, the teacher could be referring to multiple reasons for attending to a lesson on *Julius Caesar*, such as learning to appreciate a literary giant, or dealing with profound and timeless literary and political themes. However, the single purpose she gave was a test. She used it as a high-stakes strategy for gaining students' attention, but it was a double-edged sword. The test was an incentive as well as a threatening imposition, which necessitated that she be polite to compensate for it.

Ms. Goodman continued to exert tremendous effort to keep the students with her every step of the way, by making sure each person had a notebook and pen and was ready to go. She proceeded with her characteristic mix of direct commands and face-saving talk. "OK, I'm just gonna do a quick zip around the room and see how you did. Don't worry if you don't have them all; I just wanna see if you made an effort to try 'em. Good." Ms. Goodman softened the threat of checking students' homework by reassuring them, yet this implied a lack of confidence in their ability.

"Now. There will be a test, probably, I imagine it'll be Wednesday next week. OK. So why am I telling you that there will be a test?" Dennis said, "So we can write it down in our notebooks." The teacher corrected him: "No, so that you'll pay greater attention and stop fooling around. OK? So you need to keep notes, on all of this. OK?"

Ms. Goodman gave away the primary reason for the note-taking and the test, which was to solve the basic problem of control. Tests and notes became control strategies to make sure students took school seriously. In being so honest, the teacher "pulled back the curtains of her fancy talk" (C. Cazden, personal communication, September 4, 1997). Then she compensated with more politeness ("So you need to keep notes. OK?").

Ms. Goodman's mix of direct commands and redressive strategies points to commonly held views—that lower track students need structure and self-esteem building and are not interested in subject matter. Her approach served the school's values of competition and good rapport, as she tried to persuade students to engage through exerting pressure and making nice. But as hard as Ms. Goodman worked to get control, as soon as the class turned its attention to the homework on *Julius Caesar*, unrest began to bubble up and boundaries were unsettled by transgressions that raised questions about who really was in charge.

First, Malaika asked whether the opening scene occurred on a Sunday, which evoked impatience and a confusing exchange. Will, a White student who had a speech impediment, showed that he clearly knew far more than the rest of the class: "They-they-they didn't have Sundays the same way we do; they just had lots and lots of holidays all the time." Ms. Goodman teased: "Oh. I see and how do you know all this; you're that Latin scholar aren't you?" She allowed Will to share his expertise but brought him down a notch by teasing him. The lesson proceeded laboriously, as the teacher called on students to provide answers and clarified them, and students stumbled over pronunciation of names and location of quotes from the text. Will continued to actively participate in the discussion and challenged Ms. Goodman on whether Pompey, Caesar's competitor, had been killed at that point. She was momentarily stumped, asked if they could move on, and then found a footnote that resolved the issue. In the meantime, however, Will had contested her expertise, and the whole situation created an unsettled feeling in the class about the teacher's and students' ability to handle this text.

Ms. Goodman wrapped up the discussion on each question by telling students what they should have as the answer: "OK the first part of the answer to number two, how 'bout if we say, something to the effect of—" Will jumped in, and a loud protest was heard from across the room where Justine, Malaika, and Doreen were sitting: "Uhhh. Nooo." Ms. Goodman intervened: "Girls, girls. Will has an answer, let him give the answer." They responded with another cry of frustration. Over their protests Ms. Goodman reassured them, "I'm gonna translate."

Justine exclaimed openly and loudly: "I don't understand what the hell he's talking about!" I was struck by this unusual outburst; I had not observed anything like this in 7 weeks of fieldwork. Ms. Goodman repeated: "I'm gonna translate it. OK. Sh. Be patient. Go 'head. I'll listen and I'll give you a short version." Will proceeded, and Justine again yelled across to him: "What the hell are you talking about?!" Other students called out; there was palpable tension and an out-of-control feeling in the room.

Ms. Goodman stayed surprisingly calm, spoke in a moderate tone and volume, and interpreted Justine's outburst as frustration versus attack: "Shh. OK. Justine, Justine, could you be more polite and ask Will what you don't understand instead of asking—" Justine responded calmly, in kind: "OK." Ms. Goodman said, "OK. Ask Will what you don't understand." Justine removed her eyeglasses, glared across the room at Will, and unpredictably switched back into a hostile yell: "What the hell are you talking about?!" I heard someone giggle, and Ms. Goodman implored, "In a nicer way, in a nicer way." Justine rephrased her remark: "What the H-E-double hockey sticks are you talking about?" This evoked laughter from several students.

Ms. Goodman, whose low-key reaction was striking to me, tried to substantively channel Justine's question: "OK but wait a minute. About what? The slaves?" Justine, sounding very annoyed and frustrated, softened her speech to a loud whine: "What's he saying?" At this point Malaika stepped in and helped Justine clarify her question: "Where do the slaves come from?" Nikki and Malaika joined forces to explain that Caesar wasn't considered truly victorious because he wasn't bringing home slaves. Ms. Goodman affirmed their explanation gratefully: "OK. Thank you! Very good!" The class broke out in applause and cheers; the tension was broken, and order was restored.

Ms. Goodman was afraid students would not cooperate because of the difficulty of the play so, ironically, she both reassured and threatened them. At first, subtle challenges unsettled the control Ms. Goodman tried so hard to establish. The tension rose as Will challenged the teacher's knowledge, and when he took over Ms. Goodman's summary of the answer to the second question, he in effect usurped her role as teacher and authority figure. In response, Justine, Malaika, and Doreen protested against this upsetting of the social order. Ms. Goodman tried to placate them, but Justine continued to angrily express her frustration, which sparked a chaotic scene. Together, teacher and students provoked and pacified one another as they managed the pressures of success and failure in a school environment that fostered competition.

Discussion with Ms. Goodman about this episode revealed the difficulty of managing academic heterogeneity and students' anxiety with a challenging text. It also revealed a blind spot that resulted in blaming individual students rather than recognizing how the culture of schooling prompted opposition and failure. She felt it was important to allow Justine to express her frustration and that she probably spoke for other students who were also having difficulty. But she also seemed skeptical about Justine's motives, saying she "f(ound) it best not to play into" students' hostile behavior. She said, "You gotta watch it with Justine because she can be an instigator of some very negative things. It's a lot of center stage behavior. On the other hand I don't think she could read and understand much on her own." The teacher said it was not OK that students sometimes laughed at Will for "being so smart" and "so hard to understand." She said she "felt that had to be controlled" so she was:

> trying to find a balance between giving her a chance; I think it's important for them to be able to express they don't know what's going on. It's usually either Justine or Doreen who loves to play that role—"I don't get it" and then they'll chime in together and it'll be this crescendo. But then at the same time you've got Ben and Will who know everything before it's even been said.

The teacher indicated that resistance was a factor in low achievement. She viewed it as an attitudinal problem, not as a legitimate reaction against an oppressive system or problematic curriculum. Ms. Goodman told me that toward the end of the year, Doreen, during class discussion of a poem, asked "in a very hostile tone, 'How are you gonna grade us on this on the (final) exam?'" Ms. Goodman explained to me that they were "trying to get at the meaning of the poem" so they could write an essay about it on the test, and "she's getting sidetracked and trying to derail the conversation yet again." Ms. Goodman said she tried to reassure and refocus Doreen, but she became "belligerent" and muttered "four-letter words under her breath," and the teacher ignored it to defuse the conflict. She said Doreen had recently been given detention because of a missing homework packet, and she did not come. The teacher expressed defeat:

> To me that's very frustrating, you know here's a teacher who's really very willing and works very hard, to try to acknowledge African American students for their accomplishments, and really tries to motivate and push them, and be enthusiastic about when they do well, and then you get these kids who just, they ain't moving.

Perhaps Doreen was giving the teacher a taste of her own medicine, by disrupting Ms. Goodman's attempts to get at meaning with a concern about grades. But the teacher read Doreen's behavior as wanting "center stage" rather than as a valid protest or genuine concern about failure. As in so many classrooms, conflict was avoided, and underlying problems were not identified nor addressed. Like other teachers of lower track classes (Page, 1991) and subordinated minority students (Irvine, 1990), Ms. Goodman located problems in her students rather than questioning her enactment of curriculum. This may have been partially due to defensiveness about her teacher-centered, structured, skills-based style, as a veteran teacher newly placed in an English department that prided itself on an outstanding faculty. Identifying herself as an advocate of Black students, and then not feeling successful with them when she was glad to have "so many" in this class, may have made her feel particularly vulnerable. Her stories indicated fear that the Black girls on whom she was focused could be hostile when academically challenged. Although her strategies accomplished the fundamental goals of keeping order and eliciting participation, her avoidance of conflict and exploration of knowledge weakened the fundamental classroom relationship among teacher, students, and subject matter.

CONCLUSION

High school teachers face contradiction and uncertainty as they construct authority with students. They must figure out how to manage tensions over completion of assignments, student participation versus boundaries, and academic success or failure with difficult curricula, all of which have special significance for teachers' authority relations with "underachieving" Black students. Teachers are left on their own to figure out how to approach two crucial and interrelated dimensions of their practice: (a) authority and (b) enactment of curriculum.

Ms. Goodman's strategies of action in enacting authority and curriculum combined politeness, pressure, and maintenance of boundaries; they were a translation of the school's social norms and competitive values. They evoked a mix of student responses. Encouragement and face-saving fostered class participation, but emphasis on grades, rigid boundaries and control of knowledge, and uncertainty about students' intellectual ability and desire to learn contributed to limited engagement and underachievement. Limitations in the teacher's expertise—the most important basis of teachers' professional authority (Grant, 1988; Metz, 1978; Pace, 2003a)—were not addressed in a school that prided itself on a superior faculty. Genuine authority and deep involvement in learning were weakened by emphasis on order and grades rather than intrinsically valuable educational purposes (see Delpit, 1988).

The "Perspectives in Literature" class was situated in the ambiguous moral order of the high school. On one hand, Hillsdale offered many more resources and opportunities than other districts, and positive feelings about the high school among staff and students were evident. African American achievement was supposed to be a targeted concern of the district. At the same time, with its meritocratic structure, catering to privileged clientele, and attachment to the status quo, the school participated in the construction of Black underachievement.

Although confronting racial inequality is critical, it must be noted that ambivalence among Black students is linked with the broader problem of disengagement in U.S. high schools and the uncertain purposes of high school education (Cohen & Neufeld, 1981; Sizer, 1984). That problem poses a huge challenge to teachers, even as they may be unintentionally complicit (Grant, 1988; Jackson, 1968; McNeil, 1986; A. Powell et al., 1985; Sedlak et al., 1986; Singham, 1998; Sizer, 1984). While privileged students gain advantage through credentials that represent school success, the construction of Black underachievement points to cracks in a system that undereducates all students, with its emphasis on individual social mobility rather than preparing citizens for a democratic society (Labaree, 1997). Serious deliberation about the purposes of schooling, investigation of how racial inequality is framed by the culture of schooling, raised awareness about authority and its relationship to enactment of curriculum, and continuing teacher education that helps teachers develop educative strategies of action are all vital to constructing authority that disrupts insidiously harmful patterns of success and failure in high school classes.

REFERENCES

Boler, M. (1999). *Feeling power: Emotions and education.* New York: Routledge.
Brown, P., & Levinson, S. (1987). *Politeness: Some universals in language usage.* Cambridge, England: Cambridge University Press.

Cazden, C. (1988). *Classroom discourse: The language of teaching and learning.* Portsmouth, NH: Heinemann.

Chalmers, V. (1997). White out: Multicultural performances in a progressive school. In M. Fine, L. Powell, L. Weis, & L. Mun Wong (Eds.), *Off white: Readings on race, power, and society* (pp. 66–78). New York: Routledge.

Cohen, D. K., & Neufeld, B. (1981). The failure of high schools and the progress of education. *Daedalus, 110,* 69–89.

Cusick, P. (1983). *The egalitarian ideal and the American high school: Studies of three schools.* New York: Longman.

Davidson, A. L. (1996). *Making and molding identity in schools: Student narratives on race, gender, and academic engagement.* Albany: State University of New York Press.

Delpit, L. (1988). The silenced dialogue: Power and pedagogy in educating other people's children. *Harvard Educational Review, 18,* 280–298.

Delpit, L. (1995). *Other people's children: Cultural conflict in the classroom.* New York: New Press.

Dewey, J. (1902). *The child and the curriculum.* Chicago: University of Chicago Press.

Erickson, F. (1986). Qualitative methods in research on teaching. In M. Wittrock (Ed.), *Handbook of research on teaching* (pp. 119–161). New York: Macmillan.

Fordham, S. (1996). *Blacked out: Dilemmas of race, identity, and success at Capital High.* Chicago: University of Chicago Press.

Gilmore, P. (1983). Spelling "Mississippi": Recontextualizing a literacy-related speech event. *Anthropology and Education Quarterly, 14,* 235–255.

Giroux, H. A. (1983). Theories of reproduction and resistance in the new sociology of education: A critical analysis. *Harvard Educational Review, 53,* 257–293.

Goffman, E. (1967). *Interaction ritual: Essays on face-to-face behavior.* New York: Pantheon.

Goodlad, J. (1984). *A place called school.* New York: McGraw-Hill.

Grant, G. (1988). *The world we created at Hamilton High.* Cambridge, MA: Harvard University Press.

Hammersley, M., & Atkinson, P. (1995). *Ethnography: Princples in practice.* London: Routledge.

Heath, S. B. (1983). *Ways with words: Language, life, and work in communities and classrooms.* Cambridge, England: Cambridge University Press.

Howard, J., & Hammond, R. (1985, September 9). Rumors of inferiority. *The New Republic,* 17–21.

Hurn, C. (1985). Changes in authority relationships in schools: 1960–1980. *Research in Sociology of Education and Socialization, 5,* 31–57.

Irvine, J. J. (1990). *Black students and school failure: Policies, practices, and prescriptions.* Westport, CT: Greenwood.

Jackson, P. W. (1968). *Life in classrooms.* New York: Holt, Rinehart & Winston.

Johnston, R. C., & Viadero, D. (2000). Unmet promise: Raising minority achievement. *Education Week, 19*(27), 1, 18–21.

Labaree, D. (1997). *How to succeed in school without really learning: The credentials race in American education.* New Haven, CT: Yale University Press.

Ladson-Billings, G. (1994). *The dreamkeepers: Successful teachers of African American children.* San Francisco: Jossey-Bass.

Lightfoot, S. L. (1983). *The good high school: Portraits of character and culture.* New York: Basic Books.

Lipman, P. (1998). *Race, class, and power in school restructuring.* Albany: State University of New York Press.

Mathews, J. (1998). *Class struggle: What's wrong (and right) with America's best public high schools.* New York: Random House.

McCarthy, C. (1990). *Race and curriculum: Social inequality and the theory of politics of difference in contemporary research on schooling.* London: Falmer.

McNeil, L. (1981). Negotiating classroom knowledge: Beyond achievement and socialization. *Journal of Curriculum Studies, 13*, 313–328.

McNeil, L. M. (1986). *Contradictions of control: School knowledge and school structure.* New York: Routledge & Kegan Paul.

Mehan, H. (1979). *Learning lessons.* Cambridge, MA: Harvard University Press.

Metz, M. H. (1978). *Classrooms and corridors: The crisis of authority in desegregated secondary schools.* Berkeley: University of California Press.

Nieto, S. (1996). *Affirming diversity: The sociopolitical context of multicultural education* (2nd ed.). White Plains, NY: Longman.

Nystrand, M. (1997). *Opening dialogue: Understanding the dynamics of language and learning in the English classroom.* New York: Teachers College Press.

Oakes, J. (1985). *Keeping track: How teachers structure inequality.* New Haven, CT: Yale University Press.

Oakes, J., Gamoran, A., & Page, R. (1992). Curriculum differentiation: Opportunities, outcomes, and meanings. In P. Jackson (Ed.), *Handbook of reserach on curriculum* (pp. 570–608). New York: Macmillan.

Obidah, J., & Teel, K. M. (2001). *Because of the kids.* New York: Teachers College Press.

Ogbu, J. U. (1978), *Minority education and caste: The American system in cross-cultural perspective.* New York: Academic.

Ogbu, J. U. (1987). Variability in minority student performance: A problem in search of an explanation. *Anthropology and Education Quarterly, 18*, 312–334.

Ogbu, J. U. (1991). Minority coping responses and school experience. *Journal of Psychohistory, 18*, 433–456.

Ogbu, J. U. (2003). *Black American students in an affluent suburb: A study of academic disengagement.* Mahwah, NJ: Lawrence Erlbaum Associates, Inc.

Pace, J. L. (2003a). Managing the dilemmas of professional and bureaucratic authority in a high school English class. *Sociology of Education, 76*, 37–52.

Pace, J. L. (2003b). Using ambiguity and entertainment to win compliance in a lower-level U.S. history class. *Journal of Curriculum Studies, 35*, 83–110.

Page, R. (1987). Lower-track classes at a college-preparatory high school: A caricature of educational encounters. In G. Spindler & L. Spindler (Eds.), *Interpretive ethnography of education: At home and abroad* (pp. 447–472). Hillsdale, NJ: Lawrence Erlbaum Associates, Inc.

Page, R. N. (1990). Games of chance: The lower-track curriculum in a college-preparatory high school. *Curriculum Inquiry, 20*, 249–281.

Page, R. N. (1991). *Lower-track classrooms: A curricular and cultural perspective.* New York: Teachers College Press.

Pollock, M. (2001). How the question we ask most about race in education is the very question we most suppress. *Educational Researcher, 30*(9), 2–12.

Pope, D. (2001). *Doing school: How we are creating a generation of stressed out, materialistic, and miseducated students.* New Haven, CT: Yale University Press.

Powell, A. G., Farrarr, E., & Cohen, D. K. (1985). *The shopping mall high school: Winners and losers in the educational marketplace.* Boston: Houghton Mifflin.

Powell, L. (1997). The achievement (k)not: Whiteness and "Black underachievement." In M. Fine, L. Powell, L. Weis, & L. Mun Wong (Eds.), *Off white: Readings on race, power, and society* (pp. 57–65). New York: Routledge.

Price, J. (2000). *Against the odds: The meaning of school and relationships in the lives of six young African-American men.* Stanford, CT: Ablex.

Roth, P. (1994). *Portnoy's Complaint.* New York: Vintage. (Original work published 1967)

Rutter, M., Maughan, B., Mortimore, P., Ouston, J., with Smith, A. (1979). *Fifteen thousand hours.* Cambridge, MA: Harvard University Press.

Schwartz, G. (1987). *Beyond conformity or rebellion: Youth and authority in America.* Chicago: University of Chicago Press.

Sedlak, M., Wheeler, C., Pullin, D., & Cusick, P. (1986.) *Selling students short: Classroom bargains and academic reform in the American high school.* New York: Teachers College Press.

Simon, K. (2001). *Moral questions in the classroom: How to get kids to think deeply about real life and their schoolwork.* New Haven, CT: Yale University Press.

Singham, M. (2003, April). The achievement gap: Myths and realities. *Phi Delta Kappan, 84*(8), 586–591.

Sizer, T. R. (1984). *Horace's compromise: The dilemma of the American high school.* Boston: Houghton Mifflin.

Spindler, G., & Spindler, L. (1982). Roger Harker and Schonhausen: From familiar to strange and back again. In G. Spindler & L. Spindler (Eds.), *Doing the ethnography of schooling* (pp. 20–46). New York: Holt, Rinehart and Winston.

Spring, J. (1998). *American education.* Boston: McGraw Hill.

Steele, C. (1992, April). Race and the schooling of Black Americans. *The Atlantic Monthly,* 69–78.

Swidler, A. (1986). Culture in action: Symbols and strategies. *American Sociological Review, 51,* 273–286.

Swidler, A. (2001). *Talk of love: How culture matters.* Chicago: University of Chicago Press.

Tatum, B. D. (1997). *"Why are all the Black kids sitting together in the cafeteria?": And other conversations about race.* New York: Basic Books.

Valenzuela, A. (1999). *Subtractive schooling: U.S.-Mexican youth and the politics of caring.* Albany: State University of New York Press.

Varenne, H., & McDermott, R. (1997). *Successful failure: The school America builds.* Boulder, CO: Westview.

Waller, W. (1961). *The sociology of teaching.* New York: Russell & Russell. (Original work published 1961)

Willis, P. (1977). *Learning to labour: How working class kids get working class jobs.* Farnborough, England: Saxon House.

Chapter 5

Authority in Detracked High School Classrooms: Tensions Among Individualism, Equity, and Legitimacy

Janet S. Bixby
Lewis & Clark College, OR

During the last two decades, proponents of the detracking movement have tried to fundamentally change the structure and culture of high schools by reducing curricular differentiation within them (Oakes, Wells, & Jones, 1997; Wells & Serna, 1996). Prior research speaks to the influence of tracking on authority (Metz, 1978; Oakes, 1985; Page, 1991), but no studies have focused on authority relations in detracked classrooms. The detracking reform movement derives from an egalitarian impulse and challenges the individualistic values that reformers believe drive the organization and management of high schools and reproduce an inequitable social order (Page, 2000). Cultural values, including individualism and egalitarianism, have great bearing on the authority relations between teachers and students that shape classroom life (Pace, 2003b). Thus, an examination of detracked classrooms provides new insights on the interrelated cultural and structural factors that influence authority.

   In this chapter, I investigate authority relations in two detracked U.S. history classrooms that were part of a ninth grade, detracked "House" program within an academically competitive, college preparatory public high school in a moderate-sized town in the midwestern United States. Specifically, I look at the ways in which authority relations in these classrooms influence and are influenced by the nature of the academic participation of the least academically successful students who might otherwise be in lower track classrooms. They are the ones targeted to benefit the most from detracking reforms yet, having the least hope of gaining substantial benefit from schooling, they enact ambivalent and complex authority relationships with teachers (Oakes, Gamoran, & Page, 1992). They are disproportionately students of color both nationally (Lucas, 1999; Oakes, 1985) and in the school observed in this study.

My analysis identifies both cultural and structural factors within the larger school organization that influenced the authority relations in these detracked classrooms. Despite detracking, a very competitive academic environment persisted, along with hierarchical levels of academic participation among students in these classrooms. Specifically, the conflict between the egalitarian push of the school administration's reform agenda and the pull of the competitive academic culture of this overwhelmingly college-oriented high school privileged traditionally high-achieving students and disadvantaged the lower achieving students whom the reform was intended to benefit. Additionally, the students in these classes were, for the most part, quite compliant with the teachers' expectations for classroom behavior. However, some students, parents, and administrators challenged respect for teachers' legitimacy. In response to these challenges the teachers solidified their commitment to their academic departments and the status quo of their pedagogical practices, despite acknowledging that low levels of academic achievement among students of color remained a problem in the school. These dynamics undermined professional authority relations in the school and ultimately raise questions about the limited power of detracking reforms that change the structure but not the culture, curriculum, and pedagogy of classrooms.

STUDY SETTING AND METHODOLOGY

This chapter is drawn from a larger interpretive study in 1995–1996 on detracking reform. It took place in a medium-sized, predominantly White, middle-class, midwestern city called Springfield.[1] There are four large, public, comprehensive high schools in the school district. Hillside High School, where this study was conducted, had a student population that was 80% White; 11% African American; and 9% combined Hispanic, Asian, and Native American. Seventy-one percent of its graduates go on to 4-year colleges and universities. Teachers and administrators reported that Hillside served a predominantly upper-middle-class student population. Prior to the study, the district had developed a high-profile concern about race and

---

[1] All names of people and places are pseudonyms.

academic achievement, an issue that the district referred to as "minority student achievement."[2] As part of this larger reform effort to raise minority student achievement, the district pressured high schools to eliminate lower track classes and funded the House program at Hillside.

The House program was designed to distribute all ninth-grade students into heterogeneously mixed houses for their consecutively scheduled English, social studies, and science classes. The three teachers in each house thus shared the same students and had an extra preparation period in which to do team planning.

Hillside High School had a strong college preparatory reputation. Teachers were accustomed to working with students whom they thought were expecting to go to 4-year colleges or universities after high school. They had generally counted on most of their students arriving at ninth grade with, at a minimum, ninth grade level academic skills. They had also counted on most of their students being motivated to achieve in the college preparatory curriculum and in response to the instruction they offered at least to a level needed attain the grades that symbolized to prospective colleges their success in this endeavor. There was a feeling among faculty members and the community that they succeeded at this goal. I consistently heard the refrain from teachers, and witnessed it myself, that alumni returned from competitive colleges to report that they had been very well prepared for their college classes. As assistant principal Kate Simons explained:

> They have long been a college preparatory curriculum and they pride themselves in that. They still remain a comprehensive high school. We try to meet needs beyond just the college track but the bulk of the energy and the bulk of the pride I think goes into how we prepare kids for schools and the kind of feedback that we get back from kids who leave here and go and come back and say boy everybody in my English class just sat there with their mouth open. I knew what they were talking about. You guys have just done a marvelous job for me. The—they don't like to acknowledge that the college entrance requirements drive the curriculum but they do.

Similar to Pace's (2003b) Hillsdale High School and Page's (1991) Southmoor High School, the moral order of Hillside High School was characterized by its emphasis on individual students' eligibility and preparation for success in prestigious colleges and future socioeconomic success in life.

The House program, however, drew the competitive, individualistic values of this dominant school purpose into question. The House program grew out of an egalitarian impulse that foregrounded the small but growing

---

[2]The district and most of the school staff quite consistently used the terms *minority students* and *minority student achievement* in reference to students of color. Because these were the terms in use throughout the school and district cultures, I frequently use them here in an attempt to capture best the language of the staff members I studied.

percentages of students who were not succeeding academically at Hillside and the fact that students of color were overrepresented among these students.

I collected data for my study of Hillside High School from December 1995 through May 1996 and from September through December 1996. During spring of 1996, I observed one of Mr. Karl's and one of Ms. Thomas's ninth-grade detracked U.S. history classes twice a week on average and observed their other sections of the same course a few times. I observed House team meetings during that spring once a week and observed other, related meetings, such as department meetings, department chair meetings with administrators, meetings held for all House teachers, and occasional district meetings.

I recorded the apparent racial composition, based on observation and teacher comments, of the social studies classrooms that I observed. At Hillside the classes had, on average, 20 White students, 2 African American students, 1 to 2 Asian American students, and 1 to 2 Hispanic students.

I interviewed House teachers, counselors and other support staff, and school administrators. The interviews were semistructured. I had a set of topics that evolved as my research developed. In each interview I used a combination of types of questions, such as descriptive questions, structural questions, and contrast questions (Spradley, 1979). I tape-recorded and transcribed the interviews with key participants. Although I offered each participant the opportunity to read the transcript of his or her interview, no one chose to do that.

AUTHORITY RELATIONS IN TWO SOCIAL STUDIES CLASSROOMS

Covering the Content

The two ninth-grade social studies House teachers that I studied at Hillside, Ms. Thomas and Mr. Karl, had very similar teaching approaches. This similarity was in line with the philosophy of the social studies department and the school administration, both of which put a high priority on providing consistent instruction to all students in the same course. During a typical unit, each teacher would lecture to students for part or all of the period approximately every other day. The lectures were mixed with recitation: The teachers also asked questions that asked students to draw on their knowledge from the reading or to make educated guesses about the material at hand. The lectures covered complex historical concepts. A typical review sheet for a unit test listed 50 to 80 historical terms. Both teachers used pop quizzes to press the students to do the assigned textbook readings.

Once a week or so, each teacher showed a history video for part or all of a period and included information from them on the unit tests. The teachers assigned projects—often collaborative—once or twice per quarter.

Ms. Thomas and Mr. Karl were able to cover the curriculum and test students on major concepts and facts about U.S. history at a rapid rate. Their teaching approach was rooted within the larger departmental and school culture and was regarded by faculty and community members as college preparatory. Given the rapid coverage of complex concepts, teachers did not spend much class time presenting information in different ways to ensure that all students understood it. Neither did they spend much class time reviewing the concepts covered in the readings for homework.

Mr. Karl, expressing the sentiment of most of the teachers I studied, explained his approach to homework during an interview:

> *Mr. Karl:* Some freshman House teachers assign specific pages to be read for specific days and then they assign questions to be written. Um, I don't. I mean in the first quarter I assigned pages for particular days and I give a quiz but after the first quarter I simply tell them in each unit what they are supposed to read and leave it at that and they rise or fall on the tests. I don't ordinarily give much written homework except when there is an inquiry paper or a research assignment of some sort. And I don't feel guilty about it. (chuckles)
>
> *JB:* Why is that?
>
> *Mr. Karl:* Well there is the sense that you know that somehow there's some benefit in assigning more homework and I've never believed that. It seems to me bright students get sick and tired of doing what they consider busy work and it doesn't do the less able students any good unless it's directly related to what you're going to test on or unless there is some genuine connection with your goals, your teaching goals. And so I've never thought it was important. And I discovered in Japan they give far less homework than we do. It's just not a function of the quantity of the homework.
>
> *JB:* Un hunh. So do your grades rest quite heavily on tests?
>
> *Mr. Karl:* Yeah they do, I mean it depends on—again—it depends on the unit. In the last unit probably all of the grade was the test. In the current unit it'll be probably about two thirds of the grade. In the units that we do, the second world war being one of them it will only be about one third of the grade because there will be other major assignments that they'll be doing, so it varies significantly. The tests are important.

Mr. Karl's approach to homework and grading, then, relied on his being able to quickly provide students with large volumes of complex information primarily through lectures and reading assignments and then to test them on how well they had absorbed that information. On the basis of my observations and interviews, Ms. Thomas used a similar approach.

Competitive Exclusivity in Student Dynamics

The students in the two classes I studied were, for the most part, remarkably cooperative with their teachers. Rarely during any of their classes did either Ms. Thomas or Mr. Karl need to engage in any kind of overt disciplinary tactics that were noticeable to an outside observer. An occasional pause and simple comment such as "Guys, please" from the teacher quickly quieted any minor chatting or note-passing that went on during class. The majority of the students in each class gave the appearance of paying attention to and participating in the work at hand. The few students in each class who did not seem to follow along with the teacher were disproportionately, although not exclusively, students of color. They almost never created any kind of disturbance in class, sitting passively instead. Typically, two or three of the students of color in these classes sat near each other in the back or on an end row.

Although the majority of the students in these two classes were cooperative, many of them were academically competitive. One day, Ms. Thomas asked students to work in pairs of students sitting next to each other to review for a test. One high-achieving White student was paired with a White student who was often absent and received Ds and Fs. Both students resisted moving their desks together, making eye contact or even beginning the task at hand. The high-success student quickly raised his hand and asked, in a voice loud enough for the entire room to hear, "What do you do if the person you are working with hasn't been here most of the semester?" In response to this student's public put-down of his classmate, the teacher talked to the students briefly and privately and left them to work together.

At times, the teachers encouraged a competitive environment. In one instance, Mr. Karl was lecturing and questioning students. One of the more academically successful students asked a clarification question. Mr. Karl dropped his head and shook it from side to side as if in good-natured exasperation. One of the student's friends said loudly, "Oh my God—you're so stupid!" as another friend passed him her notes. The questioning student smiled, examined the notes, and the class continued. In Ms. Thomas's class, it was not unusual for her to spend the bulk of the class period doing rapid-fire lecturing interspersed with short-answer oral questions for students. During one of these sessions she asked the class if anyone could remember what the Monroe Doctrine was. A few hands went up and a boy, when called on, responded in a questioning tone of voice: "It had something to do with land?" Ms. Thomas replied: "Well (chuckling) I can't give you an A for the day for that" and then went on to explain the concept to them. On another day there was a school announcement about an Advanced Placement club that students could join in their sophomore year to prepare them for taking Advanced Placement U.S. history in their junior year. Ms. Thomas announced to the class after that: "There are three or four of you in here who ought to think about that."

Student dynamics operating outside the public classroom interactions both reflected and shaped the competitive climate. Academically successful students operated according to a pragmatic code of "making the grade" (Becker, Geer, & Hughes, 1968), in ways that often benefited exclusive social cliques, by "helping" each other. In some instances this was as simple as a student handing another a filled in worksheet to be copied in the first few minutes of class before the homework was collected. In other instances students talked about studying for tests together; sharing strategies for writing essay assignments; and meeting at one student's house to have her father, a professional in a relevant field, explain to them the concepts behind a topic for a report they were writing. In one instance a student who consistently received As even successfully pressed the teacher to give a friend the "deserved" higher grade at the end of the quarter. In each class I observed that some students consistently provided each other with various forms of academic assistance in informal ways uninitiated by the teacher. Students outside of these tight social cliques were shut out of the collective academic benefits of these collaborative efforts.

AUTHORITY RELATIONS: PROFESSIONAL OR BUREAUCRATIC

The teachers in this study prided themselves on their disciplinary content knowledge. Heated, lively discussions about recent Supreme Court decisions, political races, and competing interpretations of historical events were not uncommon during team meetings and preparatory periods among the teachers. In sharp contrast, the teachers showed little interest in discussing anything that they saw as "teaching methods." There was even a certain degree of disdain for this topic, as revealed most explicitly by a comment made by Mr. Karl. Once, during a professional development day that the administration had organized for all of the House teachers in the school, Mr. Karl expressed impatience with the time spent talking specifically about teaching methods. He found it to be of little use and commented that the ideas "probably came from those education journals that we all quit reading twenty years ago." Thus, the teachers emphasized their disciplinary content knowledge as a central element of their professional knowledge but, as Burkhardt and Schoenfeld (2003) argued is common, they devalued educational research and the pedagogical expertise examined therein.

The school placed a high value on academics. Hillside teachers were widely respected by administrators and community members as disciplinary content experts. The students granted the teachers legitimacy and cooperated with their directives. This suggests that teaches enacted professional authority. However, as in Pace's (2003a) study, classroom interactions suggests bureaucratic authority. The curriculum at Hillside was heavily influenced by the commitment to prepare students for admission to and success in college. Although a strong school culture oriented around college admissions might have created a classroom environment characterized by rigorous and open-ended intellectual inquiry, this emphasis led to a curriculum based on transmission rather than critical thinking. This is typical of high schools that are highly college oriented (Cohen, McLaughlin, & Talbert, 1993). Mr. Karl and Ms. Thomas taught U.S. history in a traditional way based on incorporative conceptions of teaching and learning (Metz, 1978). Teachers maintained tight control over knowledge (McNeil, 1986) creating social studies classes with a narrow focus on comprehension and recall (Thornton, 1994). The work that students actually did in classrooms revolved around memorizing and reciting information in a competitive, grade-oriented, environment with very little higher order thinking (Newmann & Associates, 1996).

This competitive classroom dynamic, which Mr. Karl promoted explicitly and Ms. Thomas promoted at least implicitly, was shaped by highly scripted notions of "the right answer," the students' focus on these right answers and getting good grades, and students' collaboration within exclusive social cliques. Within this classroom context teachers "gave" students formalized knowledge and grades, both deemed necessary for college entrance, in exchange for students' compliance with classroom practices and some level of academic engagement. In these classrooms, authority relations took the form of a relatively jovial exchange between students and teachers. Although there was little overt student misbehavior in class, and the focus remained relatively fixed on disciplinary content matter, the authority relations in the classroom, based on this exchange, were bureaucratic in nature. Grades infused all aspects of classroom interactions. As Pace (2003a) explained:

> They are symbolic wages exchanged for students' compliance to the system and their demonstration of ability and effort. Based on a contract in which fulfillment of obligations is exchanged for grades, authority resembles the bureaucratic relationship between managers and workers, resting on legal–rational legitimacy and the existence of sanctions to motivate continued cooperation. (p. 39)

The majority of students appeared in classes to be academically motivated to receive the preparation and credentialing that good grades in these classes promised.

Contrast: The Honors Class

In contrast to the bureaucratic authority relations in the detracked classrooms, there was a palpably different tone in the one honors integrated ninth-grade class. This class was composed of 20 students from across the ninth grade who took this course in addition to their House classes. The class met only twice a week during a lunch period and was team taught by Mr. Karl and his two teammates. Mr. Karl lectured, as in his detracked classes, most of the time. However, he focused more exclusively on historical, political, and philosophical concepts than he did in his regular lectures. He asked students consistently what they thought about the ideas he was presenting and pushed them to further refine and defend their ideas. They had to write papers about these ideas. His only major assessments took the form of essays, as opposed to his usual multiple-choice unit tests based on review lists of 50 terms.

Mr. Karl's choice of conceptually complex curricular materials demonstrated his respect for the honors students' academic and intellectual abilities. In this class, students were introduced much more frequently and explicitly than they were in the detracked classes to competing conceptualizations of historical and political events and trends. In this way historical knowledge was presented as much less scripted and more open to contestation. Although this critical approach to the study of history is common among professional historians, it is uncommon in schools (Gabella, 1994). One typical essay exam, given to students after they had been studying the French Revolution and the political philosophy of Edmund Burke, presented students with the poem "The Second Coming" by William Butler Yeats. Following a brief paragraph discussing Burke's philosophy, written by Mr. Karl, students were given the following assignment instructions:

> Use specific events from the French Revolution to illustrate why conservatives came to their conclusions about revolution. After you have explained the conservative position, react to it from your own point of view. As you develop your argument be sure to include reference to the concepts of "human nature," and "progress."

This assignment had no single right answer that students needed to produce; instead, the teacher expected students to construct original critiques and understandings of these complex ideas.

Mr. Karl and his teammates thoroughly enjoyed teaching this class and these students. During class they joked with each other in front of and often for the benefit of the students, often jousting over intellectual issues. They gave students breaks from normal routines by allowing students to eat and drink during class (which was during a lunch period) and showed two feature-length films during the semester that I observed them. One day, Mr. Karl and his two teammates offered to provide the students, who had no exam for that class, with juice, sweet rolls, and a quiet place to study in their classroom during exam week. He told the students, "We would enjoy seeing you too. We have enjoyed this class."

In this honors class, selected students were treated to a classroom atmosphere in which there was less overt academic competition and focus on grades and where knowledge was recognized as being contested, socially constructed, and intrinsically valuable. It is ironic that the intensely individualistic, competitive orientation of the detracked classes gave way, in the honors class, to a more intellectual, less grade-oriented atmosphere made possible by the fact that students took the honors class in addition to their regular subject area classes. The pull of individualism, in the form of academic competition, was reduced, because these elite students had already gained access to the gateway to upper track classes in the 10th through 12th grades. The tone in this class, with the easy, informal rapport between the teachers and students, the intellectual discussion of abstract ideas, and the lack of focus on grades suggested professional authority relations based on teachers' disciplinary content knowledge and students' ability and desire to learn, which enabled a more open-ended approach to teaching. This stood in stark contrast to the bureaucratic authority relations of the detracked classes.

CHALLENGES TO AUTHORITY IN DETRACKED CLASSES

Low-Achieving Students

Although the House classrooms that I observed did not exhibit the same "heavenly" (Page, 1991) teaching environment that the honors class did, the classroom interactions that I studied were, as I have discussed, quite cooperative. There were signs, though, that the teachers in the study did face some challenging behavior in their other House classes. During team meetings, which took place typically twice per week, the teachers talked about the distracting classroom behavior of a few students who were, I knew, low achieving. These students' behavior impeded the teachers' ability to keep the classes focused on academics. Although the students created relatively minor distractions, such as continually talking to the students around them, the distractions were still very frustrating to these teachers, who were accustomed to more compliant student behavior.

For the most part, the teachers were able to quell the negative influence of a few students relatively easily. One student, though, Susana, proved to be a more formidable challenge to Mr. Karl and his teammates and their control of the classrooms. Susana's name came up repeatedly during team meetings. Mr. Karl and his teammates expressed great frustration at her ability to "pull other kids off track" with her "manipulative" ways. They were mystified as to why, as they saw it, even otherwise academically oriented students in the class got pulled into her anti-academic antics. Despite their best efforts, the teachers found it difficult to run their classrooms as they wanted to, given Susana's influence. When they had had enough, the team took action. Taking advantage of the structure of the House program, they changed her schedule. They removed Susana from the class that she was in and placed her in one of their other House classes that had a much more achievement-oriented classroom climate. The teachers hoped that by placing her in a new class full of academic "thoroughbreds," as the teachers called the students in that class, Susana and her anti-academic antics would look foolish and her influence would be muted. They were right. The students in her new class appeared to be unimpressed with her behavior and ignored her. Her in-class behavior improved dramatically, as did that of the class from which she had been removed.

In this example, Mr. Karl and his teammates used the structural elements of the House program, which allowed them to easily shift Susana out of one class and into another within their team, and the intensely academic climate of one of their classes to offset her undesired influence. In this way the teachers were also able to maintain control over the tone and focus of their classrooms.

The students in the House classes were, for the most part, academically oriented. Their expectations of credentialing rewards in exchange for compliance formed the foundation of the generally smooth functioning bureaucratic authority relations in these classrooms. Susana's ability to pull an entire class of students off task revealed cracks in that foundation. It showed the vulnerability of the detracked classrooms to anti-academic student influences.

Teachers expressed some concern that they were getting higher percentages of students who were not "academically motivated." Mr. Karl and I talked about this perception and the impact of changing attitudes on classroom dynamics. Speaking about students, he explained:

> *Mr. Karl:*　Historically at Hillside . . . the group that wanted to succeed
> 　　　　　　over the long term, was always quite a bit larger than the other

group, and so that then would create the classroom climate, and the environment, and the expectation. But we're getting enough high-risk kids now that I am not sure that that's going to happen naturally anymore and that's a matter of some concern for the long term.

JB: Can you say more about that?

Mr. Karl: Yeah, Hillside has always been a school where the normal expectation was to go to college. I mean just about everybody went on to some form of higher education when they got out of here. And I think that we're getting more and more kids who don't have that as their normal expectation and I think that's beginning to affect kind of the group sense of themselves and that's going to change the dynamic I think of managing a class, of getting kids to do what you think is important, persuading them that what you think is important, is important to them.

JB: How do you see that in the classroom?

Mr. Karl: More passivity. A much less long-term sense, that is they will not respond to persuasion that's based on the idea that if you don't do this and if you don't do this then these are going to be the consequences, and they're not consequences you want. It's less effective.

These comments reveal Mr. Karl's clear recognition that within that school culture he had come to expect that his ability to run the classroom as he saw fit depended on the great majority of students being motivated to comply with their teachers' directives in exchange for college-bound credentials. However, it also reveals his belief that his ability to use this bureaucratic exchange to maintain compliance of their classrooms was declining.

Although Mr. Karl expressed concern that more students were coming to school with less motivation, I observed that the competitive climate of these classrooms, which generally promoted student compliance with teachers, created a very difficult environment for low-achieving students. These students, who generally had significantly lower reading and writing skills, were disadvantaged in gaining the credentials that their classmates were confident about gaining. They received little structural, academic scaffolding from the teachers and faced serious barriers to academic achievement. The focus on transmitting content gave these students little opportunity to demonstrate the skills, knowledge, and strengths that they did have, and the exclusive cliques in which peers gave each other academic assistance operated independently from the formal classroom organization and appeared to exacerbate their marginalized position in the classroom.

Parents of High-Achieving Students

I observed only a few low-achieving students actually disrupting the smoothly functioning bureaucratic authority relations in these detracked classrooms. However, whereas low-achieving students did not pressure teachers to change their practice, parents of motivated students did. In nearly every team meeting that I observed, the teachers mentioned some contact that they had had with one or more parents. Typically, the parents initiated the contact. Often the teachers discussed amicable conversations with parents about grades and/or classroom behavior. Other times, they shared stories of aggressive, grade-oriented parents pressuring them to change a grade. The perceived pressure from parents to give their children good grades influenced decisions about how to teach and grade students.

For example, the teachers made sure that their grading systems were highly accurate and defensible. Ms. Thomas's language arts teammate said to me, unprompted, during one team meeting, "Our kids have more and more pressure on them for the exactness of their grades. I use a point system to be exact, and I have never had a parent or student successfully challenge me on a grade in all the years I've been teaching." This statement suggests that parents were at times successful at having teachers' decisions about grades overturned. Indeed, during one team meeting one of Mr. Karl's teammates told a story about the assistant principal backing him up in a disagreement with a parent, an event that he called "breathtaking" for its rarity.

As teachers discussed these challenging encounters with parents, their frustration was palpable. They took many of these encounters, and the administration's reluctance to support them, as an affront to their professional legitimacy and pride. Mr. Ashton, Mr. Karl's teammate who taught science, told the most compelling story of this phenomenon. Enormously frustrated, he recounted the story of two parents who had challenged him on their daughter's quiz grade. Although the student was receiving over 100% in his class so far, she had stumbled on one minor quiz in which the teacher had given her no credit for a science test item in which she had made, in essence, a data entry mistake. The mother started off, Mr. Ashton explained, by "introducing herself as a lawyer, as if I was supposed to fall over impressed." As the three of them discussed the teacher's grading, the father challenged his methods. According to Mr. Ashton's telling of the story, the father said that he was a social scientist and that in his line of work one enters data all day long and thus a certain amount of error is expected. "You are docking her pay for a day for a data entry error," he told Mr. Ashton. When Mr. Ashton vigorously defended his grading, the father, still unsatisfied, left saying that he would check in with the math department to see how they handled partial credit. Mr. Ashton immediately checked in with his colleagues in the math department and received assurances from them that they did indeed hold to the same grading policy that he did. He ultimately prevailed in this situation, and the student's grade on the quiz stood. His relief about being supported by the math department policy was evident.

Ms. Thomas's efforts to avoid parental objections influenced group work in her classroom. She was concerned about both the achievement and the behavior of some of the students in her classes, and one of her primary teaching strategies for addressing these issues was group work. However, she did not often assign group grades because, she argued, this was problematic, especially in a detracked classroom:

> When you're in the academic setting there's still a sort of basic set of skills and some kids have them a lot of them and some kids don't. And no matter how much you try and force the other kids—no matter how much the peers try and force their peers to come up to speed there's only so far they can get with it.

She had found, through experience, that an excessive reliance on group work and group grades was likely to cause student and parent objections about grades. As a result of this, as well as her own sense that group grades were not quite fair, she made sure that student grades even on group projects were based on individual rather than group work.

THE IRONY OF COMPETITIVE INDIVIDUALISM AND AUTHORITY

The teachers relied on the competitive grade orientation of the students in their detracked classes to keep the classes running smoothly and to provide validation of their teaching. Individualistic values promoted compliance, and in the Susana incident had even pulled a socially influential and academically resistant student and the class she left back into smooth functioning. However, the excessive focus on grades by students and parents could, at times, prove disruptive to the teachers' prerogative to run their class as they saw fit. Despite the fact that the teachers saw themselves as professionals with strong disciplinary content knowledge, it was not uncommon for elite parents to treat them as mere functionaries in a larger credentialing game. In these grade-oriented interactions teachers often felt that their professional legitimacy was not recognized or respected appropriately by the parents and even their own administrators when they did not come to their defense.

Competitive values, along with the detracked structure of these classrooms, which put high- and low-achieving students together, created a complex environment in which students and their parents, with widely varying commitments to and faith in schooling, challenged teachers' rights to control the classroom in powerful, and often contradictory, ways.

AN EGALITARIAN REFORM AND CONFLICTS OVER AUTHORITY

The detracked House program had originated in large part out of concerns about what the district termed "minority student achievement." The program provided each House teacher with an extra preparatory period each day to meet with his or her teammates to discuss teaching, curriculum, and the students on their team. This extra preparatory period made the program a very expensive reform, funded by district monies set aside specifically to address minority student achievement. Both the district and the school administrators were publicly committed to increasing the academic achievement of students of color. However, although the teachers in my study did acknowledge that minority student achievement was a problem, they expressed that there was little they could do to increase the academic achievement of the least successful students, including low-achieving students of color. During team meetings, teachers on both teams suggested that they saw low student achievement as stemming primarily from individual factors such as the student's motivation; maturity; family support; intelligence; and, to a lesser extent, their susceptibility to negative peer influences. Although in interviews they discussed the low academic skills of many of the least successful students, during team meetings that I observed they did not discuss possible impacts of the teaching, curriculum, or classroom climate on the academic achievement of these students. The school principal explained how teachers in the building felt about changing their teaching: "Overall our kids are still doing very well. Most of them are doing very well and our group is unwilling to change for the small group that needs more, that's not making it. They're still feeling like it's not broken. Why do we need to fix it?"

According to Little (2003), recent research on the factors that contribute to improved teaching practices indicates the importance of professional collaboration within schools. When teachers collectively question old practices, develop new understandings of teaching and learning, and continually support each other's growth, changes that benefit students can occur. Critical professional dialogue was not evident in my observations and interviews at Hillside. Given the low value that the teachers placed on knowledge from the field of education, this lack of discussion was not surprising.

Although Ms. Thomas and Mr. Karl expressed little interest in examining their pedagogy or curricula as part of the House detracking reform, they were supportive of the reform in general, for two reasons. First, it gave them more control over students within their classes, as exemplified by the Susana incident. Second, it made it easier for them to refer students to tutoring and other support services in the building, which Ms. Thomas's team particularly appreciated. The teachers saw the House program as increasing their ability to be effective with struggling students without changing their teaching. At the same time, they viewed student success and failure as primarily a function of students' individual attributes. Their resistance to engaging in serious discussions about changing their pedagogy or curriculum reflected this view.

The school administration supported the House program as well, though for different reasons. Their goal was to increase minority student achievement. They approached this goal with a more systematic organizational analysis and egalitarian emphasis than the teachers in my study did. Whenever the issue of tracking came up in meetings, they staunchly supported the egalitarian rationale behind the elimination of lower track classes that had been mandated by the district a few years prior. They had vigorously defended the effort to fully detrack the House program to parents and staff and had invested enormous administrative time and resources to hand-schedule every single ninth-grade class to make sure that they were de facto detracked, and they voiced a subtle but consistent refrain that the pedagogy and curricula in the House classes were not working for low-achieving students and needed to change to increase minority student achievement. For example, the administration made it clear that they wanted teachers to create curricula for their House classes that were more interdisciplinary and multicultural because they believed that such changes would benefit low-achieving students and students of color.

The teachers, for their part, resisted and resented the administration's stance that their teaching and curricula were not meeting the needs of low-achieving students and students of color. Mr. Ortiz, Mr. Karl's teammate who taught language arts, spoke to me bitterly about the professional development of recent years:

> *Mr. Ortiz:* My impression—and this is just an impression which is a composite of several years of coming in on in-service day and being in-serviced by whomever, is given that we were overall failures—socially, academically, everything—that you come in and what do you learn at in-service is that you are an overall failure, that you're probably a racist, that the whole thing is all screwed.
>
> *JB:* That's pretty demoralizing.
>
> *Mr. Ortiz:* Well, it's in-service. We are required to attend it. They used to be fun but they seem to have changed the nature over the years.

Other teachers on both teams also expressed frustration with the nature and quality of the professional development that they had been receiving in recent years. Ms. Thomas, like Mr. Ortiz, found much of the professional development related to minority student achievement unhelpful. Speaking about the issue of minority student achievement, she said:

> I think kind of the feeling of throwing up our hands at a situation that we would like to see fixed but don't really know how to and our feeling a lot of pressure to but don't really have the tools to. We've had a number of people come and talk about how perhaps African American learning style is differ-ent, but then perhaps it isn't, you know and it's just kind of like "OK is it dif-ferent or is it not and if it is different how do we deal with it? Is there an across the board standard that we can and should enforce in terms of behavior and academic expectations?" So, I would say most of the discussions [are] fairly frustrating, at this school particularly.

As teachers talked about the pressure that they felt from both school and district administrators to raise minority student achievement, it became evident that they felt they were being asked to alter teaching practices and curricula in ways that ran counter to their professional judgment and/or were beyond their professional knowledge. These demands seemed to di-rectly challenge their legitimacy and classroom authority. For example, Mr. Karl and Ms. Thomas repeatedly referred to the widespread faculty concern that they were being asked to "water down the curriculum."

Teachers were ultimately aware that there was an increasing percentage of students, among whom students of color were overrepresented, who were failing ninth grade. They supported the House program, including detrack-ing as a means of addressing this issue, even as they staunchly defended both the quality of their teaching and curricula and their professional authority over these matters. However, they were caught in a tight political and professional bind. On the one hand, they worked within a school culture that was driven by the strong pull of individualism and credential-ing. Within this context, parents, students, and their colleagues expected them to teach college-bound curricula in a competitive, grade-oriented, academic environment. The perception of academically aggressive parents' power to intervene threatened the teachers' right to control key classroom practices, pressured them to maintain bureaucratic classroom authority relations based on grades, and displayed a lack of respect for their profes-sional expertise.

At the same time, the growing percentage of students who were not suc-ceeding in their classrooms and administrative concern about this issue put pressure on teachers to change. Teachers worried that higher percentages of students who were "not academically motivated" and had low academic skills would struggle in and disrupt their classes. The school administration's strong egalitarian stance, made manifest most clearly in their advocacy of the House detracking and related professional development efforts, sent the message that their teaching and curricula needed to adapt to meet the needs of these students. However, from the teachers' perspective, the changes that the administration expected them to make either contradicted their professional judgment, were not spelled out in enough detail to be helpful to them, or were simply not politically feasible given the competitive academic pressures put on them by parents.

TEACHERS' COLLECTIVE RESISTANCE

These tensions were a source of enormous frustration to the teachers. Two strong collective groups, the union and the academic departments, buffered them from these pressures to a certain extent. The contestation over authority between the teachers and the school administration were most evident in these contexts.

The conflict between the House teachers and the principal reached a climax when the principal requested that the following fall each team of House teachers call the parents of each of their students at the beginning of the school year in order to start the year off with a positive sense of connection between parents and the school. Although some of the House teachers, including Ms. Thomas and her team, willingly complied, many of the House teachers refused to do it. In response, the principal mandated that the teachers make the calls home. Some teachers, including Mr. Karl and his team, worked through the union to take the mandate to a formal grievance hearing, which they lost. Mr. Karl and his teammates, after the hearing, spoke bitterly about the conflict. Mr. Ashton, the science teacher, complained that calling home "is not necessarily professional work. It's PR work." Later, he went on to say that the principal's ability to mandate that they do this was based on an "old factory model. I'm the boss, you're the worker." To these teachers, at least, both the nature of the work of making these calls and the fact that they were forced to do it demonstrated a lack of respect for their professional legitimacy.

In addition to the union, Hillside teachers operated from within a very strong departmental organizational structure that reinforced the teachers' broad collective authority over pedagogy and curriculum. They based the legitimacy of their decisions on their disciplinary content knowledge. These strong departments established powerful norms for curriculum and teaching that had, according to House teachers and school administrators, changed little since the implementation of the House program, even though teachers readily acknowledged that these were not effective with low-achieving students, among whom students of color were overrepresented. Both Mr.

Karl and Ms. Thomas spoke approvingly of the departmental norms for teaching and curriculum and kept their own teaching and curriculum in line with these departmental expectations. The administrators, on the other hand, expressed great frustration with their unwillingness to reexamine their practice to help struggling students. Tom Smith, an assistant principal, spoke about the teachers' control over the curriculum and the administrations' attempt to encourage interdisciplinary curricula:

> It's wonderful on the one hand because they really are experts with it and really feel ownership and they believe in it and that conveys to the students and makes them better teachers. But you try to pry it away from them and then there it is, twenty years later, it's still their curriculum that they made that one year, you know. That's not to say that they don't continue to update and change, but when you say well let's just stop for a week, let's pull this week out and let's do something that's science and English and social studies. "Well, I won't get my curriculum done!" It's not that we're trying to water it down, even though that's the first thing that comes out when you say lets try interdisciplinary. "You're going to water it down! I won't get through my stuff!" And you know we believe they will get to their stuff better if they do that. That's still a long way from happening as much as we'd like to see it happen.

The departmental discussions around teaching and curriculum and the House program, then, remained firmly defensive in nature (McNeil, 1986). Such departmental resistance to interdisciplinary curricula may be common. Grossman and Stodolsky (1994) argued that "The subject matter specialism inherent in departmental organization, and possibly even more characteristic of strong departments, presents an enormous challenge to efforts to create and sustain interdisciplinary courses" (p. 188).

CONCLUSION

Evidence that tracking plays a negative role in the reproduction of inequitable student academic outcomes has been a widely accepted element of school reform agendas for the last two decades. Although a reform effort, based on these findings, to structurally detrack high schools has gained momentum across the United States, surprisingly little research has focused on what goes on inside high school classrooms once they have detracked. None of that research has focused on authority relations in these classrooms.

This study suggests two key findings relative to authority relations in detracked classrooms. First, to understand authority relations better and to enhance the quality of teaching and learning in detracked classrooms, it is important to examine the interrelated nature of authority relations at multiple levels within schools. At Hillside, the teachers were continually negotiating authority relationships not only with their students but also with parents and administrators. Each of these ongoing negotiations had an impact on the nature of teaching and learning that went on in classrooms. Furthermore, how these authority relations played out was tightly linked to how the players involved understood the teachers' professional legitimacy and responsibility. Any conflict between how the teachers and one of the other parties understood professional legitimacy and responsibility challenged the teachers' rights to determine classroom pedagogy and curricula.

The second key finding relative to authority relations in detracked classrooms is that, given that there are competing conceptions of what constitutes teachers' professional legitimacy, and that these competing conceptions have great bearing on the nature of authority relations in classrooms, shifting the basis for professional legitimacy within a school without adequate attention to larger cultural and structural school issues can lead to the retrenchment rather than the transformation of authority relations in classrooms and schools. This has important implications, because shifting the bases for legitimacy is often an explicit goal of educational reform movements. For example, a goal of educational reform in recent years has been to hold teachers increasingly accountable for the academic success of even traditionally low-achieving students, as was evident at Hillside. However, the increased pressure that school administrators at Hillside put on teachers to teach more effectively to low-achieving students in the very same classrooms where teachers were still accountable for preparing academically competitive students for college broadened the expectations placed on teachers to such an extent that the teachers resisted and resented the reform effort as articulated by the administration. Teachers found that, in practice, the expectation that they raise the academic achievement of low-achieving students was contradictory to the college-bound, individualistic orientation that shaped the nature of classroom dynamics. This felt conflict between a notion of teachers' professional legitimacy that stemmed from preparing academically competitive students for college on the one hand and one that stemmed from ensuring the academic success of all students, on the other hand, manifested itself as a conflict between teachers and administrators over who had the authority to control the teaching and curricula of classes. Furthermore, this felt conflict, and the threat that it posed to the teachers' sense of control over their own teaching, contributed to their reluctance to reexamine, let alone transform, their pedagogy or curricula, even as they acknowledged that their teaching and curricula were not effective with low-achieving students, among whom students of color were overrepresented.

Ultimately, the intention of the detracking reform was to improve the academic achievement of students of color. However, the values of individualism, credentialing, and the bureaucratic authority relations that flow from them formed the foundation of classroom culture and created difficult contexts for students with low academic skills and weak academic records. Although implementing the structural reform of detracking may indeed bring these students into classes that exhibit higher levels of on-task academic behavior, which is to their advantage, structural change alone is not likely to enable the kind of academic engagement and success for these students that educators and policymakers seek. To create classrooms where struggling students and even successfully college-bound students engage in more sophisticated forms of higher order thinking than is common in high schools today requires a more fundamental cultural shift in schools. Schools and communities must look beyond individualism and credentialing as central goals if classrooms are to become more thoughtful and egalitarian places.

REFERENCES

Becker, H., Geer, B., & Hughes, E. (1968). *Making the grade.* New York: Wiley.

Burkhardt, H., & Schoenfeld, A. H. (2003). Improving educational research: Toward a more useful, more influential, and better-funded enterprise. *Educational Researcher, 32*(9), 3–14.

Cohen, D. K., McLaughlin, M. W., & Talbert, J. E. (Eds.). (1993). *Teaching for understanding: Challenges for policy and practice.* San Francisco: Jossey-Bass.

Gabella, M. S. (1994). Beyond the looking glass: Bringing students into the conversation of historical inquiry. *Theory and Research in Social Education, XXII,* 340–363.

Grossman, P. L., & Stodolsky, S. S. (1994). Considerations of content and the circumstances of secondary school teaching. In L. Darling-Hammond (Ed.), *Review of research in education* (Vol. 20, pp. 179–221). Washington, DC: American Educational Research Association.

Little, J. W. (2003). Inside teacher community: Representations of classroom practice. *Teachers College Record, 105,* 913–945.

Lucas, S. R. (1999). *Tracking inequality: Stratification and mobility in American high schools.* New York: Teachers College Press.

McNeil, L. (1986). *Contradictions of control—School structure and school knowledge.* New York: Routledge.

Metz, M. H. (1978). *Classrooms and corridors: The crisis of authority in desegregated secondary schools.* Berkeley: University of California Press.

Newmann, F. M., & Associates (Eds.). (1996). *Authentic achievement: Restructuring schools for intellectual quality.* San Francisco: Jossey-Bass.

Oakes, J. (1985). *Keeping track: How schools structure inequality.* New Haven, CT: Yale University Press.

Oakes, J., Gamoran, A., & Page, R. N. (1992). Curriculum differentiation: Opportunities, outcomes, and meanings. In P. W. Jackson (Ed.), *Handbook on research on curriculum* (pp. 570–608). New York: Macmillan.

Oakes, J., Wells, A. S., & Jones, M. (1997). Detracking: The social construction of ability, cultural politics, and resistance to reform. *Teachers College Record, 98,* 482–510.

Pace, J. L. (2003a). Managing the dilemmas of professional and bureaucratic authority in a high school English class. *Sociology of Education, 76,* 37–52.

Pace, J. L. (2003b). Using ambiguity and entertainment to win compliance in a lower-level U.S. history class. *Journal of Curriculum Studies, 35,* 83–11.

Page, R. N. (1991). *Lower track classrooms: A curricular and cultural perspective.* New York: Teachers College Press.

Page, R. N. (2000). The tracking show. In B. M. Franklin (Ed.), *Curriculum and consequence: Herbert M. Kliebard and the promise of schooling* (pp. 103–127). New York: Teachers College Press.

Spradley, J. P. (1979). *The ethnographic interview.* Fort Worth, TX: Harcourt Brace Jovanovich.

Thornton, S. J. (1994). The social studies near century's end: Reconsidering patterns of curriculum and instruction. *Review of Research in Education, 20,* 223–254.

Wells, A. S., & Serna, I. (1996). The politics of culture: Understanding local political resistance to detracking in racially mixed schools. *Harvard Educational Review, 66,* 93–118.

Chapter 6

Moral Order in High School Authority: Dis/Enabling Care and (Un)Scrupulous Achievement

Annette Hemmings
University of Cincinnati

According to Metz (1978), *authority* in schools is a relationship between teachers and students that "exists for the service of a moral order to which both owe allegiance" (p. 26). Presumably, this order comprises shared understandings and practices that hold school actors together and essentially guides the proper or right way to realize institutional goals (Metz, 1978; Selznick, 1992). Although there may be common public expectations about what ought to constitute the moral order of high schools, the particular ones that prevail in particular sites vary (Hemmings & Metz, 1990; McNeil, 1983, 1986; Metz, 1993; Pace, 2003a, 2003b; Page, 1991). Rather than being clearly articulated and staunchly enforced in a manner that fosters the allegiance of school actors, moral orders are highly negotiable and subject to varying degrees and kinds of commitment. The forms they take have implications not only for individual teachers and students but also for society at large. Ideally, a school's moral order empowers school actors and ensures equitable educational opportunities. In actuality, however, there may be countervailing aspects that are educationally debilitating and implicated in the perpetuation of social inequalities. In the cases of the high schools in this study, moral orders were rife with paradoxes that had positive and negative consequences for individuals and society.

In examining moral orders, it is important to note how they are formed and ultimately enacted during the course of everyday school relations, especially relations of authority. As Pace (2003b) observed, authority relations are "complex and dynamic, created in moment-to-moment negotiations over academic and social matters, and shaped by many factors both internal and external" (p. 84). Among these factors are the ethical commitments that teachers themselves make to the students and communities they serve. Other, more powerful factors include an array of external and contextual pressures that often test the capacity of teachers to manage them.

In this chapter, I present ethnographic accounts of the moral orders that emerged in two urban and suburban public high schools. Central City High,[1] the urban school, enrolled mostly Black youths residing in an impoverished, socially insular inner-city neighborhood. The suburban school, Ridgewood High, was located in a predominantly White, upper-middle-class community. I spent over 2 months at each site during the 1996–1997 school year conducting fieldwork with the assistance of graduating seniors who volunteered to participate in an ethnographic study originally designed as an exploration of how diverse students were coming of age in U.S. public high schools (Hemmings, 2004).[2] I recruited three seniors at Central City High and four at Ridgewood High. I went to school with each of them for at least 2 weeks (3 days a week) to observe them and document their schools' day-to-day social and cultural patterns. I accompanied them to class, traveled with them through corridors, ate lunch with them, and hung out with them and their friends before and after school. I also conducted one-on-one, semistructured interviews with them and arranged group interviews with their friends and several of their classmates. Although the primary focus was on seniors' perspectives and experiences, several teachers allowed me to observe their classes on a periodic basis. Teachers also answered my questions about their schools, students, and approaches. Finally, I gathered brochures, handbooks, and other relevant documents.

When I analyzed these data for this chapter, I found that although there was significant variation between sites, dimensions of both schools' moral orders were replete with paradoxical understandings and practices. The paradoxes were due in part to differences in the ethical commitments of teachers, but they also were a product of the student and community pressures and their effects on authority relations. As will be explained in some detail, these commitments and pressures and the paradoxical orders they spawned had mixed implications for the fulfillment of institutional goals.

---

[1] The names of geographic locations, schools, and research participants have been changed to ensure anonymity and protect confidentiality.

[2] The original intent of this research was to explore how graduating seniors representing diverse racial, ethnic, social class, and gender social locations were coming of age in three urban and suburban U.S. public high schools. Coming-of-age processes were conceptualized as a two-pronged process of identity formation and community integration in economic, kinship, religious, and political domains of American life.

DEFINING MORAL ORDER

Building on the work of Metz (1978), Selznick (1992), and others, I have developed a broad definition of the moral order of schools which I then break down into three analytical dimensions: (a) worthwhile curriculum, (b) proper pedagogy, and (c) good character. I discuss each dimension in a manner that can be used to frame and analyze data and that also recognizes the dynamics of authority relations.

Broadly defined, *school moral order* is the socially constructed set of understandings (i.e., values, norms, mores, and rules) and practices that are meant to fulfill institutional goals. Sometimes these orders are intentionally built, much like the "moral contracts" that Sizer and Sizer (1999) promoted in their agenda for school reform. More often than not, they are constructed in unplanned ways during the course of day-to-day social interactions in classrooms and corridors. Intentional or not, there usually are moral overtones sensed by school actors as they absorb, create, and/or contest understandings and practices that are supposed to make sure they really are good teachers, students, administrators, and staff. These overtones may cause teachers to believe they have done something wrong if they fail to instruct a certain way, or cause students to feel guilty if they cheat on assignments or otherwise violate conventional norms of achievement, or they may be toned down by school actors in their own individual pursuit of the educational aims that they regard as right for them.

School actors infuse their own personal ethical commitments into their responses (and allegiance) to the particular understandings and practices that constitute the school moral order. They also react to pressures from peers, the surrounding community, and other external sources. These pressures are experienced most directly in authority relations, especially those enacted in classrooms.

In the ensuing discussion of dimensions of the moral order, I emphasize moral overtones through the use of adjectives such as *worthwhile, proper,* and *good* and auxiliary verbs such as *should* and *ought.* In the curriculum dimension, there is general agreement about what ought to constitute worthwhile content. People across the United States expect public schools to offer similar academic curricula to all students regardless of their background. It is widely believed that teachers, by following common curricular scripts, are in the best position to provide students with the "symbols of participation in cultured society and in access to opportunity" that guarantee unity and equity in American education (Metz, 1990, p. 83). Although teachers have leeway in deciding what knowledge and which skills are most worthwhile for the particular students they are assigned to teach, most feel they have a moral obligation to deliver curricula that are universally valued across society. They thus attempt, in their relations with students and others, to establish themselves as authorities entrusted with the transmission of worthwhile curricula.

Teachers also are expected to abide by norms and rules that structure the standards, practices, and processes of what can be characterized as proper pedagogy. One component of pedagogy includes instructional understandings and practices that are deemed proper if they fulfill formal educational goals by upholding high achievement standards, effectively conveying worthwhile curricula, assessing students' performance fairly, and ensuring successful learning processes. There are long-standing debates about whether direct instruction, progressive student-centered education, critical pedagogy, or other kinds of pedagogies are better and/or are more socially just than others, but defenders of all of these approaches make implicit (sometimes explicit) claims that they are the most morally defensible way to educate American school children.

Pedagogy also has a disciplinary component aimed at meeting the "instrumental goal" of maintaining order "among a student body which is only half socialized, comes and remains by legal compulsion, and frequently includes persons with radically different educational and social expectations" (Metz, 1978, p. 17). The rules, norms, and other understandings intended to foster an orderly, disciplined classroom environment are supposed to be such that teachers in their authority relations with students actually are able to exercise control. As Benne (1986) explained, these understandings should define for students proper "working relations" in adult institutions:

> The authority of these norms and rules defines for students the working relations of young people to adult-organized and adult-led institutions established for youth—in short, authority relations between the generations—more powerfully than do choices of subject matter to be studied and learned. (p. 16)

Without such relations, there is disorder that makes it difficult if not impossible to fulfill instrumental and formal educational goals.

The last dimension embodies accepted cultural values regarding what it means to have and express *good character*. Ideally, these values foster the cultivation of character marked by "goodness and excellence, stability and discipline" and other "virtuous" traits (Rosario, 2000, p. 39). Such traits not only make individual students and teachers better people, but they also are necessary for maintaining school relations that are civil, mutually respectful, and responsible. Good character also may be distinguished by expressions of care that Noddings (1984, 1999) has long recognized as a "primitive good" at the heart of all relations that are morally interdependent and genuinely responsive.

Although there are common public expectations attached to all of these dimensions, the moral orders that actually take hold in schools are anything but common both in terms of the forms they take and the outcomes they produce. Such was the case at Central City High and Ridgewood High.

DIS/ENABLING CARE AT CENTRAL CITY HIGH

By all accounts, Central City High was an urban high school plagued with problems. The vast majority of students, 81.23%, were Black teenagers, many of whom were living in poverty, growing up in single-parent families, dealing with the constant threat of crime and violence, and otherwise struggling to survive in deteriorated neighborhoods. Dropout rates at the school were high (officially, 30%; unofficially, over 60%), and students' scores on standardized achievement tests were among the lowest in the district. The situation was dire, but certainly not hopeless, especially from the point of view of teachers, who felt they had a moral imperative to help the youth who attended their school. Most teachers made a concerted attempt to institute what can be characterized as a communitarian moral order driven by an overarching commitment to an ethic of care. A *communitarian moral order* is one that fosters a sense of community and the type of individual character that encourages school actors to "respect one another, treat each other as equals, but never stray too far from the idea that [they are] first and foremost a class, a community of learning" (Rosario, 2000, p. 30). The hope at Central City High was that if a communitarian moral order of care were to prevail, then teachers would be in a better position to enable students to surmount the enormous economic and social obstacles that confronted them.

Ideals associated with the communitarian moral order of care permeated Central City High's stated philosophy as well as the language and approaches of teachers and support staff. According to a pamphlet distributed to students and parents, the school promoted "community and care" through teams of teachers who "work with the same group of students in all courses to assure a united approach to teaching." The pamphlet also spelled out ideal character traits for members of the school community in terms of how individuals should work with, and show respect for, one another:

> When you work with others, you understand what the group needs to do, your part of the job, and how others can help you and how you can help them. Respect others and they will be respected. Knowing and accepting people different from ourselves makes life more interesting.

To enact this order, teachers organized themselves into teams that met on a regular basis to plan their classroom approaches and to consider strategies for assisting students with academic and personal problems. I observed some of their meetings during which they discussed students who were cutting or failing classes, experiencing difficulties at home, being detained in juvenile detention, dealing with pregnancies and child care responsibilities, and experiencing other difficulties. They would divvy up students who, in a team member's words, needed "a huge dose of TLC"—tender loving care—along with whatever tangible help teachers were able to provide. Doses of TLC meant calling parents; tracking down absent students; counseling kids who were troubled or in trouble; and, on occasion, providing transportation, clothes, and other things.

Administrative support staff in the main office backed up teachers' commitments with their own expressions of care. Their job was largely bureaucratic as they processed students who were absent, tardy, or transferring in and out of the school. They would listen to students' excuses, fill out paperwork, and mete out official consequences for minor violations. After their official business was done, they often would shift into unofficial roles as advisors or counselors. On one occasion, I heard one of them tell a group of students about a girl who had "blown her chances for a good life" because she refused to go to a good high school. The girl, she explained, had passed the test to get into the school but purposefully failed her freshman year so she could be with her friends in another school. One of the students said, "I don't see nothin' wrong with pickin' a school full of friends." The administrative staffer said, "Like this school, huh?" "Yeah," the student responded, "Like this school." Then the staffer turned to me and said with a smile, "We got to love these kids 'cause everybody else would like to slug 'em. We hug 'em, not slug 'em."

Central City High also had a cadre of what were known as "youth advocates" hired as part of a school-to-work program. Youth advocates were supposed to help students with job internships and other program-related activities but, like teachers and administrative support staff, they expanded their activities to help students with a broader range of problems. Youth advocates felt they were in an especially unique position to offer care, as is evident in a remark one of them made during an interview:

> When you're a teacher and have hundreds of kids you have to deal with sometimes you don't have the time nor the strength to teach them and then get into their personal lives whereas we have the flexibility to go into the homes. We actually see where kids are coming from 'cause, see, if you see a child in your classroom that's not functioning you might think "that child is just lazy." That child is this or that whereas I may have gone into that home and know that the kid has no food to eat, has to go out and work or hustle on the street to even take care of Mom 'cause Mom can't take care of the family. So to me this program is a last-ditch effort to help these kids, you know, take care of them.

The communitarian values and ethic of care that teachers and staff espoused and enacted were enabling in a number of ways. They were part of the foundation of a moral order that caused socially marginalized Black students to feel they were genuinely welcome and cared for in the school. Nay, a research participant, explained how teachers and support staff often went out of their way to help kids:

> Kids can go to them anytime and talk about their problems. They can talk about any problem they want. If a kid does somethin' real bad, teachers will set them straight. It's like they see it as part of their job to be nice to us and help us with everything that's going on.

However, there were paradoxical understandings within the moral order that were disenabling, especially with regard to the promotion of academic achievement and good character. Although teachers demonstrated their commitment to communitarian care for students as disadvantaged youth, they acted in the classroom as if they did not care about students as capable learners. With some notable exceptions, teachers as they related to students in their classes greatly compromised their positions as authorities who are morally obligated to offer worthwhile curricula, use proper pedagogy, and cultivate good character. In other words, they did not go far enough to establish themselves as professional authorities who foster the intellectual and moral development of their students (Hurn, 1985; Pace, 2000a).

With regard to worthwhile curriculum, most teachers at Central City High drastically reduced the variety of knowledge sources available to students by drawing content almost exclusively from textbooks. They would trivialize this content by simplifying and eliminating substantial portions of it and transmit it through less-than-proper means. Teachers would deliver 10-minute lectures and then have students spend the rest of the period answering textbook questions, completing fill-in the-blank worksheets, or doing other kinds of rote seatwork. Students would do some or none of the assigned work, and teachers would evaluate whatever was turned in with point systems based on minimal standards of performance. I did not observe any attempts to facilitate intellectually stimulating discussions, projects, or experiments or promote higher quality work. The use of computers and other instructional technologies was rare or nonexistent. Such understandings and practices were exceptions to the ones that prevailed.

Teachers also were prone to adopt what McNeil (1983, 1986) has referred to as "defensive" teaching techniques to ensure some minimum order in the classroom. The techniques are often used by teachers in response to students who appear resistant to schooling. Resistance may be passive (putting heads down on desks or refusing to do assignments) or active (making fun of lessons or talking back to teachers), but they always pose a challenge to teachers in ways that affect everyday classroom authority relations. In the case of Black high school students, it may be incited by historical inequalities. Black students may display what Ogbu (2003) described as "low effort syndrome" and other expressions of opposition because of decades of social and economic discrimination in their relations with Whites and "White" schooling. "How minorities interpret their history," he explained, "together with the impact of societal treatment or mistreatment shapes the pattern of the collective solutions they forge for their collective problems in society at large and in education" (Ogbu, 2003, p. 51). Many Black students at Central City High did limit their efforts in the classroom, but rather than address the root causes of students' resistance, or take a stronger approach to raising achievement, most teachers settled into a defensive posture by letting students do whatever they pleased so long as their activities did not get too out of hand.

In classroom after classroom, I observed students spending most of their time socializing with their friends rather than engaging in meaningful learning activities. Such was the case with a Spanish teacher who would begin each class by assigning questions out of the textbook and then sit at her desk while students talked and laughed. She explained how her "loose standards" were necessary to make class "as pleasant as possible" so that students would not drop out of school.

> I used to feel guilty about the loose standards but then I came to the realization that these kids, you know, the kids in this neighborhood won't come unless you make things as pleasant as possible. Parents don't push them so if kids come it's because they want to.

However, not every student was resistant to schooling, nor were they coming to school because of classroom pleasantries. Many of them showed up to be educated, and they wanted teachers to assume their rightful place as professional authorities. They were critical of teachers who related to them as if they really were hopelessly at-risk Black teenagers who could or would not achieve in high school. Amber was a youth advocate who summarized their sentiments. "Teachers," she said, "have their hearts in the right place but they won't own up to what they're doing to kids."

> They try to be cool with kids so that classes are comfortable. They get buddy, buddy and lower standards so that classes are a joke. Even Advanced Placement classes are a joke. They have pretty much written kids off even though they'll tell you they haven't. Kids know what's going on and it really bothers them. They don't like being treated like that.

Amber told me how she organized a group of students into a petition drive to force an especially lax teacher to do a more professional job. Rather than change his approach, though, he "got mad and blew the whole thing off." To add insult to injury, the petition drive drew no response from administrators, and other teachers refused to get involved.

What this and other educational slights did do was fuel a mounting crisis of respect for teachers and damaged authority relations even further. It was a crisis that very much counteracted the ideals of communitarian care at Central City High. Because teachers in their defensive authority relations with students did not appear to be respecting students as capable learners, students responded by displaying more blatant disrespect for teachers as incompetent educators (Hemmings, 2003). The fact that students did not respect teachers who appeared not to respect them was evident in a science class that I observed. Like the Spanish teacher, the science teacher assigned a lot of seatwork. Students would ask classmates for answers to questions in voices loud enough for the teacher to hear. On one occasion, I heard one of them boasting about how she never read anything assigned in English class and had "a big pile of Cliff notes" in her locker. Students laughed as their teacher sat in seemingly oblivious silence at his desk. The unspoken understanding that shaped relations in this and other classrooms was, simply put, that teachers do not have to respect, or care about, Black students as young people who deserve a good education. The understanding was a paradox in a school where teachers insisted that they did indeed care about students.

Paradoxes within the school's moral order also had consequences for the cultivation of good character. I found that many of the students at Central City High were torn between opposing discursive pressures of respectability and reputation encountered in the streets (Gordon, 1997; Hemmings, 2002, 2003). According to Anderson (1998), to be *respectable* is to be well mannered, hard working, law abiding, and committed to the welfare and upliftment of family and community members. *Reputation,* in contrast, is acquired by showing up rivals, controlling weak people, and making sexual and other conquests. Pressures on young people to develop a reputation arise in places where the influence of teachers and other adult authorities ends and where personal responsibility for one's safety begins. Central City High was such a place, despite teachers' acts of caring for students. It was a school where adult controls were lax (defensive) and students often had to fend for themselves. Many felt that in order to survive in the streets and at school they had to cultivate a reputation rather than the kind of character associated with respectability. One of the students who participated in the research told me how most "kids don't want to hurt nobody but sometimes they got to. If they do, you know, if they do hurt people it's because there's pressure on them, 'cause they wouldn't hurt nobody on their own. They aren't like that. Most people aren't like that." When kids are treated with disrespect, she went on to explain, "they can't just go in the house and sit down." They have to come out and fight for respect, even if it means foregoing their own ethical principles.

So although students at Central City High were enabled by caring teachers and school staff, they were simultaneously disenabled by a lack of professional authority where it seemed nobody cared about whether or how students learned and behaved. Authority relations at Central City High were a product of competing ethical commitments and pressures that ultimately gave rise to paradoxical moral order of (dis)enabling care that had both beneficial and detrimental consequences for students.

(UN)SCRUPULOUS ACHIEVEMENT
AT RIDGEWOOD HIGH

Ridgewood High was located in an upper-middle-class, predominantly White suburban community. The school had an excellent reputation, especially with regard to how students were prepared for college. In the school year prior to my fieldwork, 88.9 of students were White European American; 4.5% were Black; and the rest were Asian, Hispanic, and multiracial. Ninety-eight percent of students who were enrolled as seniors in October graduated in May. Eighty-one percent of graduates entered 4-year colleges and universities, 3% (12 out of 402) were National Merit finalists, and 23% were awarded scholarships.

Teachers, as a matter of professional ethics, felt obliged to maintain these percentages along with the overriding emphasis on college preparation. They did not, as one of them told me, regard themselves as people who "teach morality, feed kids, are counselors, doctors, parents, and everything else." First and foremost, they were educators who felt morally bound to transmit college-preparatory curricula; ensure successful learning; and otherwise groom students for higher education and high-status, middle-class occupations. Their commitments and the pressures exerted on them spawned understandings and practices in the school's moral order that encouraged scrupulousness in the promotion of academic achievement.

Ridgewood High teachers were, in fact, quite scrupulous in how they instructed the "preppies"—students' own self designation—in their classes. Most did their best to convey worthwhile college-preparatory curricula through recognizably good pedagogy. I observed a chemistry teacher who taught his classes in a manner that resembled the laboratory work of real scientists. Students would set up sophisticated experiments, record data, and calculate results by solving complicated equations. In a U.S. government class, I watched as the teacher facilitated students' participation in an actual election. She began class by asking students if they would work as poll volunteers. "If you don't want to volunteer at the polls," she said, "then I strongly encourage those of you who are eighteen to vote." She proceeded to hand out newspapers with detailed information about candidates and issues published by the local chapter of the League of Women Voters. Students spent the rest of the period in small groups reading and engaging in lively debates about the issues based on the information they received. Many students told me how much they learned in this and other classes and described their teachers as "great," "qualified," and "smart 'cause they know a lot of stuff." They generally regarded teachers as quite professional in their relations with them, especially in how they used authority to foster intellectual development.

As exemplary as the school was in terms of curriculum and instruction, there were competing understandings that were rooted in what Page (2000) described as a *paradoxical cultural imperative* in schooling. On the one hand, teachers are to endorse individualism and competition whereby individual students are to be treated differently and, on the other hand, egalitarianism in service to the common good where students are to be treated the same. The endorsement in the case of Ridgewood High was skewed toward the former pole as teachers committed themselves to promoting the individual interests of students, often at the expense of considerations for how to promote egalitarian ideals for the benefit of the community. There was, in fact, enormous pressure on teachers from students and the local community to cater to self-interested ambition, and many did so in ways that were quite unscrupulous.

There was a definite sense among students that the emphasis on individualism had a very negative effect on the sense of community at their school. "Kids," one boy explained in the lunchroom, "have to have a distinguishing mark." He then pointed his finger at students around the room. "That guy is the quarterback of the football team. That guy is a genius. That girl is a cheerleader. If you don't have a distinguishing mark like that, you're a nobody." Then the boy described the social consequences of what happens when everyone wants to be distinguished from everyone else: "Kids at this school get into themselves to the point where they can be really unfriendly. Sometimes you think you have a friend and then they turn on you because you're no longer good enough to be in their presence."

I spoke on another occasion with a group of girls sitting in the hallway. When I asked them to describe kids in their school, one of them said they were "very snotty. . . . They are rich and are competitive about grades and things. They all plan to go to college and like the attitude is whatever it takes to get there, well, go ahead and do it!"

I observed a number of students in classrooms who did appear to be doing whatever they could "to get there." They put enormous pressure on teachers to make sure they were being distinguished as academic achievers. When teachers did not respond to the pressure, students would challenge their authority in no uncertain terms. I observed an English class taught by a teacher who was notoriously stingy with her grading. One day, she handed back an essay that students had been assigned to write. Most of the students received a B or worse. A boy in front of me was so outraged that he balled up his paper and threw it over the heads of other students into the trash can. A livid girl marched up to the teacher's desk and complained about how "unfair" the grading was. "I asked you for help," she yelled. "I did everything you told me." The teacher did not budge. "You did not do that well," she said. "Try harder next time."

Although the English teacher refused to give in, other teachers relented and were more prone to be unscrupulous in their accommodations to students' demands for unblemished report cards. They would inflate grades, accept questionable excuses for unacceptable work, or otherwise relate to students in a manner that undermined the ethical underpinnings of more scrupulous achievement standards. In doing so, they reinforced academic achievement as a form of opportunistic ambition where the goal is to fulfill one's self-interests as easily as possible while avoiding the hard work of learning and applying knowledge in the service of others.

One example was an algebra teacher who adopted a step-by-step approach that facilitated students' journey through the curriculum. Although the teacher's instructional methods were deemed to be proper, he had a habit of awarding high grades whether they were deserved or not. On one occasion, the teacher evicted a boy because he cursed loudly during a test. The boy met the teacher after school and proceeded to talk him into allowing him to finish the test. A few days later, I overheard him tell some classmates about how he had "sweet-talked" the teacher and gotten a "damn good grade" in the process. He was obviously proud of himself and had no apparent compunctions about his boorish behavior in class much less his use of tactics spurred on by ruthless ambition.

There was another, more insidious consequence of teachers' responses to student pressures that had ramifications for good character. I found that many teenagers at Ridgewood High had an overinflated sense of their privileged status and power over others. Two boys in separate conversations explained how they used their eyes to manipulate people. "There is a sucker born every second," one of them told me. "Just look at their eyes. You can read people by looking in their eyes. That's how you find out how to get what you want out of them." The other boy told me how he controlled people by making eye contact, locking them in, and letting them know with an intimidating gaze that "they're mine." He also used "charisma" to make people believe what he wanted them to believe:

> Give me twenty-five kids that are younger than me or a bunch of insecure people and give me something to talk about and I've got enough charisma to make them believe anything. They don't make decisions for themselves. I tell them "this is good and this is bad" and they believe it.

I conducted an interview with a group of students who confirmed what the boys were saying, that is, that a number of students were intentionally asserting personal power and manipulative influence over others. One of them told me how he was "afraid of [the] individualism" that had been unleashed in his school. "I'm afraid of it just because if you give individuals so much power, I mean, any one person . . . that, that can hurt everyone."

Teachers were well aware of these tendencies among students. One of them felt that students had changed over the years and not necessarily for the better. "They are," he said, "a lot more self-centered" and, he implied, less moral. "They use the 'f' word like it means nothing to them. They don't think twice about sleeping with girlfriends and boyfriends. They see it as a personal choice and nothing wrong with that."

Another teacher said the kids who attended Ridgewood High are not as good as everyone thinks: "They're told from day one they are special and they actually believe it."

Despite their awareness, these and other teachers did little or nothing to curb the excesses of student's self-interested, other-controlling individualism. In their commitment to using their professional authority to ensure student achievement, many of them essentially surrendered their moral authority to consider what might be really good for students' character with sensitivity to larger egalitarian ideals. They thus played a part in the production of a paradoxical moral order of (un)scrupulous achievement.

REORDERING MORAL ORDERS

Although the moral orders that emerged at the two high schools were notably different, both were rife with paradoxical understandings. The enabling communitarian ethic of care for disadvantaged students at Central City High was juxtaposed against a disenabling lack of care for students as capable learners. At Ridgewood High, the dualism of scrupulous and unscrupulous achievement stemmed from the imperative to endorse individualism and competitive advantage, often at the expense of egalitarianism in service to the common good. There were social consequences: Ridgewood High's moral order affirmed White middle-class privilege and power, whereas the one that emerged at Central City High perpetuated patterns of racial inequality in educational opportunity.

The particular ordering of these understandings in each school's moral order was partly the result of teachers' own ethical commitments as they assumed positions of authority in their relations with students and the surrounding community. Teachers at Central City High viewed themselves as authorities on the plight of inner-city Black youth. They were keenly aware that many of their students' basic needs were not being met and that upward mobility was obstructed in the economically impoverished neighborhoods that surrounded the school. As Amber, a youth advocate, noted, teachers' hearts were in the right place as they did what they could to provide care that extended well beyond their responsibilities as educators. However, they also showed a paradoxical lack of care as their professional obligation to ensure equitable education was subsumed by their determination to alleviate hardships rooted in socioeconomic and racial inequalities.

Teachers in their relations were quite circumspect in their efforts to be professional authorities who engaged students in worthwhile curricula through proper pedagogy and also cultivated good character. Some, like the Spanish teacher, convinced themselves that students would drop out of school if such an order were imposed. Others were apprehensive that student resistance would escalate, or their caring stance would be diminished, if they were too authoritarian. Whatever their justification, teachers were inclined to adopt defensive teaching tactics and lax behavioral controls even if it meant that students were not learning society's most valued knowledge, skills, and behavioral norms. Students were quite cognizant of mixed educational consequences as they complained about caring teachers who appeared to care less about their education.

The paradoxical understandings of scrupulous and unscrupulous achievement at Ridgewood High also had mixed educational consequences. Teachers, in keeping with their professional ethics, felt obliged—indeed, pressured—by students and the surrounding middle-class suburban community to be scrupulous in how they addressed the cultural imperative to foster individual academic achievement. Most of them used effective instructional methods and did their best to deliver worthwhile, universally valued curricula, yet many of them were unscrupulous in how they reacted to students' opportunistic ambition during day-to-day classroom interactions. What many students essentially did was assert manipulative personal power in their relations with teachers in much the same way as they did with peers. In doing so, they successfully challenged several teachers' authority to uphold educational standards as well as ethical standards anchored in egalitarian ideals. Understandings in the school's moral order were thus ordered in a manner that prompted teachers, with some notable exceptions, to be scrupulous in their promotion of individual achievement yet unscrupulous in how they allowed the students in their classes to undermine their authority to determine what was truly good for young people and for society.

So, how might paradoxical understandings and practices be resolved in a manner that gives rise to a school moral order that yields good educational outcomes? The answers are complex and not likely to be the same for every high school, and they must involve the teachers, students, and other school actors who are directly affected by them. In future research on the nature of, and solutions to, the dilemmas of school moral orders, emphasis needs to be placed on how teachers' own ethical commitments and reactions to external pressures affect their exercise of authority, including their moral authority. Attention also must be paid to how students respond to conflicting understandings and practices and the powerful roles they play in classroom authority relations. Perhaps then it would be more possible to reorder paradoxical moral orders so that teachers can enact authority relations that allow them to convey worthwhile curricula, use proper pedagogy, and foster good character in a caring and scrupulous manner. Such reorderings should ultimately empower young people to realize their individual potentials; overcome or ameliorate socioeconomic inequalities; interact in a civil, respectful manner; and work together on behalf of the common good.

REFERENCES

Anderson, E. (1998). The code of the streets. In L. C. Mahdi, N. G. Christopher, & M. Meade (Eds.), *Crossroads: The quest for contemporary rites of passage* (pp. 91–97). Chicago: Open Court.

Benne, K. D. (1986). The locus of educational authority in today's world. *Teachers College Record, 88,* 15–21.

Gordon, E. T. (1997). Cultural politics of black masculinity. *Transforming Anthropology, 6*(1–2), 36–53.

Hemmings, A. (2002). Youth culture of hostility: Discourses of money, respect, and difference. *International Journal of Qualitative Studies in Education, 15,* 291–307.

Hemmings, A. (2003). Fighting for respect in urban high schools. *Teachers College Record, 105,* 416–437.

Hemmings, A. (2004). *Coming of age in U. S. high schools: Economic, kinship, religious, and political crosscurrents.* Mahwah, NJ: Lawrence Erlbaum Associates, Inc.

Hemmings, A., & Metz, M. H. (1990). Real teaching: How high school teachers negotiate national, community, and student pressures. In R. Page & L. Valli (Eds.), *Curriculum differentiation: Interpretive studies in U. S. secondary schools* (pp. 91–111). Albany: State University of New York Press.

Hurn, C. (1985). Changes in authority relationships in schools: 1960–1980. *Research in Sociology of Education and Socialization: A Research Annual, 5,* 31–57.

McNeil, L. M. (1983). Defensive teaching and classroom control. In M. W. Apple & L. Weis (Eds.), *Ideology & practice in schooling* (pp. 114–142). Philadelphia: Temple University Press.

McNeil, L. M. (1986). *Contradictions of control: School structure and school knowledge.* New York: Routledge and Kegan Paul.

Metz, M. H. (1978). *Classrooms and corridors: The crisis of authority in desegregated schools.* Berkeley: University of California Press.

Metz, M. H. (1990). Real school: A universal drama amid disparate experience. In D. Mitchell & M. Goertz (Eds.), *Politics of education yearbook* (pp. 75–91). London: Taylor & Francis.

Metz, M. H. (1993). Teachers' ultimate dependence on their students. In J. W. Little & M. W. McLaughlin (Eds.), *Teachers' work: Individuals, colleagues and contexts* (pp. 104–136). New York: Teachers College Press.

Noddings, N. (1984). *Caring: A feminine approach to ethics and morality.* Berkeley: University of California Press.

Noddings, N. (1999). Two concepts of caring. *PES Yearbook.* Retrieved February 21, 2004, from www.edu.uiuc.edu/EPS/PES-Yearbook/1999/noddings_body.asp

Ogbu, J. U. (2003). *Black American students in an affluent suburb: A study of academic disengagement*. Mahwah, NJ: Lawrence Erlbaum Associates, Inc.

Pace, J. L. (2003a). Managing the dilemmas of professional and bureaucratic authority in a high school English class. *Sociology of Education, 76,* 37–52.

Pace, J. L. (2003b). Using ambiguity and entertainment to win compliance in a lower-level U.S. history class. *Journal of Curriculum Studies, 35,* 83–110.

Page, R. N. (1991). *Lower-track classrooms: A curricular and cultural perspective.* New York: Teachers College Press.

Page, R. N. (2000). The tracking show. In B. Franklin (Ed.) *Curriculum and consequence: Herbert M. Kliebard and the promise of schooling* (pp. 103–127). New York: Teachers College Press.

Rosario, J. R. (2000) Communitarianism and the moral order of schools. In B. M. Franklin (Ed.), *Curriculum and consequence: Herbert M. Kliebard and the promise of schooling* (pp. 30–51). New York: Teachers College Press.

Selznick, P. (1992). *The moral commonwealth: Social theory and the promise of community.* Berkeley: University of California Press.

Sizer, T. R., & Sizer, N. F. (1999). *The students are watching: Schools and the moral contract.* Boston: Beacon Press.

Chapter 7

Standards and Sob Stories: Negotiating Authority at an Urban Public College

Randi Rosenblum
Columbia University

> *Hi Professor: I know I did poorly on the midterm but I wonder if you can give me an extra assignment to bring up my grade. I really need to pass this class or I will lose my financial aid.*

> *Dear Professor: Please forgive my absences this week. I have been unable to make it to class because my child is in the hospital. I will bring you a note from the doctor in case you need it. I would be so grateful if you could tell me what I missed so I can catch up.*

> *HELP! I know you said you don't accept late papers, BUT! I'm taking 5 classes and working full time! I am SO stressed out! I'm usually good about deadlines, but I have two other papers due this week and things have heated up at my job. PLEASE! Can I give you my paper next week? Just this time? I'm begging you!*

> *Prof. D———: I need to meet with you to talk about my grade on the exam. I think the B you gave me is unfair. I studied very hard and never missed class. I'd also like to know why the students who never come to class got A's.*

The above e-mails are based on real stories recounted by professors and students in interviews conducted at an urban public college (UPC). These student pleas for exemptions, exceptions, and grade changes reflect an inescapable problem for faculty at UPC: the ongoing attempt by students to negotiate academic standards outside the classroom. When students ask for flexibility, they demand that faculty be sensitive to their individual circumstances while at the same time manage large numbers of students within a set of institutional demands. Such requests ultimately force teachers to grapple with the inherent tensions between accommodation and control, uniform standards and individual needs, and objective and subjective measures of student performance. At UPC, and probably in contemporary college life more generally, the extent to which academic requirements are negotiated is most visible in the one-on-one interactions between faculty and students that occur outside of class.

These student appeals to professors to bend the rules raise a new set of issues regarding authority relations in schools. As researchers, administrators, and teachers, we tend to think of dilemmas of authority as belonging to the dynamics of the classroom, particularly in terms of the ability of teachers to command students' attention. In this chapter I examine authority by focusing on the less familiar issue of standards negotiation in one-on-one encounters. Specifically, I address instances where faculty may or may not adjust their standards of performance (e.g., deadlines, workload, grades) for individual students.

As Hemmings explains in chapter 6 of this volume, school actors' variable understandings of educational goals and roles, shaped by cultural and practical institutional conditions, constitute the *moral order* of the school. Many UPC students perceive standards as up for grabs because the moral order is uncertain (Hurn, 1985): rather than defined by institutional policies, learning objectives, rules of classroom conduct, and expectations of student accountability are left up to individual teachers. School standards are not uniform because faculty members have varying teaching styles, modes of evaluation, and attitudes regarding the value of sanctions. In one-on-one negotiations, students push professors to take a stand on flexibility and defend their standards. Faculty then exercise their institutionally backed authority to control students' adherence to the educational goals they regard as worthwhile and just (Metz, 1978).

This chapter sheds light on enactments of authority by outlining three general strategies that UPC faculty use to manage student appeals for exceptional treatment: (a) flexibility (the Supporters), (b) inflexibility (the Standards-Bearers), and (c) bounded flexibility (the Ad Hoc Majority). Although not rigid categories, these ideal types capture the main differences among faculty in how they understand school roles and responsibilities. As the interviews bear out, UPC faculty view their standards as reflecting certain core values about what *ought* be expected from students. They justify their policies on standards negotiation by drawing on morally charged beliefs about the function of higher education, student accountability, and their role as educators.

How teachers and students negotiate work is an important focus of research because it addresses the informal, unsystematic aspects of standards-setting that are common to all educators, at secondary and postsecondary levels. Teachers' ability to earn student compliance with their expectations is a constitutive part of teaching and learning and is an especially pressing concern given the current climate of standards-based reform. Advocates for reform underestimate how differences among teachers in their pedagogical values, strategies, and willingness to negotiate with students mediate how reforms are implemented and received (Datnow, Hubbard, & Mehan, 2002; Oakes, Wells, Jones, & Datnow, 1997).

PRESSURES ON AUTHORITY AT UPC

Students appeal for flexibility in a variety of ways at UPC, ranging from deferential to accusatory, formal to friendly. Some students initiate face-to-face discussions with teachers in the hallway after class, or during office hours. Others communicate their problems or needs via phone or e-mail. The unrelenting student pressure for flexible standards highlights the paradoxical nature of authority in the contemporary postsecondary context. On the one hand, a key feature of college instruction is the high degree of autonomy teachers hold over the quality and quantity of demands they place on students and modes of evaluation. At the same time, the demand for flexibility at UPC shows that teachers' right to set the terms of work, and rigidly adhere to them, is frequently called into question.

The school I call "UPC" is one of the 11 baccalaureate colleges in the City University of New York (CUNY). Historically, CUNY has been home to New York's low-income minority and immigrant populations as an affordable means to status mobility. More than half of UPC students are first-generation college attendees drawn from local underperforming high schools. However, UPC also attracts many middle-class Whites, minorities, and newly arrived immigrants, of all ages, who go there to avoid the high cost of private school tuition.[1] Thus, UPC faculty teach students from a variety of educational backgrounds, who have different levels of skill preparation, English proficiency, and motivations for attending college. As is true in any college setting, students also have varying expectations regarding teacher authority and notions of what standards are fair.

Student differences in skill and commitment complicate professors' ability to manage students under a system of uniform standards. In particular, faculty emphasize their concerns about what some referred to as the "skill divide" among students. Despite recent restructuring efforts aimed at

---

[1]For example, the student population represents more than 140 nationalities and over 100 languages. More than half of the students at UPC are the first in their families to attend college.

raising admissions standards,[2] many students at UPC are poorly prepared for undergraduate-level work. For some faculty, the skill divide raises the difficult question of whether one standard really fits all. Many professors draw on the ideals of access (social uplift) and excellence (academic achievement) to describe how they manage students in need of remedial help.

Myriad personal obstacles further confound the problems posed by the skill divide. Students' difficulty with managing school requirements is most often explained by teachers and students alike in terms of the life situations of students at UPC. Like the majority of students in public colleges, most students at UPC are "nontraditional": They are older, work part or full time, and may be caring for children or other family members.[3] Uniform rules of accountability inevitably conflict with the very real pressures students are under. It is not unusual to find students at UPC who are taking four or five courses while simultaneously working full time and parenting. In addition, personal crises are always arising, related to the health of family members, immigration status, and other stressors. Many students, while acknowledging that requests for extensions and pardons cause trouble for teachers, believe that teachers should "put themselves in our shoes" and accommodate student needs.

Beyond the expectations and needs of students, negotiation is fostered by the great autonomy professors have in deciding the terms of student effort, including the quantity of assignments, enforcement of sanctions, and how attendance and participation are monitored or evaluated. Interviews with UPC students indicate that they encounter wide differences in teacher expectations of postsecondary performance. This diversity suggests to students that standards are potentially redefinable. In other words, a chief reason students challenge standards outside the classroom is that there are no official rules or shared institutional norms defining what constitutes an A or what demands can or cannot be negotiated.

According to Persell (2000), teachers' professional values and approach to authority cannot be consistent because students vary, and they must constantly use discretion to "balance professional judgments with client concerns, cost factors, and administrative considerations" (p. 398). Lipsky

---

[2]An emblematic example of recent restructuring efforts occurred in the late 1990s, when CUNY's open admissions policy, implemented in 1970, was revoked. The CUNY senior colleges no longer promised every New York City high school student 1 year of remedial coursework if they were unable to pass newly revised placement exams.

[3]Almost half of UPC undergraduates are age 23 or older. According to a 2002 report by the U.S. Department of Education, 73% of undergraduates are nontraditional. Although the majority attend 2-year programs, 67% of students at 4-year public colleges have at least four nontraditional characteristics. See Baker and Velez (1996) for a discussion of the rapid rise in the number of nontraditional students attending postsecondary institutions during the 1980s.

(1980) makes a similar point in his theory of the "street level bureaucrat":

> Street-level bureaucrats work in situations that often require responses to the human dimensions of situations. They have discretion because the accepted definitions of their tasks call for sensitive observation and judgment, which are not reducible to programmed formats. It may be that uniform sentencing would reduce inequities in the criminal justice system. But we also want the law to be responsive to the unique circumstances of individual transgressions. We want teachers to perceive the unique potential of children. In short, to a degree the society seeks not only impartiality from its public agencies but also compassion for special circumstances and flexibility in dealing with them. (p. 15)

In this quote, Lipsky (1980) draws a contrast between "programmed formats" and the "human dimension" of the client–professional relationship. This conception is especially useful to understanding the predicament of UPC professors. In one-on-one encounters, faculty must balance their feelings of compassion with impartial rules designed to make sure that student performance is accurately and fairly evaluated. Effective teaching and student learning are often facilitated by flexibility, but assessing students as individuals raises thorny interpersonal issues that obscure accountability and puts pressure on standards. Flexibility may allow professors to help students reach their "unique potential"; however, not all students who aim to negotiate do so for purposes of edification. Below I explore just how UPC faculty manage the dilemmas posed by the practical and human dimensions of teacher–student negotiations over standards.

THE STUDY

This chapter is based on a larger study that explored faculty and student expectations of work in a large, ethnically diverse setting. Between 2000 and 2001, I conducted in-depth, semistructured interviews with 70 students and 30 teachers at UPC. My interest in the negotiation of standards at UPC and public higher education more generally was not incidental: I had been working in a CUNY college as an adjunct professor in sociology since 1996. Although my "insider" status equipped me with a keen sense of UPC students' problems, it was through the research that I began to fully realize the pervasiveness of student appeals for flexibility and how they shape authority relations.

Interviews enabled access to the otherwise-unobservable expectations underlying one-on-one encounters outside the classroom. The discussions lasted on average for 90 minutes and ranged from 1 to 2 hours. Invitations to participate in the study were randomly distributed to faculty across academic departments. In choosing from the pool of volunteers, my aim was to sample the greatest variety of academic disciplines and title status.[4] Six faculty members were recruited informally through the use of snowball sampling.

The data reveal three ideal types of professors: (a) Supporters ($n = 6$), (b) Standards Bearers ($n = 9$), and (c) Ad Hoc Majority ($n = 15$). The three types highlight the central differences among faculty in how they manage student attempts to negotiate standards outside the classroom. Each group justifies the strategy they espouse—flexibility, inflexibility, and bounded flexibility—by drawing on distinct moral frameworks of authority roles and standards.

I do not use this taxonomy to suggest a neat fit between teachers' moral justifications and their actions. Indeed, negotiations with students are highly discretionary, mediated by teachers' varying personal styles, curricular demands, and student characteristics. Teachers' willingness to bend rules is also informed by practical assessments regarding time management and conflict avoidance.[5] Thus, in different situations, faculty may shift from one position to another. Drawing on Pace's (2003) notion of "authority-as-hybrid," I understand teachers' authority as complex enactments of combined strategies based on culturally influenced styles, skills, and habits (Swidler, 2001).

On the other hand, the moral salience of faculty talk provides insight into the ideologies that influence the demands teachers place on students (Gamson, 1966; Lipman, 1998; Metz, 1978). At UPC, teachers do generally base their policies of flexibility on their beliefs about why standards should or should not be negotiated and how students should be treated. Regardless of where a professor falls on the spectrum of flexibility at any given time, they aim to persuade students to adhere to the educational goals they view as worthwhile. Flexibility, inflexibility, and bounded flexibility were strategies widely acknowledged by teachers and students alike in the interviews.

The Supporters: Flexible Standards

The Supporters espouse a commitment to flexibility and negotiation in one-on-one encounters with students. These professors are always willing to accommodate individual student needs, which usually requires bending

---

[4]I use the folk term *professor* to refer to all participants, even though some did not hold a PhD at the time of the research. The sample consists of 13 senior faculty, 10 junior faculty, and 7 adjunct faculty. Status or discipline differences among faculty or age and racial–ethnic characteristics are not relevant to the data presented here.

[5]The refusal to administer a makeup exam to a student who missed the final because of a family emergency, for example, may have more to do with the teacher's schedule than any policy of inflexibility. Patterns of negotiation are further related to varying demands and conditions related to the horizontal (area of study) and vertical (level of difficulty) curriculum.

the rules established in the classroom. In justifying their general policy of flexibility, the Supporters share three defining features: (a) a claim of responsibility to address students' remedial needs; (b) belief that flexibility facilitates higher standards; and (c) a reluctance to use sanctions, which are viewed as impractical or harmful.

The pedagogical goals of the Supporters must be understood in terms of their strong identification with a particular conception of CUNY's institutional mission—a commitment to provide the opportunity of higher education to the "have-nots"—which makes their teaching a calling. For example, many of the Supporters claimed that they could easily have obtained jobs at more prestigious universities with better work conditions but that they feel more rewarded at UPC because they can contribute something to students who have never before been valued. In one example, a history professor described the importance of what he sees as the teacher's obligation to "make amends" for previous, cumulative disadvantages of public schooling.[6]

> [At UPC] we have many students who aren't prepared for college and I guess the question that we have to ask ourselves is: Is it their fault? Do we penalize them by writing them off or do we do everything we can to make amends for the lack of preparation that they received in high school? I saw this time and time again, good ideas that were just expressed in a poor way and so I would try my best—given our salary and our time constraints—to give them every chance to improve their work.

This quote expresses the Supporters' fundamental belief that teachers carry an institutional responsibility to address the remedial needs of poorly prepared students. To the history professor, teachers who "write them off" penalize students for deficiencies that are "not their fault." In this sense, the Supporters aim to compensate for what they perceive as structural barriers to many UPC students' success. The history professor went on to explain what it means to give students "every chance":

> If I see a student who is willing to try harder to do better and is willing to give it their best shot by rewriting a paper or turning in an essay three days in advance to say "Can you take a look?" I always give my students the opportunity. If you do some work up front, I will reward you by telling you where you've fallen off.

The professor's offering to help students improve their work before it is due demonstrates how he tries to attend to their individual needs. Instead of seeing such acts of support as a relinquishing of teacher control, he sees them as a way to encourage and thus persuade engagement. He believes

---

[6]For purposes of confidentiality, names of department affiliations have been changed. In instances where subject matter is relevant, the field of study has been changed to a related field, such as another social science for political science.

that rewarding students who do some work "up front" is an appropriate way to promote learning by offering students the assistance they need in order to be accountable to the collective standard.

Granting individual attention to students is a challenging enterprise at UPC, where the average class size is 40. What I call the "above and beyond" policy of the Supporters reflects their eagerness to go to great lengths to reach out to students, promoting and sometimes even inviting negotiation with students whom they view as in need of extra support. An anthropology professor described how he requires his students to perform an in-class writing exercise on the first day of class. The professor does not grade the assignment but uses it as an instrument to assess students' writing proficiency, the area of student competence most reflective of the skill divide. He explained that although the task of evaluating the writing skills of approximately 50 students is daunting, it is justified by the benefit of being able to help students early on in the course:

> If I noticed a student had severe problems, whose English was poor, I would try to say, "Please come see me" and then say "Look, obviously you have problems expressing yourself in English. Have you gone to the writing center? Have you taken any remedial classes?"

This quote demonstrates how the anthropology professor aims to manage student differences. He claims that he typically keeps "an eye on" students throughout the semester who have troubles with writing, and he rewards their progress in the final grade. His attempts to build rapport and supervise individual students are an assertion of his authority to redefine classroom standards and direct student effort. Thus, students are not expected to make it on their own; responsibility to classroom requirements is shared. In another example, an English professor said he "staged an intervention" with a student who was unable to write an essay:

> There was one student, she couldn't write. I didn't know how she got through UPC. I don't know how she got past the sixth grade and I didn't give her a grade all semester. I said, "I can't grade anything you've turned in 'cause it's that bad and I'm giving you an incomplete for the semester and I'm gonna work with you." And I said, "Look, I think UPC is doing you a disservice if they're gonna give you a degree and you can't write an essay."

In this case, it was the professor, not the student, who initiated the negotiation of an incomplete. Instead of failing the student for inadequate work, the professor deliberately withheld the grade so that he might have the chance to "work with" the student on her writing. He justifies his response in terms of the best way to avoid committing a "disservice" to the student, which connotes institutional, not individual responsibility, for what he perceives as a societal, not personal, failure. In this particular situation the student did not take the professor up on his offer and received an F for not completing the course requirements. However, the story highlights a central aspect of the way in which the Supporters morally frame their role as educators: to encourage and reach out to students whom they view as capable and deserving.

These stories paint a picture out of sync with conventional beliefs about the effects of flexibility on standards. Flexibility is often depicted as a reflection of teachers' lack of control over students, who pressure them to lower standards (Powell, Farrar, & Cohen, 1985; Sizer, 1984). Many of the Supporters' colleagues share this view and equate negotiation with giving in to students or being slack. However, the majority of Supporters were adamant in their belief that flexible standards do not indicate less work or promote grade inflation. The history professor told me:

> It's not to say that there are two standards in the class. The bar is high, and while I understand that some [students] come from backgrounds that for whatever reason [they're] at a disadvantage, the fact is, if they want an A, they have to do this level of work. So I think you can do both. You can keep your standards up and you can also give students an extra chance. I think that's part of the contract. . . . That it's a public institution that is geared towards access but it is also an institution that tries to maintain standards, and if we have to work a little harder to provide both access and excellence as the little cliché says, then I'm willing to do it.

This quote reflects this professor's belief that flexibility is necessary to fulfill the institutional responsibility to both access and excellence, which he believes can be achieved simultaneously. According to the Supporters, negotiating extra chances does not compromise standards because students are inherently different in what they need to succeed, not in their potential for success.

The supportive approach put forth by the Supporters further reflects their reluctance to use sanctions or rely on rigid rules of student conduct. A film and media studies professor was very explicit about the educational benefits of open-ended deadlines. If a student cannot get the paper in on time, he gives an extension regardless of the cause for lateness. He believes that excuses are immaterial. It is the work that counts, not the rules:

> I don't care what the reason is. I tell them in class, "If you need more time let me know." If I get lousy papers, I give them an incomplete and tell them why. Ultimately it's about producing the work. The due date is a meaningless measure. I tell them in class, "If you want a grade you have to give me a paper." If they want to deal with an incomplete, what do I care? Of course it creates a burden later on if they hand in the paper when I have an overflow of work, but I have no problem with it.

His logic rests on the belief that the quality of work students produce is more important than their adherence to classroom policies. The professor sees grades and deadlines as formalities and uses the unconditional granting of incompletes as a way to manage students' inability to hand in polished work promptly.[7] He believes sanctions are counterproductive because they undermine students' ability to express their true potential and thus lead to *lower* levels of performance. Although he acknowledges the potential burden of accepting papers that appear any time, he is willing to be inconvenienced. However, few UPC students take incompletes, even if they are dissatisfied with their grade. Given that the majority are older, have work and family obligations, and are eager to graduate, students by and large prefer to finish the work.

A math professor defended her reluctance to use sanctions not in terms of standards but by drawing on issues of trust. She views building trust as paramount to student learning and success, especially for students who "feel less about themselves" in a college environment for which they are not prepared due to their inadequate high school education:

> [The students] get the message that I care. But I will not monitor, and I think there are people in this department who give a quiz every day. I have to tell you that I think that is just terrible. It's a terrible message, "I am in charge of you. I am gonna make sure whether you like it or not."

From this perspective, faculty who give daily quizzes send students the message that they cannot be trusted to attend class or follow the material. The math professor regards sanctions as potentially writing off capable students who will internalize their failures when unable to adhere to requirements. She aims to promote students' sense of inclusion rather than maintaining conventional academic requirements through sanctions that may be regarded as punitive or intimidating.

A political science professor provided an emblematic example of how the Supporters view authority as a tool to foster trust in their relationships with students. In one-on-one encounters, she aims to treat all students' problems as legitimate and valuable. The political science professor views trust as so essential to her role that she extends flexibility to even those students who are visibly trying to deceive or manipulate her. In the interview, she made reference to the "dead grandmother" problem, a term sarcastically used by several teachers to connote students who allege to have been absent or missed an exam because of a death in the family, or a health-related emer-

---

[7]Exams are the one case where the student's excuse does matter to the professor. If a student claims to be ill, he will request documentation from a doctor, because "it's not fair to the students who took the exam at the appointed time." He thus regards flexibility as inappropriate because the exam requires that all students be prepared to take it on a fixed date.

gency more generally, but who are actually suspected of lying. Students who try to deceive their teachers by forging the existence of an ill grandparent are at once appealing to teachers' sympathetic sensibility and their desire to take students at their word. In the following quote, the political science professor describes how she makes a deliberate choice to presume that students who give excuses are being truthful:

> It never occurs to me that they're scam artists. Even when it's true. When I started teaching here my kids used to laugh at me because so many students had grandmothers who died. The grandmother who died in Puerto Rico, or wherever, a lot of grandmothers. I choose to believe it, always, I never look at a slip from the doctor. They bring it to me sometimes, they say "I was sick," "I had asthma," "Here's a note from the doctor," I say, "I don't need to see that." I choose to believe them, that's part of the way I treat them, if they're getting over, it's their loss. I think there's more benefit to them and to the relationship by my choosing to believe them even when they may be getting over.

This professor's unwillingness to look at doctor's notes or sanction students whom she suspects are lying reflects her belief that the benefit of communicating trust outweighs the benefits that may be brought from holding students to unbendable regulations. Even in cases where it is clear that the student is "getting over" she chooses to believe them because of the "benefits to them and to the relationship." In this sense, she accepts their excuses in order to communicate her support and prevent students from feeling alienated. Whether deliberate or not, an added advantage of her blanket policy of flexibility is that it enables her to avoid awkward discussions about personal problems and student dishonesty.

This approach was also evident in stories regarding cheating. The Supporters view acts of plagiarism as a serious violation of academic standards, but they do not believe sanctions are the appropriate response to the offense; this perspective sets them apart from many of their colleagues. Two Supporters told me of instances where a student was caught cheating or had plagiarized a paper. In both cases, the professor acknowledged to the students that they had violated classroom norms but did not penalize them. Instead, the students were given new assignments in lieu of the work that had not been accepted.

The preceding examples illustrate how the Supporters build relationships with students and encourage their adherence to learning demands. The Supporters are unequivocal in their identification with flexible standards, which they justify in terms of their moral beliefs about the teacher role. They see flexibility as a resource that enables them to provide the support and affirmation students need to manage the work, a goal commensurate with their ideological claims about educational access and social mobility.

Standards Bearers: Inflexibility and Sanctions

Another group of professors, the Standards Bearers, put forth a model of authority very different from the approach presented by the Supporters. Standards Bearers view student attempts to negotiate and teachers' willingness to bend the rules as reflecting the lowered standards of postsecondary institutions. This orientation is justified by the belief that negotiating with students is incompatible with the fundamental work of college professors: to maintain rigorous standards. These individuals are highly suspicious of their colleagues' flexibility, which they believe perpetuates in students a distorted sense of irresponsibility.

One chemistry professor, who defined college as an "elite pursuit," offered insight into this perspective:

> The national view of education in this country is that education is merely a device for acculturation, it is not an entrée into intellectual work. I definitely see the flip side of this, that there is an elitist attitude among many faculty. I have been accused of being that, and in many ways I am, but I understand what that accusation means. It's an elite pursuit, the same way that being a concert pianist is not going to be for every piano student that goes to Juilliard. They won't all make it.

By framing postsecondary education as an "elite pursuit" the professor draws the line between the goals of excellence and an institutional responsibility to accommodate the needs of underprepared students. The chemistry professor invokes the ideals of meritocracy—that some students are more able than others—to suggest that the work of teachers is to accurately distinguish differences among students in their ability and motivation, such that they can evaluate the difference between "every piano student" and the future "concert pianist." Meritocratic assessments of this kind are possible only under uniform standards of performance. This perspective is directly at odds with the view that undergraduate teachers should address matters of student access to achievement. On the contrary, the Standards Bearers argue that the work of preparing students for college falls exclusively on educators at the primary and secondary stages of learning, before it is too late to adequately correct student deficits. In this view, students who cannot adhere to undergraduate-level requirements simply do not belong in college.

A biology professor who teaches a 200-person introductory lecture course illustrates the Standards Bearers' commitment to non-negotiable requirements. Many students take her notoriously time-intensive class because it is a gateway to the health professions, such as nutrition, nursing, and medicine. UPC regulations dictate that students in these programs must earn a C-minus in the course in order to proceed with more advanced degree requirements. Adhering rigorously to the UPC grading code, the

163

professor grants a D or F to all students who average less than a 70 on course requirements. Invariably, the professor is approached every semester by failing and near-failing students who plead for extra chances to bring up their grade. In the interview, the professor explained that she does not negotiate grades, even in instances where a student is within a "fraction of a point" from passing. As a result, several students have filed grade appeals against her, forcing her to defend her grading practices in front of the UPC ombudsman. In our interview, she explained:

> I want it to be totally objective. No essay. No extra credit. Multiple choice. If there's a 69.8, that is a D following the code. I will not give them the C-minus. If I have to give a student 8 decimal points, then I have to give all the students, and when does it stop? There has to be a certain homogeneity.

Her question "when does it stop?" expresses concern with the arbitrary nature of grades negotiated outside the classroom, especially in large lecture classes with hundreds of students. She claims that the frequent granting of exceptions renders grades meaningless and disadvantages students who do not aggressively challenge the teacher. She feels "completely vaccinated" against student complaints thanks to her multiple-choice exams and computer grading system, which prevent any arguments over her interpretation of students' answers.[8] In encounters with indignant students, the "code" serves as a transparent symbol of students' relative efforts, allowing her to deflect the expectation that grades can be negotiated.

It is not that the biology teacher is unsympathetic to the situations of failing students. Like many Standards Bearers with whom I spoke, she expressed regret for being unable to accommodate students who have intellectual and personal difficulties in managing the work. At the same time, the professor justifies the need to fail students in terms of a professional and public commitment to standards: "What I do is think to myself, if I was in the hospital and one of my students was taking care of me, what would it mean if they were poorly trained? That is my responsibility." In addition, she feels exonerated in demanding a lot from her students because her curriculum is an introduction to coursework that will get increasingly more difficult and lays the groundwork for challenging technical graduate programs.

Many professors in this group insist that personal difficulties are not an adequate basis to be excused from course requirements. They talked at

---

[8] In general, it is easier for faculty in the natural sciences or in mathematics to quantify standards of assessment. More than their colleagues in the humanities and social sciences, they have better access to national standards of curricula, textbooks, and assessment technologies. However, teachers from a variety of academic disciplines talked about the problems posed by qualitative instruments of measurement. Aside from the time-saving advantages, quantitative standards render the evaluation process less open for negotiation and are easier to justify in the face of student antagonism.

length about the frustration caused by students' widespread expectation
that negotiation is an appropriate part of the student–teacher relationship.
In one example, a philosophy professor described how he is annoyed by
students' belief that difficult circumstances exempt them from the hard
work required to attain good grades:

> What troubles me is, they come to class unprepared, and I know there's lots
> of good reasons. You sit down with somebody and they say they're taking five
> courses and they have a full-time job and the additional family obligations,
> but still, that is not reason alone for me to give them an A just because they
> have it so hard. And then what I find gratifying is that sometimes, by being
> insistent, they finally sit down and start doing the work and they see what
> they're able [to do].

This professor understands his students' weak attachment to the work as
a problem of competing priorities. He justifies the refusal to negotiate by
describing the positive response of some students to his "being insistent."
He regards this as evidence that students are able and willing to take
responsibility for the work when they are made aware enough times that
it is the "right" thing to do. In the interview, he described how he takes
pride in emphasizing to his students that attending college is a choice, and
one that comes with certain binding responsibilities. Thus, he draws on
students' moral obligation to the work and the institutional right of faculty
to demand student accountability.

Some Standards Bearers expressed deep resentment over the problems
of student disengagement (e.g., not coming to class and avoiding assignments), which they view as encouraged by the flexible practices of other
faculty. This mistrust of colleagues is informed by clashes with students who
are indignant over, or bewildered by, inflexible policies. In interviews, they
complained about students' "sense of entitlement" to receive satisfactory
grades for less-than-satisfactory work. Like most teachers, they partly at-
tribute the problem to students' underpreparation as well as to the absence
of official guidelines that state clearly what students are expected to do.
But the Standards Bearers also believe that their colleagues reinforce in
students the false sense that "fairness" stems from "being nice" rather than
treating students equally. In the Standards Bearers' moral framework, the
true support of students starts with the message that they are just like everybody else. The chemistry professor made this point: "I have had a troupe of
gay students, Asian students, Black students, come in and say, 'Thank God
you're not treating me on the basis of the color of my skin, you know, you're
holding me to the same standards as everybody else.'"

He went on to express his regret that holding students to a uniform
standard is not the typical approach of UPC faculty: "Rather than being a
self-respecting academic doing serious work, you have to feel that you're

doing good work for a benighted group of underprivileged—it's a terribly patronizing attitude I find, but common." The "patronizing attitude" he perceives as pervasive among faculty reflects the belief among the Standards Bearers that grade inflation operates as a mechanism for faculty to address personal and political concerns about educational inequality. A drama professor made this point in more explicit terms. He believes that many UPC professors give into the social and interpersonal pressures of students who beg for higher grades, "especially if they are minorities." He claims these faculty have a belief that they can "give the student self-esteem by giving out fraudulent grades" when in fact "self-esteem is something a person obtains through their achievement."

Because they espouse a policy of inflexible standards, the Standards Bearers disproportionately face the burden of student hostility. Sanctions, warnings, and detailed information about their expectations are strategies intended to ward off student challenges before they happen. For example, Standards Bearers use the first day of classes to communicate how seriously they feel about rules of classroom conduct and make clear that appeals for negotiation will be met with opposition. Thus, they call students' attention to the specific expectations of accountability in the course, particularly regarding the standards that are most vulnerable to student challenges and transgressions: grades, attendance and punctuality, and deadlines. "Late papers will not be accepted" or "I will not give make-ups" are statements intended to command compliance while preempting student appeals for flexibility.

On the first day, some teachers even exaggerate the extent to which they are inflexible. They push their warnings about negotiation to the level of what one sociology professor referred to as "scare tactics":

> You have to let them know early on that they can't just do whatever they want. They can't just decide not to come to the exam. The key is scaring them on the first day. You have to drill it into their minds or else they'll try to walk all over you.

The syllabus is a key resource of preemption. Aside from general course information (topics of study, books to buy, office hours), some teachers use the syllabus as a formal contract that makes official the non-negotiability of their standards. Typical items on the syllabus intended to control student behavior include what one professor referred to as "civility rules," regulations of classroom conduct, such as no eating or sleeping in class and no lateness. Itemized grade distributions, which state the proportions allotted to the different kinds of student efforts and assignments, are partly aimed at helping students structure their effort but also serve the function of preventing students' attempts to negotiate the gray areas of assessment. Another strategy is the inclusion of institutional policies, such as plagiarism, that students may not be aware of or may try to evade. Finally, some professors find it useful to offer students guidelines about how to manage emerging problems. For example, they may suggest time management strategies or provide information regarding tutoring services offered by the institution. To the Standards Bearers, such instruction serves as both a support to guide students' successful managing of the work and a shield against claims that students "can't understand" or "don't know how."

Such extensive detail in the syllabus enables faculty to direct student action, avoid ambiguity, and convey to students that individual attempts to negotiate the terms of the work will not be tolerated. In addition, preemptive warnings, either communicated verbally or documented in the syllabus, serve as powerful forms of self-defense in subsequent encounters with students. In the face of students having a wide range of personal and academic difficulties, professors feel absolved by pointing to their clear and concrete standards. They can simply remind the student, "It's right there in the syllabus," or "You knew how much work the course required." This is evidence that the professor played fair, and students make the choice about how much effort they put into the course—a choice that has consequences.

Another strategy is to design assignments that have a built-in flexibility. Requirements that allow students to "drop the lowest grade" offer some leeway when they have trouble completing assignments or attending an exam. Standards Bearers can thus use optional requirements as leverage against accusations that they are inflexible or unfair, subtly directing students to *negotiate with themselves* as difficulties arise throughout the semester. For example, after several semesters marked by frequent confrontations with students over his weekly homework assignment policy, a psychology professor changed the compulsory requirement to a voluntary points system in order to preempt student pleas for extensions and pardons:

> I give them homework worth about 200 points for the semester and they need to get at least a 100 to get the whole bonus so I say, "I'm not negotiating about any dying grandmothers. I realize something can come up. If you miss one there are others. Make sure that you bring up your points early, then, if your grandmother dies later, there is no problem." So I don't negotiate any extension. This is all in the syllabus, everything is clear in the beginning.

What these strategies have in common is their intent to give students a sense of control over their fate. Such tactics make it possible for the Standards Bearers to exercise authority as they see fit while at the same time appearing reasonable and staving off hostility. The extensive use of sanctions and emphasis on uniform standards demonstrate an orientation decidedly distinct from the Supporters. Unlike the first group, they argue that students' academic and personal difficulties are irrelevant to teachers' work. To these professors, the idea that flexibility undermines standards is self-evident and indisputable.

The Ad Hoc Majority: Bounded Flexibility

Whereas the Supporters and Standards Bearers may be seen as opposing poles of the spectrum, the third type identifies with aspects of both flexible and inflexible approaches. These professors, who are the majority, reject blanket policies of uniform or flexible standards and instead adjust their responses to students on a case-by-case basis. The Ad Hoc-ers always use their discretion to grant leeway or enforce sanctions, viewing students' attempts to negotiate as sometimes warranted, sometimes not. In describing one-on-one encounters with students, these teachers expressed a range of attitudes regarding the access/excellence debate, which suggests a mixture of uncertainty, ambivalence, and the experience of feeling "caught in the middle." Their ad hoc response to students reflects their efforts to at once maintain control over their standards while being attentive to students' varying needs.

One political science professor provided a helpful description of the third type. When the issue of student requests for flexibility was raised, he told me that he thinks of himself as generally lenient when it comes to rule-setting. In the classroom, he indicates to students that he is "easygoing" by "not being overly serious or taking myself or my syllabus too seriously, or being willing to negotiate with them about things." More than just a matter of personal style, he justifies his relaxed approach to sanctions and schedules in terms of his compassion and concern for students' troubles:

> I'm very sensitive to the fact that the majority of these students work and carry other responsibilities and stuff so I'm relatively sympathetic when they do come to me personally about problems that come up during the semester that prevent them from doing work on time.

This statement expresses his view that frequent adjustments are appropriate because students encounter obstacles beyond their control. But what seemed like a straightforward Supporter-like position at this point in the interview grew more complex and ambiguous. Later on, the political science professor explained how his easygoingness is "bounded":

> There are ways in which I'm strict and there are ways in which I'm not strict. I can sometimes have a very authoritarian style in the classroom and that is a core strategy on my part, which is that sometimes intimidating them about the importance of meeting deadlines and doing the reading is a way of scaring at least a few of them into fulfilling the requirements in a timely manner.

On occasion, the political science professor presents a standards-bearing approach by calling students' attention to sanctions. Such "authoritarian" measures are necessary, he argues, to maintain conventional requirements and remind students of the importance of accountability. Above all, however, his objective in acting strict is to "curtail the folks who want to take advantage of me." Like many teachers, the professor is adamant about protecting himself against the affront and inconvenience of managing students who are trying to "get over":

> Any reasonable person is going to be sensitive to personal interruptions or problems but they have to make a commitment to the process, to the class, to the school, to whatever, and there are students for whom being in college at [UPC] is not exactly a priority in their life.

The political science professor illuminates the unavoidable dilemma posed by flexibility. Conjuring up the human dimension of teacher–student interaction, he believes that "any reasonable person" will feel sympathy for students who cannot handle the demands of school. At the same time, he acknowledges that students are not equal in their entitlement to clemency. Students who assign a low priority to school do not deserve flexibility because they dodge their responsibility, as students in higher education, to take academics seriously. Even worse, attempts to get over often involve dishonest excuses, which he regards as the ultimate violation of trust in the student–teacher relationship. His solution to the problem is to draw on sanctions only in the cases where he assumes inflexibility to be the appropriate response. His willingness to negotiate is bounded by students' demonstrated commitment to learning.

As the term *bounded flexibility* suggests, the Ad Hoc-ers fall closer to the Supporters than to the Standard Bearers on the continuum of UPC standards. These faculty share with the Supporters a willingness to bend the rules for individual students, and they similarly view such acts as consistent with high standards. We may also assume that the flexibility the Supporters grant their students is always to some extent bounded by the expectation that students will do the work. The Ad Hoc-ers are distinct in that they claim to be more discriminating in their granting of flexibility and, much like the Standards Bearers, emphasize the importance of setting boundaries in the classroom to preempt student attempts to get over.

The distinction between the Supporters and the Ad Hoc-ers therefore suggests a difference of degree rather than kind. In addition, some Ad Hoc-ers claim to promote policies that reward student progress and participation partly because they want to resolve and manage skill disparities among students. Similar to the Supporters, they believe weak students should be granted extra chances to manage the work in the face of difficulty. However, they do not share the Supporters' sense of responsibility to actively reach out to students, and they put a high premium on student commitment as crucial to their willingness to negotiate in one-on-one encounters.

To varying degrees, the Ad Hoc-ers base their responses to students on their interpretation of the behavioral clues that indicate student accountability, honesty, and a genuine commitment to school. A Spanish professor illustrated how in dealing with student excuses she tries to decipher students' deservingness:

> There are the students who call on the day of the exam and say that they're sick or that there has been an emergency with their kid. Of course I can tell off the bat from their performance in class and on exams how serious they are. Sometimes I know they're calling me with an excuse because they're just not prepared. There are the few cases where something bad has happened and then there are the students who aren't telling me the whole truth. In that kind of situation I do give make-ups, but if it seems like the student isn't really telling the whole truth I will go to great pains to make the makeup exam harder. It's only fair to the other students in the class who show up. I do make the judgment though, if it seems something really bad has happened.

As this quote suggests, she believes student excuses require tailored responses. In managing student appeals, she tries to draw a line between instances where "something really bad has happened" and lesser excuses. The student's credibility is reflected in how seriously he or she takes school demands, as indicated by prior classroom performance. In the event this professor knows too little about a student to make an assessment, she tends to give them the benefit of the doubt.

Her reaction to students who miss an exam without justification sheds light on her ad hoc authority. Rather than fail the student, she "takes great pains" to administer a more challenging exam. Unbeknown to the student, this subtle form of punishment allows the professor to avoid confrontation, all the while balancing out her standards. The more rigorous exam is the sanction she uses to reward students who are accountable and penalize those who are not.

Certainly, professors' responses to student appeals are also influenced by practical issues. For example, faculty will consider the amount of additional work or inconvenience posed by revising the terms of work. How much the negotiated standards deviate from what other students were required to do is also relevant, as is the cause of the student's difficulty and how much it could have been avoided. However, in recounting past encounters with students outside the classroom, the Ad Hoc-ers consistently drew a contrast between engaged, committed students on the one hand, and dishonest, manipulative students on the other. To one philosophy professor, managing students' requests for flexibility requires that he can discern the "sob story" from legitimate excuses, which he bases on an examination of students' overall engagement in the class:

If somebody has very spotty attendance and they don't hand their paper in, and they come to me a week later and they give me a sob story, I say quite frankly, "You never come to class," or, "You infrequently attend class and now you are doing this." What I usually do is take the paper and tell them I'm going to grade them down one grade. Now, you know, in the abstract it's so hard to figure out. I suppose it does matter that I know the student and whether the student attends class.

In this example, the professor calls on the student's weak commitment to the work to deflect the cause of the student's difficulty back onto the student and assert his right to penalize students who do not adhere to his standards. He chooses to be frank in this instance and confront the student about his or her poor attendance as justification for why the student had no real leeway to ask for a pardon. When it comes to students who miss deadlines, the philosophy professor relies on the clues that identify the quality of student participation to delineate the hardworking/deserving student from the student whose paper must be graded down.

Conversely, in the face of visibly serious students, the Ad Hoc-ers see no conflict in bending the rules or negotiating grades. One public health professor told me: "If a student who screwed up on their midterm comes to me and seems genuinely concerned then I factor that in." For this teacher, factoring in the genuine concern of the student who did poorly on the exam may mean assigning the poor grade less weight in proportion to other aspects of the student's overall performance. His choice to "give the edge" to the student is contingent on the student's genuine seriousness or interest, which may be based on the student's prior performance or promise for future performance.

Many professors argued that they can rely on impressions of student commitment because the students' classroom behavior tends to be consistent and cumulative. It is unlikely that students who ostensibly care about the work and take the work seriously will miss an exam or a deadline unless it is unavoidable. An English professor thus justified for herself the granting of pardons because students tend to follow through on their promises:

I couldn't tell you of a routine system that I use. I tend to take them at their word and let the chips fall where they may, but 9 times out of 10 a student who needs an extra chance will deliver on it, if you know what I mean. The student who tends to disappear, who comes and gives you the song and dance, chances are that student will disappear again.

A chief rationale for rewarding flexibility to students who show effort concerns what a classics professor referred to as the role of engagement in "real learning." These faculty emphasize the link between students' actual learning and their consistent engagement. If the chief pedagogical goal of teachers is to promote learning, they argue, then it follows that the process of learning should be relevant to the evaluation of student performance.

It is also the case that the Ad Hoc-ers reward commitment because they share the sentiment that, given the pervasive disengagement in the UPC classroom, students who do the work should earn something in return. Students who take the work seriously demonstrate that, like their teachers, they understand and honor the value of higher education. It is also true that professors often feel a deeper sense of responsibility to or sympathy for the student when they feel a sense of shared purpose and commitment to educational goals.[9]

Finally, professors equate student concern for learning with respect for their rules and expectations. For example, a professor's response to a student outside of class may also be influenced by the student's tone and attitude. Students who are perceived as overconfident and entitled may invoke little sympathy for their plight. An economics professor made this point:

> This student, she gets a D on the midterm, and writes me an e-mail saying she really needs this course to graduate, can I please give her some extra work, as if it was a perfectly appropriate request. It wasn't apologetic, just matter of fact, "please tell me what I can do to pass." She came to class but her work on the exam . . . it was obvious she didn't understand any of the material. But asking me to tell her what it was that she could do about her grade, it was as if it was taken for granted, that it was automatic procedure.

In this particular scenario, the professor believed the student did not deserve extra chances to bring up her grade because she had not demonstrated competence of the material, a fact the teacher used as leverage in defending her refusal to be flexible. The professor's key justification for inflexibility was based on the student's unwillingness to acknowledge her responsibility to course requirements. However, the teacher also implies that she may have responded differently had the student taken a more deferential tone.

The ad hoc orientation to authority demonstrates how the majority of UPC professors are discriminating in their use of sanctions. As a faculty type, the Ad Hoc category is most useful in that it highlights how, to adjust to the situation at hand, professors may shift between the two poles of flexibility and inflexibility. Their extensive reliance on discretion makes evident the subjective dimensions of assessment with which all teachers must grapple. All teachers use ad hoc judgments in encounters with students, because educational goals are complex, and students are variable. In tailoring their

---

[9] We can also assume that faculty are motivated to accommodate "good" students because student commitment validates their effectiveness as teachers. To a certain extent, student interests intimates that the teacher is effective and the material engaging. All teachers spoke earnestly of the importance of student interest for job satisfaction.

responses to individual students, these faculty members clearly illustrate how standards are constructed out of teacher–student interaction.

The Ad Hoc-ers' willingness to negotiate with students is primarily shaped by their perceptions of that student's level of commitment to the work, formed through interactions inside and outside the classroom. The practice of rewarding commitment gets at the core of their moral framework: Students are human and make mistakes, but ultimately they have to commit to the course.

CONCLUSION

When students ask for flexibility outside of class, they challenge professors' authority to set the terms of work. Negotiations outside the classroom are the sites where uncertain educational standards and authority relations are fought out. Flexibility, inflexibility, and bounded flexibility are the strategies faculty exercise to achieve students' compliance to the learning goals and rules of accountability that they consider appropriate and worthwhile.

Professors draw on moral frameworks of school roles to defend their willingness (or unwillingness) to accommodate individual students. Whereas the Supporters aim to be sensitive to student needs and equate flexibility with high standards, the Standards Bearers stress the importance of uniform standards and view flexibility as a breach of authority. The Ad Hoc-ers, on the other hand, do not ascribe to strict notions of either access or excellence to account for their practices; rather than relying on blanket procedures, they make discretionary judgments about student deservingness. The situational approach of the Ad Hoc Majority most clearly highlights the complexity of authority relations. In practice, all UPC faculty move back and forth on the ideological continuum of flexibility and inflexibility, support and accountability, access and excellence. Their responses to individual students are ultimately shaped by the ever-shifting moral, practical, and personal dimensions of teacher–student interaction outside of class.

Institutional standards regarding flexibility are highly variable, and the moral salience of faculty talk makes it clear that consensus is unlikely. What UPC professors do share is the desire to invoke the standards that they believe best facilitate learning. This common goal is overlooked by the many faculty who view their colleagues as purveyors of bad standards. Students too often misconstrue the motives behind certain faculty practices. The strategies of authority that some students interpret as unfair may in fact reflect a professor's profound sympathy for students or deep ambivalence about sanctions.

The faculty perspective on standards negotiation has important consequences for students that fall beyond the scope of this chapter. Flexibility and inflexibility are strategies that shape student expectations of authority, responsibility, and grades. Sociologists of education have not adequately addressed the negotiation of standards in on-on-one situations. Current debates surrounding secondary and postsecondary reform demand more research that can examine how authority is enacted outside the classroom and how such interactions shape educational standards. Comparative investigations will be crucial to understanding how varying student characteristics and institutional conditions play out in the negotiation of academic work in schools.

REFERENCES

Baker, T. L., & Velez, W. (1996). Access to and the opportunity in postsecondary education in the United States: A review. *Sociology of Education, 69,* 82–101.

Datnow, A., Hubbard, L., & Mehan, H. (2002). *Extending educational reform: From one school to many.* London: Routledge Falmer

Gamson, Z. F. (1966). Utilitarian and normative orientations toward education. *Sociology of Education, 39,* 46–76.

Hurn, C. (1985). Changes in authority relationships in schools 1960:1980. *Research in Sociology of Education and Socialization: A research annual, 5,* 31–57.

Lipsky, M. (1980). *Street-level bureaucracy: Dilemmas of the individual in public services.* New York: Russell Sage Foundation.

Lipman, P. (1998). *Race, class, and power in school restructuring.* Albany: State University of New York Press.

Metz, M. H. (1978). *Classrooms and corridors: the crisis of authority in desegregated secondary schools.* Berkeley: University of California Press.

National Center of Education Statistics, U.S. Dept. of Education. (2002). "Nontraditional undergraduates" in the *Findings from the Condition of Education Report,* Office of Educational Research and Improvement, 2002–012.

Oakes, J., Wells, A. S., Jones, M., & Datnow, A. (1997). Detracking: The social construction of ability, cultural politics, and resistance to reform. *Teachers College Record, 98,* 482–510.

Pace, J. L. (2003). Revisiting classroom authority: Theory and ideology meet practice. *Teachers College Record, 105,* 1559–1585.

Persell, C. H. (2000). Values, control, and outcomes in public and private schools. In M. T. Hallinan (Ed.), *The handbook of the sociology of education* (pp. 387–407). New York: Kluwer Academic/Plenum.

Powell, A. G., Farrar, E., & Cohen, D. K. (1985). *The shopping mall high school: Winners and losers in the educational marketplace.* Boston: Houghton Mifflin.

Sizer, T. R. (1984). *Horace's compromise: The dilemma of the American high school.* Boston: Houghton Mifflin.

Swidler, A. (2001). *Talk of love: How culture matters.* Chicago: University of Chicago Press.

Epilogue: The Sources and Expressions of Classroom Authority

David T. Hansen
Teachers College, Columbia University

"Good morning! Everyone please stand up!" The young men and women did so, although with looks of surprise and uncertainty on their faces. "OK, please sit down!" Everyone complied, while looking around sheepishly at their peers. "Now, don't ever let anyone tell you teachers have no authority!"

I know several teacher educators who have begun their courses with this exercise. They want to impress on their candidates, as starkly as possible, that not only will they have authority, by virtue of inhabiting a professional role, but that they will have to learn to use it if they are to be successful teachers. The message is important. However, these same teacher educators know they have opened a Pandora's box and that things are not as easy or straightforward as their opening gambit implies.

As the chapters collected here by Judith L. Pace and Annette Hemmings demonstrate, classroom authority is a malleable concept and an unstable phenomenon. There appear to be many sources of classroom authority and many ways of expressing or enacting it. There seem to be multiple (and often multiplying) contextual factors in schools and classrooms that variously support, undermine, vitiate, and shore up teachers' authority to educate. There are many ways of conceptualizing classroom authority—what it is, or what it should be—and there are many ways of investigating it. The chapters help us see how and why the ambiguities surrounding classroom authority contribute to the fundamental ambiguities of teaching, to why the work is proverbially "messy": unpredictable, surprising, and uncanny. The authors reveal just how difficult it can be to teach well, a fact ignored by reformers who perceive teachers as problems rather than as persons struggling to create inhabitable versions of authority in a society that constantly calls their authority into question. The chapters also illuminate why teachers need to confront, in theoretical and in practical terms, the issue of authority in education. If they fail to do so, the issue will be determined for them, either by others in the system or by the force of routine and habit.

In this epilogue, I highlight several provocative features of classroom authority the contributors identify, and I sketch some consequences of their overall project for research and for teacher education.

Classroom authority can be an expression of *roles,* of *persons,* or of both. The importance of role stands out in the exercise described at the beginning of this chapter. The candidates stood up and sat down not because they admired the character or knowledge of the teacher. They did not know him or her as yet. They obeyed because they were *students* and because a *teacher* in a *classroom* instructed them to do so. The same scene would have unfolded no matter who filled the roles of student and teacher. Long-standing cultural and societal expectations are at work. They inform the constitution of the roles and how their occupants conduct themselves. They help structure the teacher's authority. A comparable tale could be told about any society that has a formal educational system. A professor of anthropology I know once described to me what happened when he invited a professor from India to his classroom, located at a prominent American university. At one point in the class, someone asked the visitor what he thought of their seminar and how it differed from courses he taught back in India. He said he was surprised when he came in that nobody stood up and that throughout the session students were eating and drinking. The vignette reveals the fact that although educational roles are universal, their content can differ across societies. Moreover, this content can evolve within each culture. Fifty years ago, American students would never have dreamed of eating or drinking during a seminar. One hundred years ago, they would have risen when a professor came into class to begin teaching.

In short, educational roles influence the expression and dynamics of educational authority. However, individuals can not only occupy roles but also can *shape* them, sometimes so extensively that the institutionalized role metamorphoses. The consequences may be problematic, or worse, if teacher and students arbitrarily abandon their roles and fail to create something educative in their place. That possibility underscores the fact that educational roles are not in and of themselves disempowering (a romantic bias that has generated a great deal of confusion over the years). Like rituals and ceremonies, roles play crucial social functions in helping human beings dwell together. But individuals can sculpt roles and, thereby, influence their impact. Thanks to a dedicated teacher, for instance, a classroom can become a place where people genuinely engage one another in an educational adventure. I suspect most of us could describe classrooms that were so alive that both space and time dissolved into the background and ideas, projects, texts, and more, took center stage.

The teachers that Randi Rosenblum and John S. Wills describe are giving a distinctive stamp to their roles as educators. I am struck by how vividly their individual philosophies of education, and their individual visions of their authority to educate, shine through their accounts of how they work with students. As Wills emphasizes, teachers' authority to educate emerges over time, through their everyday efforts and interactions. It cannot be established by fiat or secured overnight. It has to do with earning and sustaining trust. In other words, *the authority to educate* differs from *authoritarian power* to order people about. Most of us can perhaps remember authoritarian classroom environments in which education took a back seat to control and rote routine. The very fact we could experience classrooms in the same school that were alive or dead illuminates the importance of the person in the role of teacher. The multilayered cultural expectations bound up in the role do not necessarily override individual agency, creativity, and commitment.

However, the range of social energies at work in a school can without question constrain an individual teacher's ability to shape the role—not just his or her own, but the role of student as well, especially with regard to what students should be expected or encouraged to do in the educational setting. If these energies are catalytic enough, they can lead teachers to veer away from using what several of the authors call *professional authority* and resort to *bureaucratic authority*. They move from enacting authority rooted in their educational prowess and vision as teachers to discharging authority based in the institutionalized function of moving crowds of young human beings through the socializing, sorting process called schooling.

Judith L. Pace, Annette Hemmings, and Janet Bixby illuminate the pressure institutional environments can exert on the kind of authority a teacher enacts, even as they demonstrate that an individual teacher's preparation, professional history, and career trajectory also influence what he or she does. Posed differently, their studies shed light on how roles and persons interact in school settings, with sometimes ambiguous, confusing, and contradictory results. As we learn from Pace's chapter, at one moment or phase of a school year a teacher may feel she has the reins well in hand and can work with students in genuinely educational fashion. She may feel that her work expresses all that she has learned over her years of teaching and that her philosophy of education is alive and well. At other moments or phases, however, the same teacher may feel she's lost her way and that classroom interaction is being guided by forces not only out of her control but also perhaps out of the range of her understanding. Unknowingly, and unwittingly, as Pace makes plain, the teacher may be contributing to her own predicament by subtly shifting from one source of authority to another: from her professional authority as a seasoned educator to the bureaucratic authority invested in her by the school system.

Bixby's comparative analysis of an honors class and detracked class also illustrates the differences between professional and bureaucratic authority. Education takes places in the one classroom; miseducation, or at any rate, noneducation, characterizes the other. Bixby demonstrates how that difference results, in part, from the institutional environment of the school. The moment they walk through the school door, teachers are drawn to focus on the high-achieving students and to advance their prospects. So far, so good; there is certainly nothing wrong with supporting ambitious students. But the problem is that the ethos does not *also* draw teachers into thinking of how they can assist *all* students, especially those who are less advantaged at the start. Bixby's conclusion is inexorable: It is one thing to alter school structures, quite another to alter an ethos. For genuine transformation to occur, she contends, the very culture of the school and classroom needs to change. How to accomplish that constitutes a challenging, perplexing problem in its own right, because altering cultures is anything but a straightforward engineering problem. It is a slow, unwieldy educational task, one of awakening the moral, intellectual, and aesthetic sensibilities of those who educate *and* of those in a position to support or hamper them.

Hemmings spotlights the impact of the school's moral order on how teachers interpret and make use of their authority. I take that concept to be rooted in the sociological idea of *mores,* or customary ways of regarding, treating, and interacting with others in a given social setting. The term has to do with typical expectations and presumptions about conduct. Hemmings shows how the moral order of a school can compromise teachers' intentions and hopes. In one school she examined, an ethos of caring ironically, if not perversely, leads some well-intentioned teachers to lower their academic expectations of minority youth. Their posture becomes all the more problematic because students can see through their so-called "caring." In the other school Hemmings investigated, an ethos of competition and careerism leads some teachers to overlook student dishonesty, if not downright ethical corruption. Recall the terrifying talk of one of the students Hemmings interviewed, who boldly refers to how he uses his eyes to dominate others in the school, to the point where he can say "that person is mine." His testimony brought back grim memories of individuals I still remember from high school who seemed to relish manipulating and humiliating others, with nary an adult to intervene. Some students act in *authoritarian* ways that, at times, can be challenged successfully only by educators who are *in authority.* Hemmings' data imply that the moral order of the school will influence whether teachers become professional authorities who conceive their responsibility as taking in the whole person of the student: his or her aesthetic, moral, and intellectual growth, qualities that often flourish or degrade together.

The observational work that Wills, Pace, Bixby, and Hemmings have conducted suggests that educators' authority derives its integrity, at least in part, from a commitment to all the students placed in their care. That commitment does not translate into treating students in identical ways (as if persons were robots). It does mean doing the best one can, under the circumstances and with all the resources at hand, with each student. Rather than deriving from superior power—which the system grants in a variety of ways—the authority to educate seems to spring from a sense of the significance and the necessity of education.

However, classroom authority becomes a more elusive concept, and phenomenon, when we discover that it may emerge from sources other than persons or roles. James Mullooly and Hervé Varenne sketch a classroom scene that seems to throw out the window concern about the ethos of the school, on the one hand, and a focus on the teacher's professional biography and experience, on the other hand. According to their analysis, the teacher in question and her students *play* with authority and with the whole process of schooling itself. They do not mock authority, reject it, or escape it. Instead, they enact it by eliding both roles and persons as possible sources. Authority emerges from a highly ritualized, symbolic mode of classroom life. For Mullooly and Varenne, authority constitutes a property of interaction. It is not a "possession" in the hands of teachers or students. It has the quality of a verb more than that of a noun (a point illuminated by Wills, as well). In Goffmanesque fashion, Mullooly and Varenne steer clear of any and all reification of authority. They portray classroom occupants as bound up in complicated, spontaneous modes of relating that could not possibly be duplicated in another classroom, or even by the same persons in their own classroom the very next moment. Selves, persons, subjectivity, and roles, as these are conventionally understood, disappear from the dramaturgical analytic the authors construct. Their disappearance may be no surprise given the scripted nature of the curriculum in the classroom, which the authors suggest, tongue in cheek, creates a lot of room for comedy (we might remember that tragedy is the other side of comedy).

In contrast, persons and roles may also disappear when authority becomes rooted in genuine educational experience. By that I mean instances in which teacher and students have given themselves over, metaphorically speaking, to an inquiry, whether the latter be interpreting a novel or poem, conducting a scientific experiment, resolving a math problem, painting a still life set up in the classroom, or assessing historical evidence. In these circumstances, authority can be understood to shift from the school or teacher and come to reside in the inquiry itself. Teacher and students alike heed the call to engage themselves in the inquiry, to come under the sway of its requirements to think carefully, to consider alternatives, to attend to details, and to listen to the views of others. The authority invested in inquiry differs from the authority of the academic discipline or subject, often expressed in the form of textbooks containing bodies of authorized knowledge to which teachers and students must hearken, and rightfully so if the textbook is crafted responsibly. Just as researchers should take seriously what their precursors have done, both methodologically and substantively, so teachers and students should take seriously the human experience brought together in a good textbook. However, just as a researcher is not bound by precedent in some kind of rote fashion, so a teacher and group of students can push beyond preset bodies of knowledge and examine questions that may lead to multiple and sometimes surprising answers. When this occurs, authority becomes a property of inquiry; it derives from curiosity, doubt, interest, perhaps even yearning.

The contributors' fine-grained analyses in this book convince me that there may be no limit to the configuration of sources and expressions of authority inside classrooms. Life *is* sometimes stranger than fiction. It is also more wondrous and more confusing. Teachers respond differently, or so it seems, to (a) the bureaucratic authority placed in their hands by the system; (b) the professional authority garnered through their preparation, experience, and dedication; and (c) the spontaneous authority that emerges through the unique trajectories interaction takes in the classroom. Mullooly and Varenne provide one example of the latter. I've touched on another with a reminder of the ways in which genuine educational experience can lead persons to "lose" themselves in an inquiry or project. I mean lose their selves quite literally, in a way John Dewey captured when he described how a person loses her- or himself in an activity—that is, becomes so intimately bound up in it that she or he loses self-consciousness—with the result that the person may "find" a new self, however subtly altered, a self now more perceptive, sensitive, capable, knowledgeable, insightful, and so forth (Dewey, 1916/1985, pp. 132–133, 361–362).

A third example comes to light when we attend to what the students are doing in the studies reported herein. It seems obvious they are shaping the emergence and enactment of classroom authority. Although Rosenblum focuses on negotiations outside the classroom, her study graphically displays the fantastic diversity of ways in which students influence how a teacher uses his or her authority to educate. In tacit or explicit fashion, students can support or undermine a teacher's authority. Their actions can help generate, or subvert, conditions for educational experience. Just as teachers gyrate between different sources of authority, so students move back and forth between accepting the expectations of role set by a given system, school, or teacher, and moving beyond them. I cannot number the times I have been surprised and delighted by a student who suddenly takes the reins of discussion in hand and turns the class in an unexpected and fruitful direction. I also cannot number the students I have had who seem content to interpret their role in purely passive fashion, in effect conceiving of themselves as the proverbial empty vessels awaiting new information. In the one case, students act as *persons* whose ideas and questions matter to them. In the other case, students act as *occupants of a role* whose personhood is kept on the shelf. Sometimes the same student acts in one way, then in the other. In any case, students' posture affects the enactment of classroom authority.

Like the contributors in this book, I am struck by the power of institutions and their environments to influence how people conduct themselves. I am impressed by how intricate and complicated authority becomes when we appreciate the range of actors who have a stake in it, among them teachers, students, administrators, and parents. I am equally struck by the irrepressible urge many teachers and students feel to make something meaningful out of the time they spend together. These facts raise questions for researchers and teacher educators, and I will turn to them after first providing a broader context regarding authority.

As numerous scholars and public commentators have pointed out, Americans have a love–hate relationship with authority. On the one hand, they often equate talk of authority with authoritarianism and are quick to resist the idea that somebody should have authority over them. Perhaps teachers everywhere in the land can recall moments when it seemed others regarded them as bureaucratic dictators. Roger Abrahams (1986) ascribed these sentiments to shifting societal understandings of who and what we are as human beings:

> With the growing emphasis on the individual's control over his or her own identity, the institutional ways of engineering personal transformations have lost much of their power. For such socially sanctioned transformation to occur, we must believe in the power of those invested with authority to mark these changes for us. But in many ways such authority has been undercut because of our belief that we should do such changing on our own. This is authentication substituted for authority. (p. 52)

On the other hand, in their actual everyday conduct, Americans seem all too disposed to heed authority, even when it is in fact authoritarian. Is there anyone who has never been intimidated by a forceful salesperson, police officer, bus driver, school principal or academic dean? I leave aside larger political questions regarding the expression of authoritarianism in public life and its impact on our actions and sensibilities.

These cultural responses to the issue of authority complicate teachers' authority to educate. Many teachers, or so it seems, are often unsure of what grounds their authority and are equally unsure of how to enact or express it in their work. Most are repelled by the idea of becoming authoritarian, but pressures from outside the classroom—from the current obsession with standardized testing, from the wishes of parents, from the ethos of schools, and much more—seem to lead many teachers to compromise their philosophies of education and to act out of bureaucratic rather than professional authority. Some teachers seem to abandon professional authority altogether and simply pass the time with students by assigning endless worksheets and other busywork and passively moving everyone along in the system. Still others dilute their authority by caving in to unspoken teacher codes in a school that, in some cases, license low expectations and standards. As Elizabeth Campbell (2003) recently argued, even the best intentioned teachers sometimes "suspend" their morality, as she puts it, and go along with the crowd. They substitute group norms as the source of authority and slip away from a commitment to educate all students.

From these varied perspectives, the very idea of classroom authority featured in this book becomes problematic. "The profession is unclear," write Eugene Provenzo and his colleagues, "as to the authority, responsibility, and freedom teachers have when they teach, while the [educational] system is unclear as to what authority, responsibility, and freedom society has given to it" (Provenzo, McCloskey, Kottkamp, & Cohn, 1989, p. 569). What does American society want from its schools? Should schools advance social, cultural, religious, or political aims? Or should they be places where the young prepare for jobs? Should schools pursue all these goals? Confusion about educational purpose, including the conflation of socialization or enculturation with education; uncertainty about the place of teachers in influencing lives rather than in merely transferring information; diverse and contradictory evaluation mechanisms in schools and even in the same classrooms—all of these and more reflect a climate in which the flight from authority exhibited by some educators becomes all too comprehensible.

The chapters Pace and Hemmings have assembled herein suggest a response to these circumstances other than either hand-wringing or exiting the scene. To be sure, the struggles, frustrations, and contradictions in teachers' practice they report are all too real and important to understand. Few teachers are strong enough to resist or repel unilaterally social energies that compromise their work; the realities of working in school systems are too formidable to expect teachers to be superhuman. At the same time, however, qualitative research over the last several decades has shown that very few schools are "totalizing" institutions that govern the hearts and minds of their occupants. On the contrary, research has demonstrated time and again the unfathomable ways in which teachers and their students have been creative, imaginative, and successful in their work despite any number of institutional and societal impediments. The cup is both half-empty and half-full. The studies in this book complement other classroom-based work in showing how unnecessary it is to resort to strident perspectives that all too often end up being reductive or deterministic.

In short, there remains an important research agenda on classroom authority, and I urge researchers to take up the baton extended by the contributors to this book. There remains much to learn about how classroom authority manifests itself, how it emerges over time, how it may evolve in a given educational setting, how educators themselves think about it, and more. From a substantive point of view, for example, do elementary school teachers also fall into the intriguing (and, of course, idealized) categories Rosenblum puts forward, of the Supporters, Standard Bearers, and Ad Hoc Majority? What about secondary school teachers? How do these various configurations play out in the culture of a school, or in a specific department? How do new teachers respond when they encounter old hands who conceive and enact authority in disparate ways? Is educational authority in fact being undermined in schools everywhere today, as we see in Wills's chapter, by the pressure exerted by standardized testing? From a methodological point of view, how can qualitative researchers attend to what is often a moving, unstable target, an object that seems to keep metamorphosing over the course of a school year? It will not do to define or characterize classroom authority on the run, and yet inquiry needs somehow to be responsive to the dynamics of authority in order to grasp their variety and meaning. The sheer range of sources and enactments of classroom authority remains remarkable, puzzling, and, depending on one's point of view (or state of mind) worrisome or heartening. Additional qualitative research can help us better understand the phenomenon and come to grips with what kind of standpoint we want to adopt toward it.

Philosophers of education have important contributions to make as well. There exists an ongoing tradition of philosophical analysis of authority, from Richard Peters (1959, 1966), to an edited collection by David Nyberg and Paul Farber (1986), to other more recent treatments. However, I see a need for new analyses in light of emerging qualitative research such as that represented in this book. For example, how or in what ways does the moral *order* of a school compare or contrast with the *moral* aspects of educational work? As mentioned previously, the idea of a moral order is rooted in the sociological notion of mores, associated with custom and social convention. However, the idea of the moral is rooted in issues of personal character, of justice, of virtue, of goodness itself. The moral points to persons and whatever agency they enact, whereas mores point to roles and their influence on action. As we have seen, persons and roles appear to constitute at times conflicting, and at other times complementary, sources of authority in schools.

Philosophical work will also prove indispensable when we turn to normative questions. What *should* authority look like in practice? Should one of

the many versions of classroom authority touched on here trump or lead
the others? Should the democratic experiment still underway in the United
States influence the answer to these questions? If so, how?

Philosophical questions, in turn, will trigger new questions for field-
based research. For example, *when* does authority happen? The moment
students walk into the classroom? The moment a lesson starts? Or does it
"start" over the summer when the teacher puts together her pedagogical
plans? Together, qualitative researchers operating from one or more of the
social sciences, and philosophers of education operating from traditions of
moral and social philosophy, can generate a corpus of enlightening work
on the nature and consequences of classroom authority.

This work can be invaluable in teacher education. For example, foundations courses can take up directly the question of educational authority.
They can use philosophical works and texts such as this book to help candidates engage the differences between authority and power—to discern,
for example, why the vignette that opens this epilogue may in fact say more
about power than about authority. Candidates can begin to grasp how and
why authority can emerge from multiple sources. They can begin to think
about how to be *an* authority and to be *in* authority and that taking on
this posture does not mean acting in coercive or insensitive fashion. On
the contrary, candidates can consider why authority is unavoidable and
that they can play an active role in whether its source will be primarily
professional, bureaucratic, or arbitrary. In the meantime, methods and
discipline-based courses can help candidates understand how the authority
to educate can find expression through thoughtful lesson plans, pedagogical techniques, and evaluation measures, allied with a strong command of
academic material, and all of this bound up in a sense for why attentiveness
and responsiveness to students helps distinguish the authority to educate
from authoritarianism.

I believe many veteran teachers would concur with the idea that educational authority in the classroom is emergent, fragile, contingent, and
dynamic. Given these realities, good teaching seems to necessitate vigilance:
an ongoing concern for the integrity of classroom life so that teacher
and students alike can engage in meaningful educational work. That task
requires patient effort, but many experienced teachers would say the effort
is redeemed time and again in what students end up accomplishing—suggesting, in turn, how the life of the teacher can be one of genuine accomplishment. In this light, qualitative and philosophical work on authority
can be useful for teacher candidates once they have graduated and taken
up positions in schools. This work can become an integral element in
induction and mentoring programs, assisting new teachers to keep hold of
their agency, creativity, and dignity in the face of unexpected challenge and
difficulty. It can become an important aspect of teacher learning across an

entire career, especially if teachers engage in continuing conversation with one another about the topic.

Pace and Hemmings have taken a valuable step in these directions. The studies they have assembled advance our understanding of classroom authority, even as they raise many questions for further conceptual and field-based inquiry. The project attests to how important it is for teacher education programs to take classroom authority seriously. The teachers whom we meet in these chapters would have been well served had they had systematic opportunities to think about the educational meaning and consequences of authority. Those opportunities would not have eliminated the challenges and predicaments they have faced as educators, but they might have helped the teachers respond to them in more satisfying, educationally justifiable ways and thereby experience deeper personal fulfillment as well as professional success.

REFERENCES

Abrahams, R. D. (1986). Ordinary and extraordinary experience. In V. W. Turner & E. M. Bruner (Eds.), *The anthropology of experience* (pp. 45–72). Urbana: University of Illinois Press.

Campbell, E. (2003). *The ethical teacher.* Maidenhead, England: Open University Press.

Dewey, J. (1985). *Democracy and education, The middle works of John Dewey 1899–1924: Vol. 9: 1916* (J. A. Boydston, ed.). Carbondale: Southern Illinois University Press. (Original work published 1916)

Nyberg, D., & Farber, P. (Eds.). (1986). Authority in education. *Teachers College Record, 88,* 1–106.

Peters, R. S. (1959). *Authority, responsibility, and education.* London: G. Allen & Unwin.

Peters, R. S. (1966). *Ethics and education.* London: G. Allen & Unwin.

Provenzo, E. F., McCloskey, G. N., Kottkamp, R. B., & Cohn, M. M. (1989). Metaphor and meaning in the language of teachers. *Teachers College Record, 90,* 551–573.

Author Index

Subject Index

WITHDRAWN

MAY 0 6 2024

DAVID O. McKAY LIBRARY
BYU-IDAHO